*Enterprising Women in Urban Zimbabwe*

# Enterprising Women
# in Urban Zimbabwe

*Gender, Microbusiness, and Globalization*

Mary Johnson Osirim

Woodrow Wilson Center Press
Washington, D.C.

Indiana University Press
Bloomington and Indianapolis

EDITORIAL OFFICES

Woodrow Wilson Center Press
Woodrow Wilson International Center for Scholars
One Woodrow Wilson Plaza
1300 Pennsylvania Avenue, N.W.
Washington, D.C. 20004-3027
Telephone: 202-691-4029
www.wilsoncenter.org


ORDER FROM

Indiana University Press
601 North Morton Street
Bloomington, IN 47404-3797
Telephone: 800-842-6796
Facsimile: 812-855-7931
iuorder@indiana.edu
http://iupress.indiana.edu

9 8 7 6 5 4 3 2 1

Library of Congress Cataloging-in-Publication Data

Osirim, Mary Johnson.
Enterprising women in urban Zimbabwe : gender, microbusiness, and globalization /
Mary Johnson Osirim.
    p.   cm.
Includes bibliographical references and index.
ISBN 978-0-253-35347-4 (hardcover : alk. paper)
1. Self-employed women—Zimbabwe.  2. Businesswomen—Zimbabwe.
3. Entrepreneurship—Zimbabwe.  4. Small business—Zimbabwe.  I. Title.
HD6072.6.Z55O85   2009
338'.04082096891—dc22                                    2008045631

**Woodrow Wilson
Center Press**
*Washington, D.C.*

The Woodrow Wilson International Center for Scholars, established by Congress in 1968 and headquartered in Washington, D.C., is the living, national memorial to President Wilson.

The Center is a nonpartisan institution of advanced research, supported by public and private funds, engaged in the study of national and world affairs. The Center establishes and maintains a neutral forum for free, open, and informed dialogue.

The Center's mission is to commemorate the ideals and concerns of Woodrow Wilson by providing a link between the world of ideas and the world of policy, by bringing a broad spectrum of individuals together to discuss important public policy issues, by serving to bridge cultures and viewpoints, and by seeking to find common ground.

Conclusions or opinions expressed in Center publications and programs are those of the authors and speakers and do not necessarily reflect the views of the Center staff, fellows, trustees, advisory groups, or any individuals or organizations that provide financial support to the Center.

The Center is the publisher of *The Wilson Quarterly* and home of Woodrow Wilson Center Press, *dialogue* radio and television, and the monthly newsletter "Centerpoint." For more information about the Center's activities and publications, please visit us on the web at www.wilsoncenter.org.

Lee H. Hamilton, President and Director

To my parents and foreparents—whose affection, diligence,
and determination strengthened me along the way
To my Honey, my best buddy—whose love, devotion,
and support kept me on the right road
And to my daughters, Vonnie and Briella—whose curiosity,
zest for life, and wisdom beyond their years
continue to light the path.

# Contents

# Tables and Figures

# Preface

This book was written during a devastating period in Zimbabwe's modern history—during the massive economic and political crisis of the first decade of the new millennium. The "enterprising women" about whom this volume was written, also experienced the major economic crisis of the 1990s, but they met this crisis with a strength and resilience that enabled them to maintain their families and their businesses and contribute to material culture and human capital formation, as well as to assist in the development of their communities and their nation. I wrote this book to make their lives visible and to share their experiences as entrepreneurs in the microenterprise sector—both the challenges and the successes—with the hope that their experiences might be useful to scholars, policy makers and women entrepreneurs seeking to improve their lives and the lives of millions of African and Global South women in this sector. This is especially important given that after agriculture, the microenterprise sector is the second major arena for women's income-generation in sub-Saharan Africa.

My interest in the topic of African women and work has a long history, stemming from the significant absence of women in certain segments (namely the bakery and furniture making businesses) of the Nigerian small-scale and microenterprise sectors, which I discovered during my dissertation research in the early1980s. At the end of that decade, I returned to Nigeria to find "where the women were" in these sectors and discovered them in the highly gendered activities of market trading, sewing, and hairdressing. Not only did I seek to understand the decisions made by largely poor and low-income African women to begin and operate microenterprises, but I also wanted to examine how they combined this role with their responsibilities as mothers, wives, and members of extended families. Around this same time, I became enthralled with what I was learning about Zimbabwe and the state's commitment to enhancing the status of women there, given the vital roles that women played in the nation's liberation war. I was very excited by the prospect of exploring first-hand how changes in legislation, the creation of a new Ministry for Women's Affairs, and greater access to health care, education, child-care, and microfinance had affected the position of women entrepreneurs in Zimbabwe. Before embarking on my first fieldwork visit there, however, I also discovered that the economic success of the first post-independence decade was drawing to a close. The nation was facing significant unemployment, balance-of-payments problems, and other economic woes, which was leading it into the hands of the major international financial institutions (IFIs) and the adoption of an Economic Structural Adjustment Program (ESAP). Thus by early 1991, it had become apparent to me that the one major facet of globalization that had affected many African nations by that time, in the form of ESAP, was rearing its head in Zimbabwe. This led me to focus much of my work among Zimbabwean women entrepreneurs, not only on the establishment and maintenance of their businesses and the balancing act they had to perform to meet their family responsibilities, but also on the impact of globalization on their enterprises, their families and their communities. I later discovered during my fieldwork that, in addition to the IFIs and the state, NGOs (nongovernmental organizations) and women's informal associations also played a role in the prospects and possibilities for women's microenterprises and their contributions to Zimbabwean development.

Besides the policy implications of this work, it is my intention that this study also contribute to a greater understanding of several gendered sectors within the microenterprise economy. Most of the earlier studies on African women in this sphere focused on their participation as market traders and did not engage in a comparative analysis of women entrepreneurs in a range of activities. Further, it is somewhat rare for a U.S.-born sociologist to study African women's entrepreneurship in the microenterprise sector, and I have brought to this exploration my feminist political economy gaze. It is my sincere hope, therefore, that this perspective will provide new analytical insights into the roles of the state, NGOs, and globalization on their daily lives and the operation of their firms. It is also my intention that in this difficult moment of transition, the feminist political economy paradigm and the ways in which it illuminates these women's experiences will begin to point the way forward toward the implementation of policies to improve their lives and promote sustainable development.

What is the difficult transition to which I am referring? At the time in which I am writing this, the two major leaders of the nation, Robert Mugabe of ZANU-PF (the Zimbabwe African National Union-Patriotic Front) and Morgan Tsvangirai of the MDC (the Movement for Democratic Change) have recently agreed to share power in the nation after nearly a decade of political turmoil. This power-sharing agreement, which will keep Mugabe as president and name Tsvangirai as prime minister, however, has yet to come to fruition since these leaders have not agreed on the selection of cabinet ministers. Moreover, the nation still faces a major economic storm, with inflation now running more than 100 million percent, while the population contends with major food shortages, massive unemployment, HIV/AIDS, and, more recently, cholera.

Needless to say, the past decade has been a tumultuous one, especially for Zimbabwe's poor and low-income majority. Undoubtedly, these times have been trying ones for the entrepreneurs in this study. I remain optimistic, though, that even under these very difficult circumstances, the Zimbabweans in this work remain the diligent and dedicated "enterprising women" that they were when I met them.

# Acknowledgments

This book was written during a very difficult period in Zimbabwe's post-independence history. As I wrote each chapter, however, I remembered the incredible strength and spirit of the urban women entrepreneurs whom I interviewed in the 1990s, and in many ways I felt reassured that they would likely withstand the severe economic and political crisis that the nation experienced in the new millennium. I am first and foremost extremely indebted to these women, who shared their personal and business lives with my research assistants and me. I am so grateful for their patience in participating in the lengthy interviews and allowing us to observe their enterprises in action. They made this book possible.

My colleagues and students at Bryn Mawr College played a major role in bringing this work to fruition. I was fortunate enough to have very bright and dedicated research assistants from sociology, anthropology, and political science who assisted me in conducting interviews. Camille Carraher, Amanda Garzon, Tambudzai Kamukosi, Julianna Kohler, Claudia Leiva, Niambi Robinson, and Donna Reyes served in this role and made all the difference in this project. My gratitude is also extended to two other former students, Mary Green and Mary Leasure, who provided invaluable assistance to me when I returned from the field. I extend a special note of thanks to my colleagues and friends in Sociology and Africana Studies who remained very supportive of my research and who over the years were an important audience for presentations on various subjects addressed in this book: Michael Allen, Linda-Susan Beard, Pim Higginson, David Karen, Phil Kilbride, Kalala Ngalamulume, Judy Porter, Ayumi Takenaka, Bob Washington, and Nate Wright. The many stimulating conversations with my colleague Bob Washington on African development further convinced me of the importance of my work and why I had to share the stories of these women entrepreneurs with a broader public. The Bryn Mawr Africa Fund, the Bryn Mawr–Haverford–Swarthmore–University of Pennsylvania Title VI Consortium in African Studies, and the National Science Foundation made it financially possible for me to make several fieldwork visits to Harare and Bulawayo in the 1990s. My sincere appreciation is also extended to the administration of Bryn Mawr College, which afforded me two generous sabbaticals during which most of this book was written.

I am very grateful for the assistance provided by the Sociology Department at the University of Zimbabwe and particularly by the department's chairpersons during my several visits, Victor Muzvidziwa and Michael Bourdillon. They helped me identify and hire graduate students from sociology and social work who also worked with me as research assistants. Several other Zimbabwean friends and their families facilitated our entry into the society and extended their hospitality to us. I am thus very thankful to the Culverwell, Raftopoulous, McCullagh, Kamukosi, Peel, and Gibson families for making us feel at home in their country. My work also benefited from inspiring conversations with feminists and activists in Zimbabwe, Rudo Gaidzanwa, Patricia McFadden, and the late Esi Honono.

A very warm expression of gratitude is extended to my colleague and friend, Nancy Horn, whose initial work on market traders in Zimbabwe led me on the path to discovering the microenterprise sector in that nation. Whether meeting at the Annual Meetings of the African Studies Association, at Bryn Mawr College, in Zimbabwe, or in my kitchen, we enjoyed many thought-provoking discussions about Zimbabwean development, the status of women in that nation, and microfinance that continued to motivate me to complete this work.

The Woodrow Wilson International Center for Scholars in Washington provided the perfect venue for researching and writing much of this book. I was very fortunate to spend a sabbatical year at the Center, where I was engaged in many exciting conversations about race and gender relations in the United States and gender and development in the Global South with other fellows and staff, including Jane Guyer, Sharon Harley, Peniel Joseph, Stephen King, Rachel Roth, and Philippa Strum. During my tenure at the Center, Saira Haider and Kristina Kempkey provided excellent assistance with the qualitative data analysis for my project. I was very pleased to have the opportunity to work with Howard Wolpe in the Africa Program in organizing a conference on "Women and Islam in Africa," which led to other exciting research collaborations for me regarding women and African development.

I extend my very heartfelt thanks to Joe Brinley, director of the Woodrow Wilson Center Press, to Yamile Kahn, managing editor of the Press, and to Alfred Imhoff, this book's copyeditor. They have all worked tirelessly to make this book a reality. In addition, two anonymous reviewers provided useful comments on an earlier version of the book, which contributed substantially to this volume. My very special thanks are also extended to Jodi Jacoby and Karen Sulpizio from Bryn Mawr College, who at various stages of this project assisted in the preparation of my manuscript. They remained so patient and supportive of me throughout this process.

Finally, I am so very grateful to my husband, Sam, my daughters, Yvonne and Gabrielle, my mother Margaret, her sister "Auntie," my sister Debbie, and my son-in-law Cary, who along with other members of my extended family have inspired, guided, and supported me during these many years. They are the wind beneath my wings.

*Enterprising Women in Urban Zimbabwe*

# Chapter 1

# Introduction: Why Study Zimbabwean Women Entrepreneurs in a Globalizing Era?

I have invested in this business because it has enabled me to send my children to school. I had to invest in their education because this is the one thing that I always considered seriously.

—Hilda Bizure, a trader, Mbare Market, Harare, 1991[1]

ESAP [Economic Structural Adjustment Program] retrenchment has resulted in loss of customers. With hairdressing as a luxury business, no one can make themselves attractive while the stomach growls with hunger. ESAP has destroyed so many families. Some of my relatives are out of work and people have lost property due to the inability to pay the increase in rates. They tell us it will end next year, but who knows. I see the government as being responsible for ESAP. They have cheated us. Ministers live rent free with healthy allowances, and they backdated a 64 percent pay hike by seven months. They live well and the rest of us suffer.

—Miriam, a hairdresser and seamstress, Bulawayo, 1994

The views expressed above demonstrate some of the positive and negative aspects of being a businesswoman in the microenterprise sector of urban Zimbabwe in the 1990s. During that decade, which followed the economic and political boom of the 1980s, poor and low-income populations, especially women, faced severe financial challenges due to an economic crisis and the state's establishment in 1991 of the Economic Structural Adjustment Program. This program, which had been developed at the behest of the

---

1. Pseudonyms selected by the respondents are used for all participants in this study.

International Monetary Fund and the World Bank, was one facet of globalization in the 1990s, when under the auspices of a free market, nation-states around the globe became more fully integrated into the world capitalist system.

Globalization as an economic, political, and cultural phenomenon is not new—it began several centuries ago with the processes of colonization and imperialism. There are different periods of globalization, with the latest, most recent phase emerging in the 1980s (Chase-Dunn 1998; Moghadam 2005). This period—often referred to as the "current phase" of globalization (i.e., the 1990s, the time frame for this study)—was initially characterized by the expansion of a world capitalist economy, economic restructuring, and the enactment of structural adjustment programs in Global South nations that were mandated or strongly recommended by the major international financial institutions and the Global North as a remedy for the Global South's economic problems.

Although Africa still remains the world's poorest continent, some African nations—such as Ghana, Kenya, and Nigeria—whose economies have experienced substantial economic growth, now have a different relationship with the IMF.[2] Rather than needing to adhere to strict structural adjustment requirements to obtain the necessary loans, as in the past, these African nations are more likely to turn to the IMF in its role as a consultant on economic issues (Faiola 2008).[3] But unlike these other Sub-Saharan African nations, Zimbabwe, though no longer under the auspices of ESAP as in the 1990s, is in the midst of a massive political and economic crisis and therefore does not occupy the enviable position of largely "consulting" with the IMF.

This study, however, is focused on the "enterprising women" of Zimbabwe in the 1990s—those who encountered the period of economic crisis and structural adjustment. The market trader quoted above illustrates the strong commitment of many entrepreneurs to maintain their firms despite severe economic challenges and to contribute to the development of human capital in their society by investing in their children's educations. The quo-

2. Though these African nations have experienced economic growth in the past decade, they still face major problems with socioeconomic inequality, income distribution, and their mode of inclusion in the global capitalist system. Furthermore, nations such as Nigeria still experience substantial challenges in the development of infrastructure, which I witnessed firsthand and which were frequently discussed during my recent visit to Nigeria in June 2008.

3. This is not to diminish the role of the IMF, which remains a powerful international institution on the world stage, particularly for Global South nations.

tation from the hairdresser-seamstress exhibits some of the most debilitating effects of the economic crisis and ESAP on entrepreneurs and the society at large, such as massive unemployment. It also demonstrates the stark contrast between the living conditions of government officials and those of most low-income Zimbabweans during this period.

This book seeks to document the business experiences and personal lives of Zimbabwean women entrepreneurs in different segments of the microenterprise sector in order to examine "who they are" and also to explore the impact of the nation's economic crisis and structural adjustment on their lives. On the basis of in-depth interviews conducted with 157 seamstresses, hairdressers, crocheters, and market traders in 1991, 1994, and 1997, this study reveals that in the maintenance of their businesses and families, they contributed to community and national development. They reinvested profits in their enterprises, engaged in innovation, contributed to the development of material culture, and provided employment in their communities. They also contributed to—or fully supported—the upkeep of their households and extended families, and they made major investments in the education of their children. As they say in their own words, these Zimbabwean entrepreneurs accomplished these feats while facing the many challenges posed by the economic crisis and structural adjustment of the 1990s, including massive layoffs and underemployment, which significantly increased prices for both business inputs and household goods and increased competition in the marketplace.

Moreover, interviews with the major leaders of both governmental and nongovernmental organizations (NGOs) throughout the 1990s (with the latter, especially in 1999) revealed that very few of the poor and low-income women entrepreneurs in this study benefited from the business assistance offered by these bodies. Among the reasons they did not benefit were their lack of knowledge about business support programs and social-class discrimination in the allocation of loans and other forms of assistance. Working within a paradigm of feminist political economy, this study engages in an intensive examination of these businesswomen's lives and demonstrates that they are, in fact, "enterprising women."

## Why Study Zimbabwean Women Entrepreneurs in the Microenterprise Sector and the Impact of Globalization?

Most social science scholarship on African women and work over the past two decades has focused on women's participation in the microenterprise (informal) sector of the economy (Darkwah 2002, 2007; Snyder 2000; Clark 1994; Horn 1994; House-Midamba and Ekechi 1995; MacGaffey and Bazenguissa-Ganga 2000; Osirim 1998, 2003a, 2003b; Robertson 1984, 1997). Feminist scholarship has paid particular attention to this sector because it is, after agriculture, the largest area of income generation for women on the continent. Interest in the microenterprise sector has expanded even further due to the economic consequences of structural adjustment programs, which were established in more than forty African nations during the 1990s (Darkwah 2002; Munguti, Kabui, and Isoilo 2002; Osirim 2003b; Pheko 1999). In Zimbabwe, ESAP caused massive layoffs and underemployment, especially among men in the formal sector, and the state strongly encouraged both women and men to begin microenterprises as a poverty alleviation strategy. In some African nations, women own the majority of microenterprises (about 64 percent in Zimbabwe), which produce many "gendered" goods and services, among other items.

Zimbabwe also serves as a very interesting test case in which to study the development of women's businesses and their contributions to the broader society, because the state made a commitment after independence in 1980 to reduce social inequalities by advancing the position of women. Because women were major participants in the Liberation War, the postwar government of Robert Mugabe promised to promote equality between women and men. Before independence, women in Zimbabwe had been legally categorized as minors completely under the jurisdiction of their husbands, fathers, or brothers. In the first postindependence decade, the state established a women's ministry; expanded social services, job training, and loan programs; and changed the status of women from legal minors to full citizens. By the end of the 1980s, women had achieved parity with men in primary school enrollment and had benefited from the expansion of child care programs and free health care for the poor (Stoneman and Cliffe 1989). Therefore, Zimbabwe provided a good test case for exploring how advances in women's status could actually be realized in a state that appeared dedicated to promoting equality.

Zimbabwe's position as a settler colony under British colonialism makes it an interesting site in which to study the role of intersectionality in the lives of black businesswomen from a feminist political economy perspective. (See figure 1.1—a map showing Zimbabwe's major cities and its position in Southern Africa.) In Zimbabwe (formerly Southern Rhodesia), the British established a system of strict separation of the races, similar to the one in South Africa. During colonialism, due to their race, gender, and social class,

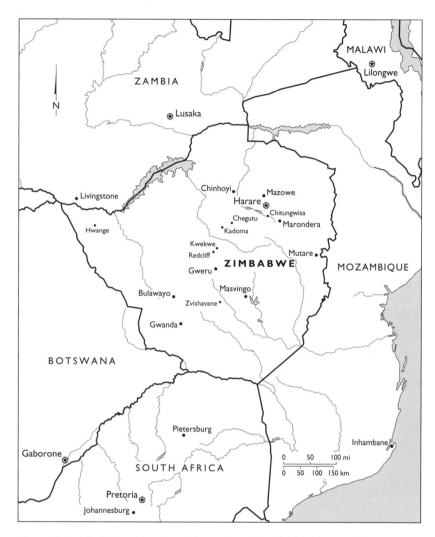

Figure 1.1. Zimbabwe's major cities and position in Southern Africa

black women were at the bottom of the Rhodesian socioeconomic hierarchy. As a result, black women received the least amount of formal education compared with all other groups in society, were restricted to the least arable land on which to farm, and were assigned to remain in the rural Tribal Trust Lands allocated by the British. Most educational offerings, formal-sector jobs, and opportunities to live in cities were off limits to black Zimbabwean women. Thus, given this legacy of ninety years of British rule, what was to become of black women—and, indeed, black businesswomen—one to two decades after independence?

As the second most developed economy in Sub-Saharan Africa after South Africa at the end of the 1980s, Zimbabwe also provided an interesting case for studying the impact of economic crisis and structural adjustment on low-income populations in an economic environment that until then had been relatively stable (Sylvester 1991; Stoneman and Cliffe 1989). (See figure 1.2—a map showing Zimbabwe's position in Sub-Saharan Africa.) Precisely because of this more positive economic history, Zimbabwe was one of the later nations on the continent to establish a structural adjustment policy. When the state implemented this policy with ESAP, along with removing tens of thousands of state workers, it also reduced subsidies for vital social services such as education, housing, transportation, and health care. These reductions eroded much of the progress toward gender equality that had been realized in the first postindependence decade and took an especially harsh toll on poor and low-income women and children. For example, in the early 1990s, UNICEF ranked Zimbabwe second in Sub-Saharan Africa for its immunization of children against measles (UNICEF 1993; Kamidza 1994). But by 1993, due to the decline in the number of children receiving immunizations in the first years of ESAP, measles had become a killer disease.

This study demonstrates in many ways how devastating such an economic crisis and structural adjustment can be for an African nation, especially when a country once as strong as Zimbabwe can essentially be brought to its economic and political knees on the world stage as a result. This is not to say that the personalities in power in Zimbabwe do not bear major responsibility for the nation's current severe maladies, but rather that the international financial institutions and the Northern hegemonic powers are not blameless in this strife, especially given their past and to some extent continuing actions.[4] For example, in late 1999, when the present political crisis began, one major problem still confronting the nation was the lack of significant land reform—a legacy partly due to the Lancaster House Agreement at the end of independence. Although the Zimbabwean state was very slow in its land reform efforts of the 1980s and 1990s, and some of the results of these programs were questionable, the conditions of the land reform

---

4. Multinational mining companies, such as Anglo-American, are still doing business in Zimbabwe. As of June 2008, the company still planned to proceed with new platinum mining, despite severe political crisis in the country.

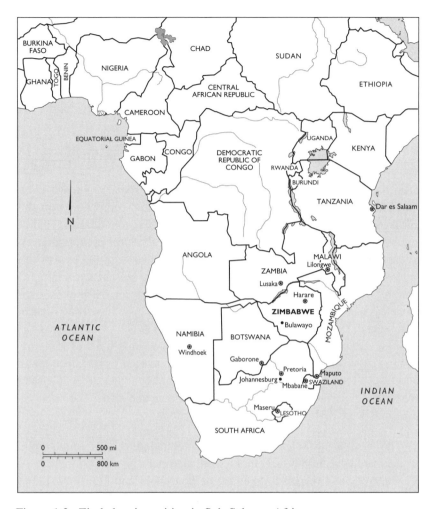

Figure 1.2. Zimbabwe's position in Sub-Saharan Africa

program negotiated with the British government in the Lancaster House Agreement also limited what the Zimbabwean state was likely to accomplish in the first fifteen years after independence.[5]

Because Zimbabwe was not alone in Sub-Saharan Africa in experiencing economic crisis and structural adjustment under the globalization process in the 1990s, this study can hopefully shed some light on the problems

5. See chapter 2 for a more detailed discussion of the Lancaster House Agreement.

encountered by a large proportion of the population—poor and low-income women in the microenterprise sector—and the agency and empowerment demonstrated by these women in response. Perhaps the lessons learned from their experiences can assist other businesswomen and other low-income African women more broadly in their responses or resistance to unwelcome state policies and to some of the asymmetric effects of globalization.

## Research Methods and Sites Selected in This Study

Over the past few decades, feminist scholars in the social sciences and the humanities have been committed to identifying and projecting women's authentic voices in examining their positions in their communities, in their societies, and in the global economy. Questions about the appropriate way to capture such voices have been open to much debate in the past twenty years (Reinharz 1992). I would argue that such concerns are especially important when attempting to examine the lives of women in the Global South, as well as women of color around the globe, whose voices have been silenced or marginalized for centuries (Osirim 2003a).

In an attempt to document Zimbabwean women's lives as entrepreneurs, I chose to engage in intensive, in-depth interviews using open-ended questions. These interviews were more exploratory than other interview schedules, especially those based on fixed-choice questions. The interview measures were divided into three major sections:

1. The personal attributes of the entrepreneur, including basic demographic data and educational and employment histories.
2. The roles and responsibilities in the household and family, including marital status and attitudes about the union; the number, ages, and sexes of children; the household division of labor and changes over time; decision making in households; and responsibilities for extended family members.
3. The operation of the business, including the reasons for starting it, the amount and sources of start-up capital, changes in its employment size and production methods over time, its financial history, the role of state agencies, nongovernmental organizations, and the private sector in assisting their businesses, and the impact of the economic crisis and globalization.

Each interview measure contained 130 open-ended questions on these subjects. Market traders, crocheters, hairdressers, and seamstresses were selected for this study because these are some of the major economic activities in which women are involved as entrepreneurs in Zimbabwe, indicating the gendered nature of activities in the microenterprise sector (Horn 1994; Saito 1991; Downing 1990). Interviews were conducted with 61 market traders, 57 crocheters, and 39 hairdressers and seamstresses.

The leaders of some state and about 25 NGOs were also intensively interviewed. Directors of government agencies—such as the head of the Ministry of Community and Cooperative Development and Women's Affairs, and the head of the Women's Bureau for the Zimbabwe African National Union–Patriotic Front (ZANU-PF)—were interviewed in 1991, whereas most leaders of NGOs were interviewed in 1999.[6] The leaders of governmental organizations and NGOs were asked about the purposes and goals of their groups; which population(s) they served; the cost (if any) for their services; the impact of their services on the targeted populations; their sources of funding; how their agencies were organized; and changes over time and plans for the future.

Gender studies scholars have often insisted that for a woman to be best understood in a research project, it is best for her to be interviewed by a woman (Reinharz 1992). Some researchers have argued that because of the gendered nature of language and to establish the optimum comfort level for women respondents, women interviewers are likely to be more successful in studies of women. Such scholars have maintained that the trust level of participants is enhanced when women interview women. There is some controversy surrounding this idea, however, with respect to the African case. In her study of market traders in Harare, Horn (1994) employed both women and men in her interviews with market traders. Local informants advised her that jealousies and superstitions among some Zimbabwean women might compromise the veracity of the study if women conducted all the interviews. In some Zimbabwean settings, female respondents interviewed by women might accuse the interviewers of witchcraft.

In my study, primarily women undergraduate and graduate students, as well as some male graduate students, were hired as research assistants to conduct some of the interviews. I interviewed many of the 157 women interviewed over the course of the project. On each fieldwork visit, I employed one or two undergraduate students from Bryn Mawr College; these juniors and seniors, majoring in one of the social sciences, served as research

---

6. A few leaders of major NGOs in this study—e.g., the Zimbabwe Women's Finance Trust—were interviewed in 1994 and later in 1999.

assistants. I gave these students background reading materials on women in Zimbabwe (and African women entrepreneurs) and trained them in interviewing techniques. In one case, a student also included supplemental questions in the interview measure, which she used in her senior honors thesis. On some occasions, I also employed graduate students from the sociology and social work departments of the University of Zimbabwe to work as research assistants. Two of these students were women, and two were men. My research revealed that mature, university-trained students from different communities than the participants appeared to obtain the most comprehensive responses from market traders, crocheters, hairdressers, and seamstresses. These students did not seem to pose a threat to the confidentiality of the respondents or elicit any fears of witchcraft.

Most of these interviews were conducted in English. Several market traders and some crocheters, however, felt more comfortable speaking in their first languages, either Shona or Ndebele; in these cases, graduate students from the University of Zimbabwe and a Zimbabwean student from Bryn Mawr assisted me in conducting the interview.[7] All the entrepreneurs were interviewed at their businesses, with interviews ranging from about two to three hours. Participant-observation was also conducted at their work sites. Either a Bryn Mawr student or I interviewed the leaders of governmental organizations and NGOs.

How were the entrepreneurs, government organizations, and NGOs identified and chosen for inclusion in this study? Preliminary lists of some crochet markets, beauty shops, and sewing enterprises were obtained from government offices, such as the Women's Bureau of ZANU-PF. A wide range of local informants—including city council members, professors, and other government and private-sector employees—also identified markets and sites where entrepreneurs in the selected fields were located. Beauty shops and sewing enterprises were the most difficult businesses to find, and my research assistants and I spent a great deal of time walking along the downtown streets of Harare and Bulawayo searching for them.

Because the focus of this work was urban entrepreneurs, I decided to interview businesswomen in the two largest cities in the country, Harare (formerly known as Salisbury, under British rule) and Bulawayo. These urban areas both epitomize colonial cities in settler colonies. During the colonial period, the downtown city centers were largely off limits to blacks. The

---

7. On one or two occasions, I also obtained the assistance of a local informant in Bulawayo to assist with some interviews in Ndebele.

Figure 1.3. A downtown pedestrian mall, Harare, June 1994

downtown areas are the major commercial districts, in which one now finds department stores, food markets, the major post office, restaurants, cinemas, nightclubs, and City Hall (see figures 1.3 and 1.4). As one moves toward the outer ring of the city center, one finds commercial strips, which today include black-owned businesses, such as hairdressers and fabric shops, as well as a major bus depot that provides transportation to the black residential areas, which are known as the high-density suburbs. The white residential areas, called the low-density suburbs, spread in a circular fashion away from the city center. Single-family dwellings with large lawns and trees dot the low-density suburbs, whereas multistory, barracks-like housing and small bungalows typify the high-density areas (see figure 1.5). In some high-density suburbs, such as Mbare, the location of the largest market in this study, cardboard shanties have been erected next to many small bungalows to frequently accommodate the poor, newer migrants from rural areas.

At the time of these interviews, Harare's population exceeded 1 million, while Bulawayo's was more than 600,000. Harare is located in the region of the Shona speakers, the country's major ethnic group, which makes up about 80 percent of its population. Bulawayo is the major city in the region

Figure 1.4. A downtown Harare street scene, June 1994

of the Ndebele speakers, who make up about 16 percent of the population. Bulawayo is located in the southern part of the nation, closer to the South African border, and thus it is not unusual to find South African, as well as Malawian and other Southern African traders, working in its food markets. Harare is located in the northern part of the country, and thus one often finds Zambian traders in its food markets. Traders from other nations found in Zimbabwe have generally been longtime residents of the nation and are not

Figure 1.5. Barracks-type housing in a high-density area, Bulawayo, Zimbabwe, July 1994

recent migrants. In general, the Southern Africa region has been and continues to be an important locus of international labor migration.

To the extent possible, I decided to concentrate interviews in a few sites for each activity studied. Therefore, the food sellers were interviewed in two markets—one in the high-density suburbs of Harare, Mbare Market; and one in the high-density suburbs of Bulawayo, Manwele Market. Mbare Market is the largest in the nation, with more than 1,000 vendors selling just about any imaginable object, from food and clothing to housewares and electronics. It is also located across from the major bus depot providing transportation to other high-density suburbs and the rural areas. Manwele Market is quite small in comparison. It houses about 40 traders—20 working inside under protective covering, and 20 working outside in makeshift quarters that provide little or no protection from the elements. Other black Zimbabweans are most often the major customers of these market traders who, in addition to selling basic Western-style foodstuffs, also sell products used in African ethnic cuisines.

Unlike their sisters in market trading, the crocheters' markets were generally found in the downtown areas of major cities and in shopping centers in the low-density suburbs. In Harare, the crocheters were interviewed at the Newlands Shopping Center, the major crochet market in the city with more than 80 businesswomen, and at the Kamfinsa Shopping Center, with about 15 to 20 crocheters. Both sites were located in Highlands, an upper-middle-class suburb of Harare. Bulawayo crocheters were interviewed at the crochet market at City Hall and at Ascot Shopping Center. The former location is the major market for crocheted goods, flowers, artwork, and other crafts in Bulawayo, with 20 to 30 crocheters working on the sidewalk in front of City Hall. About 15 to 20 crocheters could be found at the Ascot Shopping Center. The crocheters catered to a largely white, expatriate clientele, including dealers and tourists from South Africa and the Global North. Cross-border traders of crocheted goods and other clothing served the needs of both black South Africans working and shopping in downtown Johannesburg and the townships as well as white South Africans shopping in flea markets located in the city's more elite areas.

The seamstresses and hairdressers were often found in independent establishments in the downtown sections of the cities, with some concentrated in a few buildings, such as Broadwell Lodge and Robin House in Harare. Their customer base was largely composed of black Zimbabweans.

## Telling Their Stories

This study thus looks in depth at women market traders, crocheters, hairdressers, and seamstresses in urban Zimbabwe. But before investigating their roles as entrepreneurs, mothers, and wives, and before considering the impact of globalization on their lives, the study examines the theoretical underpinnings of their experiences as businesswomen in the national and global economies. Chapter 2 presents an overview of the major paradigms in the sociology of development and perspectives on the role of the microenterprise sector in national economies. The chapter defines the perspective of feminist political economy as the central construct for understanding the statuses and roles of women in contemporary societies, particularly those in the Global South.

Against this backdrop, chapter 2 also provides a discussion of the labor history and general historical development of Zimbabwe from the colonial period to the time of this study in the 1990s and the changes in the position of black Zimbabwean women (and men) throughout this period. In this investigation, close attention is paid to the role of the state and the national and global economies in the construction of women's identities as manifested in the worlds of work, home, and the broader society. As a key aspect of this perspective, the concept of intersectionality aids in understanding how the interactions of gender, race, and class shape the experiences of black Zimbabwean women. In addition, the chapter introduces the reader to the important role of agency in the lives of these women.

Chapters 3, 4, and 5 focus, respectively, on the activities of Zimbabwean women entrepreneurs in three major subsectors of the microenterprise economy: crocheting, market trading, and hairdressing and sewing.[8] Each chapter includes a comprehensive examination of the personal attributes of these entrepreneurs, their roles and responsibilities in their households and families, and their methods in operating their enterprises. For each activity, I delineate how the women learned their craft, their educational and occupational histories, and the division of labor in their households and families. With respect to their firms, I investigate the history of their businesses from the start-up period to the time of their interview, including a focus on employment generation, production and innovation, and financial performance over time. Each chapter also includes a discussion of the impact of globalization on their enterprises, in the form of ESAP. These three chapters also document the problems and successes that these entrepreneurs have experienced as well as their aspirations for the future. All these issues are explored in the participants' own words.

The existence of support services provided by the state and NGOs for small enterprises and microenterprises is investigated in chapter 6. In the early years after Zimbabwe gained its independence, the national government created several programs to enhance the performance and spearhead the growth of such microenterprises, particularly among poor and low-income women. The state also engaged in some efforts to support the poor after the imposition of ESAP. At the same time, substantial growth in the number of NGOs was also observed in Zimbabwe, especially in those activities targeting women's needs for microfinance and training. Though only a few of these efforts, such as the Zimbabwe Women's Finance Trust and the Zambuko Trust, directly benefited the entrepreneurs in this study, chapter 6 also presents examples of women's informal strategies for coping with the economic crisis and ESAP. Rotating credit schemes and cross-border trade are

---

8. Because of hairdressing and sewing enterprises' similar sizes and characteristics, the similar attributes of hairdressers and seamstresses as entrepreneurs, and the smaller number of hairdressers and seamstresses interviewed, this study groups hairdressers and seamstresses together as one "type."

two notable strategies used by entrepreneurs to maintain their businesses and even enable them to grow during the period of economic crisis and structural adjustment.

Chapter 7 provides a summary and a comparative analysis of this study's major findings. Though pointing out some of the differences among the three occupational categories of businesswomen, the chapter mainly highlights their many similarities. The chapter also offers policy recommendations to improve the position of women entrepreneurs in the microenterprise sector—considered from the micro level of the local community (e.g., the building of new comprehensive urban markets), the national level (e.g., changes in the education system), and finally the macro level of the global economy (e.g., establishing international fair trade networks to support production from women's microenterprises). The chapter also gives an overview of the recent crises in the Zimbabwean state and economy, which make it highly unlikely that the suggested policy changes will be implemented in the short term. However, given the able contributions of the nation's businesswomen to their firms, families, communities, and nation during the 1990s, the chapter suggests that they will continue their quest as enterprising women.

# Chapter 2

# Shaping the Discourse on Women and Development: Theory and History in the Study of Women and the Microenterprise Sector

In the past two decades, scholarship on the role of the microenterprise sector in societies of the Northern and Southern hemispheres has grown exponentially,[1] with the major emphasis placed on understanding the position of this sector within the developing economies of the Global South (MacGaffey 1987, 1990, 1998; MacGaffey and Bazenguissa-Ganga 2000; Portes 1998; Portes, Castells, and Benton 1989; De Soto 1989; Macharia 1997). More recently, feminist scholars of development have paid particular attention to the roles of women as entrepreneurs in this sector and to their contributions to the development of local economies and communities (MacGaffey 1987, 1990, 1998; Robertson 1984, 1997; Clark 1994; Horn 1994; House-Midamba and Ekechi 1995; Darkwah 2002, 2007; Pheko 1999; Snyder 2000).

Much of this research has been done by feminist historians and anthropologists who focused their studies on women's participation in one segment of the informal sector (e.g., market trading) within specific ethnic groups and societies. Though some of these studies (MacGaffey 1990, 1998; Robertson 1997; Darkwah 2002) emphasized the role of the state in the development of informal-sector activities, few of these works really focused on the combined roles of nongovernmental organizations, the state, and the global economy in shaping the terrain for women's entrepreneurship.

1. The microenterprise sector is commonly referred to as the informal sector. For reasons that will be discussed below, I prefer to use the term "microenterprise"; however, the term "informal sector" is occasionally also used in this chapter, especially if I am describing the work of other scholars.

This study aims to do just this—to examine the development of women's informal-sector activities in urban Zimbabwe and their abilities as entrepreneurs within the context of the state, nongovernmental organizations, and globalization. This chapter intends to situate the many scholarly debates surrounding these issues theoretically: How can we understand the "gendered" nature of the work that women do in this sector? How is women's work shaped by local institutions and global processes? How does this work affect the nexus of responsibilities that they experience in their families and their communities? What impact does globalization have on identity construction for women entrepreneurs in Zimbabwe and on their contributions to economic, political, and cultural development? In exploring these questions, this chapter first reviews some of the major contributions to the theoretical literature in two specific areas that are most relevant to this study: the sociology of development and the study of the microenterprise sector. In discussing theories of the sociology of development, this chapter pays close attention to those paradigms that best explain the contemporary position of Southern nations within a global economy. Second, this chapter situates Zimbabwean women's work and their role as entrepreneurs within the historical development of the nation—from the precolonial to the contemporary periods.

## Modern Theories in the Sociology of Development

Theories in the sociology of development emerged from the social change literature of the nineteenth century, taking their inspiration from scholars such as Auguste Comte (1875). Until very recently, the vast majority of theory-building in the field of development had been exceedingly masculinist, with this bias viewed as most apparent in the work of the modernization theorists (Scott 1995). Within both the structural-functionalist and psychocultural perspectives in this school, women's roles within the broad public sphere of development were largely ignored. In fact, functionalist theorists of modernization maintained that women's roles were circumscribed to those of primary nurturers within the private sphere of home and family (Parsons and Bales 1955). What was most important to functionalists was that developing societies adopt the structures that were responsible for development in the West, such as significant migration from rural to urban areas to facilitate the development of industry; the adoption of democratic processes such as voting to create a broader sense of identity as citizens of a polity and a sense of nationhood; and a shift from extended to nuclear family forms to facilitate the entry of men into formal labor markets in the cities (Eisenstadt 1966, 1973; Parsons 1966). Psychocultural theory noted that in order for societies to develop, it was essential to adopt those personal characteristics of the modern man that were regarded as pivotal to development in the West. Included among these characteristics were such features as rationality, creativity, "future-time orientation," and appropriate risk taking—all of which were associated with male behavior in the West (Inkeles and Smith 1974).

The emergence of conflict theories within the sociology of development proved to be of far greater significance in explaining the problems that nations in the South were experiencing that restricted the positive growth of their societies. Conflict perspectives—which draw on the works of Marx, Lenin, and many neo-Marxist theorists—have encouraged us to move beyond the boundaries of the particular nation-states in question if we want to understand the challenges to development faced by Southern nations. Thus, within the conflict approach, the paradigms of dependency, world systems, and comparative political economy focus our attention on the relationships that exist between the "developing" nations of the South and their so-called more "advanced" neighbors in the North. Though individuals and groups are acknowledged as important agents of change in such perspectives, the emphasis has moved away from individual personal characteristics as essential for economic development. Early conflict theories also ignored the roles of women in the development of societies,[2] but more recent theorists have acknowledged the pivotal roles occupied by women (Nash and Fernandez-Kelly 1983; Young, Wolkowitz, and McCullagh 1984; Elson 1992; Moghadam 1999, 2000, 2005; Chow 2002).

Within the conflict perspective, world systems theory begins to explain the contemporary problems of development faced by nations in Asia, Africa, and the Caribbean and Latin America. World systems analysis—initially developed by Immanuel Wallerstein (1974) in his work *The Modern World System*—maintains that an exploitative relationship exists between core and peripheral nations, as also explained by the dependency theorists in the 1960s and 1970s. Unlike scholars in the dependency school, however, world systems theorists argue that an identifiable system exists and extends

---

2. The noted exception here is Engels's (1902) work, *The Origins of the Family, Private Property and the State,* where he does note the ways in which men oppressed women within the context of marriage.

beyond the boundaries of individual states. This system is global capitalism, which emerged in its modern form in Western Europe during the sixteenth century. Unlike some of the earlier paradigms in the sociology of development, world systems theory is historical in its approach—it postulates that we can only understand the dynamics of social change and the contemporary problems of development if we explore the roots of these dilemmas in the emergence of the modern capitalist system (Chase-Dunn 1998).

According to Jan Knippers Black (1991), rather than emphasizing the interactions among the governments of the North and South, world systems theory focuses on the actions of nonstate actors, namely, multinational corporations and financial institutions. The economic organization of the world system consists of a single division of labor that unifies the multiple cultural systems of the world's peoples into a single, integrated system. Each geographical area of the system has acquired a specialized role producing goods that it trades with others to obtain what it needs. The global economy is driven by international elites, particularly in Northern societies, whose governments usually do their bidding. The control centers of the world economy are therefore the financial rather than the political capitals. The essential struggle for Wallerstein, then, was between rich and poor classes rather than rich and poor states (Wallerstein 1974; Black 1991).

At this juncture, world systems theory can clearly be seen to occupy a major role in sociological theorizing about globalization (Chase-Dunn 1998; Sassen 1998; Moghadam 2000), which, in this sense, refers to the movement of populations, capital, and ideas to form an international, integrated economy. Production, trade, banking, and communications are some of the most salient activities in the creation of this unified global economy. In the modern period, there is no doubt that major advances in technology and transportation have been central in facilitating the growth of such a system. The boundaries between nation-states have become increasingly flexible and porous in the process of globalization. As noted by world systems theorists, in a globalized world, power is concentrated less and less in the hands of individual heads of nation-states (especially in the South) and more and more in the hands of the leaders of multinational corporations, international financial institutions, and, to some extent, multilateral organizations. The actions of such institutions are particularly noteworthy as we ponder the position of women entrepreneurs in urban Zimbabwe, because this population bears an undue share of the consequences of the major debt burden in the form of structural adjustment policies implemented at the behest of the International Monetary Fund and the World Bank.

Comparative political economy, a more recently developed approach within the conflict perspective of development, enables us to see both the negative and positive effects of globalization on populations in the South. This perspective expands the parameters of early world systems theory and aims to uncover, interpret, and explain distinctive patterns of development as they manifest themselves throughout various societies. The global capitalist system remains a key variable in the analysis, but at the same time, the autonomy of the state and the strengths of dominant and subordinate classes are considered critical factors in charting a society's development. Unlike the early dependency theorists, international political economists argue that the penetration of foreign capital does not necessarily result in the contraction of the economic role of a state in the Southern Hemisphere (Evans 1979; Evans and Stephens 1988). The local bourgeoisies and workers directly connected with the multinational corporations might benefit from the latter's activities. Evans (1979), however, indicated that the expansion of the state's role—for example, its involvement in the triple alliance with foreign capital and the indigenous bourgeoisie in Brazil and Nigeria—does not necessarily advance other indices of development, such as improving living standards for the majority.

Conversely, the perspective of comparative political economy (also referred to as the political economy of the world system) enables us to explore the roles of subordinate classes in creating social change (Evans and Stephens 1988). For example, this theory allows us to investigate the roles of various actors in civil society and their responses to the negative consequences of globalization. With regard to this study, comparative political economy helps us account for the resistance of market-trading women (and their organizations) to structural adjustment programs in Southern nations. For example, the closing of urban markets and demonstrations in city streets by these women, students, and other workers against massive state layoffs; and the removal of price controls and bans on imports have led groups of these individuals to organize against the state.[3] In this process, they are demonstrating not only their antagonism for government policies but also their empowerment as individuals and members of groups. Comparative theories of political economy have encouraged us to consider how the growth of nongovernmental organizations and increasing acts of resistance against

---

3. Market-trading women in such nations as Nigeria and Ghana closed city markets as a form of protest against structural adjustment and other state policies during the 1980s and 1990s.

the policies of states and multilateral agencies demonstrate a positive out-come of globalization (Margolis 1993; Eckstein 2002; Portes and Fernandez-Kelly 2003; Moghadam 2005).

Most recently, feminist scholarship has broadened the parameters of the theories of world systems and of comparative political economy. Whereas the latter acknowledges the existence of an international division of labor, feminist scholars within this tradition have continued to draw our attention to the gendered nature of this segmentation (Fernandez-Kelly 1983, 1994; Sassen 1989, 1998; Moghadam 2000; 2005). Precisely because an under-standing of political economy is central to this perspective, I have chosen to call this a "feminist political economy perspective," as opposed to sim-ply a gender analysis. Building on world systems theory, this paradigm argues that both internal factors (e.g., specific problems within states) and external factors (e.g., the relations that exist between states in the Global South, the Northern hegemonic powers, and international financial institu-tions) must be considered in assessing a nation's prospects for development. The global capitalist system then, in combination with domestic factors, reinforces inequality between the rich and poor as well as between women and men. As many manufacturing and high-technology service activities are transferred from the high-wage core nations of the North to the Southern periphery, feminist theorists draw our attention to not only how particular regions or nation-states become the producers of these goods and services but also to the differential access to and returns from such activities based on gender. For example, women, especially young women, have become the major laborers on the many global assembly lines for electronics, textiles, and footwear found in East Asia, South Asia, and the Caribbean and Latin America—particularly given the stereotypes about women's quick, nimble fingers. Moghadam (2000) points out that though we are witnessing in-creased levels of labor force participation for women (which might be con-sidered a positive consequence of globalization), this growth is occurring largely in low-paying, low-level manufacturing and service positions. Thus, we have also witnessed an expansion in transnational care work for women, including domestic work and sex tourism (Parrenas 2000; Osirim 2003b).

The perspective of feminist political economy also forces us to consider the critical roles that women now play in labor migration. Economic crises, the enactment of structural adjustment policies, the dislocation of many male workers from traditional labor markets, and the growth in low-level service activities in the North and the South—all have resulted in more women traveling abroad in search of income-generating opportunities to maintain their families and communities. Though many women migrants have pursued care work in some form(s), long-distance trade in global consumer items has also been a sphere of economic activity for some women. Darkwah (2002, 2007) illustrates how Ghanaian women, many of whom were former civil servants, such as teachers, began trading in East Asia and Southeast Asia in response to structural adjustment and trade liberalization in Ghana. Globalization had both positive and negative consequences for these women, who purchased gendered consumer items such as makeup, hair products, and kitchen goods in nations such as Thailand for sale in Ghana. On the one hand, these businesswomen were active agents responding to the increased opportunities for enhancing their incomes posed by the removal of past trade barriers. On the other hand, they experienced a downturn in their activities with the devaluation of the Ghanaian cedi (Darkwah 2002; Adomako Ampofo et al. 2004). To make such travel feasible also meant the development of social capital in their "home" and "host" nations— they developed relationships with the wholesalers and retailers of such goods and, at the same time, strengthened their social networks at home that provided care for their children and families while they were away. Feminist political economy provides us with the tools to study such shifts in women's and men's lives—transitions that take us far beyond the domains of classical and neo-Marxist theories of development centered in the nation-state to analyses at the global level in which we can closely investigate transnational connections and women's (and men's) agency. How does labor migration affect relations among women and men in households, families, communities, nation-states, and the global economy? Do transnational opportunities for women reduce or exacerbate inequalities between the genders? What impact does gendered labor migration have on community and national development?

These scholars have further drawn our attention to the intersections of race, class, and gender in the lives of women of color in the South (as well as in the North) in both the historical and contemporary periods. Thus, these researchers have identified women's roles in the process of development, while recognizing the connections among capitalism, colonialism, and patriarchy in structuring their life experiences (Hennessy 1993; Scott 1995). As Lewis (2002) indicates, stratification based on the intersectionality of race, class, gender, and imperialism was noted in the early 1980s by African feminists, even before the noted contributions of U.S. feminist sociologists such as Margaret Andersen and Patricia Hill Collins (1992) and Elizabeth Higginbotham and Lynn Cannon (1988). Through their structural analyses, these scholars have acknowledged women's agency in their families, communities, and nations, as well as their acts of resistance to colonial and postcolonial states and to globalization (Okonjo 1976; Van Allen 1976; Osirim 1995; Mama 1996; McFadden 2001; Pereira 2003; Adomako Ampofo et al. 2004; Moghadam 2005). Feminist scholars on Africa have also largely brought the public/private sphere split noted among the modernization theorists and early feminist researchers to a close and have revealed that this discourse is not applicable to the lives of most African women. Further, an area of more recent investigation is the impact of global economic processes on social relations, identity, and family formation.

In addition to the effects of these relocations on the status of women in the labor market, feminist political economists are generally concerned with the consequences of the international division of labor for social structure and on culture. Therefore, in response to the negative effects of globalization on women in the labor force around the world, many women have formed transnational feminist networks—such as Development Alternatives with Women for a New Era (DAWN) and the Women's Environment and Development Organization (WEDO)—in an attempt to resist further growth in inequality and deterioration of their status (Moghadam 2005). Moreover, these networks have joined with others in demonstrations against some of the international financial institutions, such as the World Trade Organization, to call for both economic and social justice. The response and resistance to the current phase of globalization, manifested in women's establishment of these networks, was also revealed at the state level. Sub-Saharan African nations witnessed a massive increase in the number of non-governmental organizations focused on addressing women's material and strategic gender interests as a result of economic crisis and globalization. For example, the organization Niger Delta Women for Justice joined with many other women from Delta State in Nigeria to express their resistance to corporate malpractice by Shell Oil and Chevron/Texaco in that region. Pipeline explosions, oil spills, and petroleum fumes from these multinational corporations have seriously impeded women's abilities to provide for their families in this area. Most rural women in this state depend on seafood from the surrounding wetlands, the processing of palm oil, and the growing of vegetables to feed their families and provide them with income. Not only have these oil corporations destroyed much local production, but they have also polluted the local water supply (Turner 2001). In addition, these corporations have failed to provide gainful employment for the recent schoolleavers in these communities. In response to this myriad of problems, Niger Delta Women, along with other groups in the region, have staged many protests of these oil corporations, ranging from barricading the gates of companies to singing protest songs. These protests have often resulted in violent backlashes from the Nigerian authorities (*The Guardian* 2002). Such organizations, created locally in Global South communities as well as those imported from the North, attempted to close some of the socioeconomic gaps created by economic crisis and globalization. As a theoretical framework, feminist political economy is best able to analyze and explain women's organizing to protect their material interests and to resist the power of the state and multinational corporations.

Feminist political economy, then, provides us with three major issues to consider in understanding the position of women (and men) in Global South societies: (1) the role of internal and external factors in national development; (2) the intersectionality of gender, race, and class, which positions the life chances of individuals and groups and positions them in national socioeconomic hierarchies; and (3) the role of women's resistance and agency to state policies and to contemporary globalization. To what extent is economic globalization creating a world culture or, at the very least, new transnational cultures?

## Theorizing about the Microenterprise (Informal) Sector and Entrepreneurship

In studying the processes of social change and economic development in Southern nations, scholars in this field began more than three decades ago to focus on the role of the informal sector or "second economy" in these societies. This sector, which functions outside the purview of government regulations, was viewed as separate and distinct from the formal economy. Early investigations of the informal sector took their lead from the work of the International Labor Organization in research on Kenya in 1972:

> This sector can be characterized by its ease of entry, reliance on indigenous resources, family ownership of enterprises, small scale of operations, labor-intensive and adapted technology, and skill acquired outside of the formal school system, and unregulated and competitive markets. (ILO 1972, 6)

Given this definition of the informal sector, many social scientists observed that such activities were prevalent in Southern nations, where very-small-scale enterprises, such as trading, often proliferated. In Sub-Saharan

Africa, for example, it was relatively easy to begin such activities with small amounts of capital and utilizing family labor, especially among those populations that experienced structural blockage in the formal labor markets (often due to low levels of education, capital shortage, ethnicity, or gender).

Much of the early literature on the second economy, however, could be faulted on at least three grounds. First, a relationship did exist between the formal and informal sectors. Early research on this topic maintained that these were separate, autonomous entities, operating in totally different labor markets (Mazumdar 1976; Souza and Tokman, 1976; Feldman 1991). Yet there is no doubt that throughout the Southern Hemisphere, these two sectors do interact; low-status laborers frequently work in both sectors simultaneously. The informal sector offers an opportunity for workers to supplement their incomes and for individuals to strengthen their family ties, and it serves as a form of "employment insurance" in case of formal-sector layoffs. In addition, workers in both the formal and informal sectors frequently participate in both sectors as consumers of goods and services. Thus, the considerable relationship between the formal and informal sectors is demonstrated by the activities of workers and consumers on a regular and, for many, a daily basis.

Second, the so-called informal sector is a major area of economic activity for many in Sub-Saharan Africa. After agriculture, the informal sector is clearly the major source of income for women on the continent, as well as for many men. The fact that most urban and rural families are dependent on income, goods, and services derived from the informal sector suggests that this *is* the major economic sector in Sub-Saharan African nations. The formal economy still employs at most only about one-third of all women of working age, so informally employed women thus clearly constitute the majority in African nations.

Third, the informal sector was largely regarded as a persistent feature of developing nations in the late twentieth century that had essentially disappeared from societies in the Global North. On the contrary, however, the work of many social scientists over the past two decades has demonstrated that, indeed, the informal sector is still a present and functioning entity in the North.

One of the major scholars to highlight the important role of the informal sector in both Northern and Southern societies in the contemporary period is Alejandro Portes (1994, 1998; also see Portes, Castells, and Benton 1989). In fact, Portes and his colleagues drew our attention to the expansion of informal-sector enterprises in both regions as a result of worldwide economic restructuring. Large corporations, in an effort to increase their profitability, particularly in the 1980s and 1990s, have been downsizing their salaried workforce and expanding their subcontracting arrangements with informal-sector enterprises to avoid taxes, minimum wage and health regulations, and the attempts of unions to improve wages and benefits. Portes's work strongly suggests that it is a mistake to simply characterize enterprises in the second economy as "survival" activities, because many of these businesses are dynamic and yield incomes for their entrepreneurs that surpass some of their formal-sector counterparts. Of course, Portes does acknowledge that the informal sector contains a very wide range of activities—both legal and illicit. At the same time, he notes that for the workers in such industries, conditions are frequently very exploitative (Portes, Castells, and Benton 1989).

In his work on the informal sector, De Soto (1989) has also maintained that the stereotypical images of chaos and inefficiency have to be dismissed when considering activities in this sector. He suggests, like Portes, that the development of the state (or lack thereof) is of major importance in understanding the creation and expansion of very small enterprises. Rather than focus on the factors of size or tax evasion, De Soto (1989, xii) stresses that the second economy is the "people's creative and spontaneous response to the state's incapacity to satisfy the basic needs of the impoverished masses." If anything, he argues that during the past forty years in Peru, urban migrants have developed specific interests and have established their own organizations and rules to help them "navigate around" the institutional barriers created by the state.

In recent years, however, feminist researchers have strongly advised that the word "microenterprises" be substituted for "informal sector" or "second economy" for some of the precise reasons cited above. This is an attempt on the part of scholars in feminist and gender studies to remove the pejorative connotations, such as "inefficient" and "marginal," that seem to accompany the term "informal sector" and to consider women's ventures as beyond the level of "survival" activities (Otero 1987; Downing 1990; Horn 1994; Osirim 1995, 1996, 1998, 2003a, 2003b; Robertson 1997). With respect to Sub-Saharan Africa, many of these researchers have turned their attention to an examination of women's microenterprises, the major way that women earn income on the continent after agriculture. Their studies have explored the size of operations, the legal status, the nature of production, and, in some cases, the role of the state in this process (MacGaffey 1987, 1998; Clark 1988, 1994; Horn 1990, 1991, 1994; Saito 1991; Schoepf 1992; House-Midamba and Okechi 1995; Osirim 1995, 1997, 1998, 2003b; Darkwah

2002). These and other scholars have noted the long history of many African women in this sector, particularly the noted position of West African women involved in market trading significantly predating colonialism. Such opportunities enabled some West African women to achieve economic independence and to make major contributions to the maintenance of their families and to community and national development (Sanday 1974; Johnson-Odim 1982; Robertson 1984; Clark 1994).

These feminist researchers have been involved in an ongoing debate with researchers who see microenterprises as part of larger growth-oriented strategies in the South. Many of the latter scholars have been based at Michigan State University, where they have maintained that attention and support should only be given to the most dynamic elements in the small enterprise and informal sectors that demonstrate the greatest potential for growth. Microenterprises owned by women are often viewed by such researchers as inefficient and stagnant and thus as not appropriate for support from the state. Feminist scholars have cautioned against narrow theoretical and policy analyses that ignore women's contributions in these areas. They acknowledge that women's activities are often clustered in low-growth, low-return ventures but argue that they should be supported by the government because they assist in family maintenance and contribute to development (Buvinic 1989; Downing 1990; Osirim 1998).

In the contemporary period, women in various regions of Sub-Saharan Africa engage in local and long-distance trade, which, in the latter case, frequently involves the crossing of international borders (MacGaffey 1998; MacGaffey and Bazenguissa-Ganga 2000; Darkwah 2002, 2007; Osirim 2003a, 2003b). For example, MacGaffey (1998) has demonstrated the existence of major trading routes for Congolese women that stretch from the continent to Europe. She has also noted the critical roles that marriage to foreign husbands played in obtaining foreign exchange and inputs for production and sales—resources to which these women and their male counterparts often did not have access within the Democratic Republic of the Congo (MacGaffey 1986). Darkwah (2007) illustrated that women who work at the apex of the trading economy in Ghana initially reaped the benefits of trade liberalization in their purchasing of global consumer items from such far-off locales as China, Dubai, and Thailand. The gendered nature of this trade can be noted in the types of items they purchased—light industrial goods such as women's cosmetics, kitchen utensils, and children's clothing and toys. This work holds both intrinsic and instrumentalist value for these women, whose earnings provide them with higher incomes than their peers in the public sector and whose global trading activities develop and strengthen their social capital and establish their identities as transnationals (Darkwah 2007).

Feminist researchers have also drawn our attention to the gendered nature of women's microenterprises in Sub-Saharan Africa. Their firms are usually service oriented and are viewed as an extension of their domestic duties. They are generally clustered in a small range of activities, including market trading, hairdressing, dressmaking, soap making, baking, handicrafts, food processing, and domestic work. Partly because of their domestic origins, these activities are sometimes not considered "real work" deserving of adequate remuneration. Because the majority of these activities are home based, women have difficulty in attracting customers (Downing 1990). So, despite the many painstaking hours of work that women invest in their businesses, the majority of their enterprises are hampered from achieving significant growth and profitability.

Conversely, there has also been evidence to suggest that some of the typically gendered activities in this sector can be profitable for women. In Zimbabwe's urban areas, for example, food-related activities have proven to be good investments for women entrepreneurs. Food processing, such as the production of peanut butter and sunflower oil, as well as bakeries, take-away food shops, and catering, have succeeded in meeting the growing demand for ready-to-eat foods by the growing urban population (Saito 1991). Feminist scholars have also suggested that catering to the local urban and tourist markets are potentially thriving areas for women's enterprises. Included among such areas are handicrafts, garment making, batiks, and rattan and hand-woven rugs (Downing 1990; Osirim 1998, 2003a). Furthermore, as noted above, the activities of market traders in global consumer, albeit gendered, items have proved profitable for Ghanaian businesswomen (Darkwah 2002, 2007).

The persistence of gender-role socialization patterns, the structural blockage that women experience in the labor market, and the resulting division of labor by gender has meant that most women in contemporary Sub-Saharan Africa, however, are still concentrated in the low-growth, low-wage segment of the microenterprise sector. Coupled with these factors, most women in this sector in Sub-Saharan Africa have experienced difficulties in maintaining their businesses, given the economic crises that have beset most of the continent over the past twenty years. Unlike many previous works, this study explores women's participation as entrepreneurs in some of the various types of microenterprises in which they are clustered. But before embarking on this investigation, let us first examine how a paradigm of feminist political economy applies to the study of women entrepreneurs in urban Zimbabwe.

## Women, Gender, and the State in Zimbabwe's Precolonial and Colonial Periods

The emergence of feminist political economy as a theoretical paradigm within the sociology of development and the contributions of feminist researchers to the study of the microenterprise sector in Sub-Saharan Africa provide us with a framework within which to situate the contemporary analysis of women entrepreneurs in urban Zimbabwe. Such an investigation requires us to consider how the colonial and postcolonial states, as well as patriarchy and globalization, have played key roles in structuring women's (and men's) experiences in this sector. At the same time, it is essential to understand women's agency in shaping their identities and experiences in this sector and in creating "vehicles of empowerment" through which they have responded to state and global policies, maintained their families, and contributed to development.

This theoretical paradigm, along with the world systems perspective, enable us to understand how Zimbabwe (Rhodesia) entered the world system as a colony of Britain and what this meant for the status of women and men in the process of national development. Thus, Zimbabwe's early development was significantly limited by its relationship with Britain as a colonial power and its mode of incorporation within the world economy as a producer of primary products, most notably tobacco, maize, wheat, coffee, tea, gold, coal, asbestos, and chrome. To more fully comprehend the contemporary position of low-income women entrepreneurs, it is essential to briefly review Zimbabwe's economic history, particularly with respect to the relationship of black African labor to capitalist development and the state. What roles did black women and men occupy in the colonial period?

The area of Southern Africa that came to be known as Southern Rhodesia (and later Zimbabwe) was first of particular interest to British colonists who were in search of the second Rand. Under the auspices of Cecil Rhodes' British South Africa Company, British settlers began to enter the colony in the late nineteenth century to begin gold mining in the region. In fact, even before the British raised the flag over Mashonaland in 1890, trade in cattle and ivory from the Ndebele had already developed in exchange for horses and guns from whites. Although South Africa surpassed Southern Rhodesia in overall gold wealth, the latter also held promise for British settlers because it had coal and iron deposits and the potential for substantial agricultural development. However, during the early 1890s, the discovery of rich gold deposits in Southern Rhodesia had not materialized for many whites, and as a result, the latter began raiding the Ndebele for their cattle and later labor. The ensuing Anglo-Ndebele War led to many deaths, although the Ndebele did resist. In fact, such resistance was also noted on the part of Ndebele women who "refused to reveal where cattle were hidden and were shot in cold blood" (Phimister 1988, 16). Thus, even from the earliest days of the colony, women and men resisted white colonial authority, although they were not successful in ending British authority. During this period, the British stepped up their control of the region through the creation of a hut tax and the extension of forced labor in the mines. Confrontations between the British South Africa Company and the Shona later ensued, leading to the "First Chimurenga" (Rising) among the Shona. Although the Shona fought vigorously, with the power of European weaponry, the British were also able to subdue them by 1897 (Phimister 1988; Raftopoulos 1997).

By the end of the nineteenth century, British settlers in Southern Rhodesia had also created infrastructure to support their mining endeavors. They had developed a railway, which extended from Southern Rhodesia to South Africa, and had established Bulawayo as a colonial city. By the mid-1890s, Bulawayo already had more than 100 stores, several solicitors' offices, banks, and hotels and was home to about 2,000 white settlers who were enjoying newfound wealth (Phimister 1988). Throughout this period and beyond, Southern Rhodesia and South Africa were particularly linked as a result of British settlement in both regions, the promises of gold wealth, and the railway. Moreover, in the aftermath of the Anglo-Boer War in 1902, increasing numbers of white immigrants from South Africa settled in Southern Rhodesia in search of good farmland and a more hospitable "British" climate in which to live and work (Phimister 1988). Southern Rhodesia's ties to the broader Southern African region can also be seen in the actions of the Rhodesian Native Labour Bureau. This organization, which was begun in 1903, recruited labor for the new colony widely throughout Northern and Southern Rhodesia (now Zambia and Zimbabwe), as well as Nyasaland (now Malawi), Mozambique, and South Africa.

From the earliest periods of forced and/or recruited labor, black male miners were clearly residents of "internal colonies," where their daily lives were strictly controlled by British capitalists and the state. The large mining establishments were organized around compounds in which accommodations and meals were provided for the workers. Employers organized black workers in the residential areas by skill levels and marital status, whereby those with the fewest skills, who were more likely to be temporary workers, were placed in the inner section of the compound where they could be most closely watched. Those on the higher skill levels and married workers, both of whom were believed least likely to desert the mines, were located on the outside of the inner section (Phimister and van Onselen 1997). Even in the early twentieth century, however, black laborers occupied a range of positions in the mines, including engine drivers, drill sharpeners, and boiler attendants (Phimister 1988).

Not only were the miners closely watched, but they also experienced very harsh living conditions and were subject to severe discipline. White managers, or black "police boys," proffered severe punishments in the form of beatings, fines, and/or imprisonment for workers who did not adequately complete their tasks in the mines (Phimister 1988; Phimister and van Onselen 1997). Thus, not only were black male workers forced to engage in the most difficult labor imaginable in the mines, but they were also subject to significant violence in the workplace. In addition, life was very difficult in the compounds and in the various types of barracks-style housing to which migrant male laborers were subjected throughout the colonial period. White employers tightly rationed the staple food, maize meal, as well as meat, and the workers thus frequently went hungry. In fact, black workers were typically underfed and overworked, resulting in such diseases as scurvy. Pneumonia, influenza, tuberculosis, dysentery, and syphilis were some of the other maladies that frequently plagued miners. Phimister (1988) estimated that, at best, 34,000 miners died between 1900 and 1950 as a result of these diseases. Despite all the severe challenges that mining posed for black workers, they continued to resist the power of the employers and the state in their strikes against the mines and the railways in the first half of the twentieth century (Raftopoulos 1997).

The effects of colonialism on the development of the local population were compounded by the fact that Zimbabwe was a settler colony with a race-based system of stratification. Therefore, not only were black Africans subordinated by the Europeans resident in the colony, but the former were also treated as "internal colonies," by which they were effectively denied basic civil rights in their country and were banned from their own land and access to resources (Blauner 1972; Bonacich 1991). Though white settlers began farming in Matabeleland even before the rising in 1893, commercial agriculture really took off in Southern Rhodesia in the early twentieth century. From this period until independence in 1980, black Africans had very limited access to land and to the rich mineral resources of their country. By 1902, European settlers occupied the best, most arable lands in the country—they effectively controlled three-fourths of the best land.

The Land Appointment Act of 1930 ratified this de facto condition by reserving 20 million hectares of land for whites, while 9 million hectares were set aside as the black reserves (Sylvester 1991). Though there were some difficulties in the early days of farming, growing maize and tobacco eventually turned out to be especially profitable for white commercial farmers. These farmers proletarianized the black peasantry whom it hired away from the reserves (Tribal Trust Lands) to work their large-scale farms. Black men had little choice because the colonial state imposed taxes on them, which they had to pay (Horn 1994; Osirim 1998, 2003b). To further control black labor and to ensure their limited social and geographical mobility, the colonial state later passed the Native Registration Act, which "compelled black men to have permission to seek urban work or visit urban areas" (Sylvester 1991, 35). Given this system of internal colonialism, this period from the 1920s to the end of World War II came to be known as the era of racial noncompetition.

What happened to women under British colonialism in Southern Rhodesia? As explained by feminist political economy, a racial and gendered system of stratification was developed by the colonial state. This system differed substantially from most practices within families and communities that predated colonialism. In precolonial society, women's and men's roles were not equal, although they were certainly complementary. Women had power within their husband's family and within their brother's family (Cawthorne 1999). During this period, both women and men were involved in agricultural production and the overall maintenance of the household (May 1983; Horn 1994; Osirim 1998). Among the Shona-speaking people, the largest ethnic language group in the country, a gender-based division of labor existed whereby land for cultivation was allocated to married men by village headmen (Holleman 1951; Horn 1994; Osirim 1998). Married men in turn would allocate land for garden plots to their wives, and these plots would be used to feed the family, with any surplus left for trade. Men were responsible for clearing the land, felling trees, and soil preparation, while women were engaged in planting, weeding, and harvesting the crops. Clearly, then, both women's and men's activities were central to the maintenance of families.

Within the colonial system, black men generally occupied more privileged positions (although far below the level of their white counterparts) than black women. The race-based system of stratification ensured white Rhodesians' control over access to valued resources, such as education that further enabled them to regulate the supply of labor, thereby ensuring their hegemonic control in a land where they were vastly outnumbered by blacks. Internal colonialism was exacerbated for black women, who were expected to eke out a living in the Tribal Trust Lands, which were characterized by poor, infertile soils. Poor, black peasant women shouldered the heaviest agricultural burdens and worked longer hours than their male counterparts (Phimister and van Onselen 1997). Black males were drawn to the large, white-owned farms to work on cash crops, as well as to the towns and cities to work in the mines and factories. The system of migratory labor that developed meant that, with few exceptions (e.g., in some of the mining compounds mentioned above), black men frequently resided for most of the year in barracks-like conditions and occasionally were able to visit their wives and families in rural areas. Wages earned by black men were so low that they barely covered their living expenses in the towns, with very little remaining to provide for their families at home. Therefore, through their efforts in subsistence agriculture, women were expected to be the major providers for their children and other relatives, even though the quality of the land on which they farmed made this exceedingly difficult.

Feminist political economy also assists us in understanding how colonialism combined with African patriarchy to significantly oppress black Zimbabwean women (McFadden 2001). Phimister and van Onselen (1997, 46) explain:

> Valued primarily as labour units whom chiefs, husbands or fathers could transfer or use for their own benefit, black women lived and worked in an oppressive nexus sanctioned by custom and aggravated by colonialism. While women had rights of disposal over "women's crops" and . . . earnings acquired through the exercise of such skills as pottery and healing, they were collectively excluded from political authority and direct access to the means of production. . . . This generally subordinate relation to men subsequently hardened under colonial rule into one of permanent legal minority.

Black African men were also more likely than black women to receive formal education. Because black men were expected to "serve" the colonial state in mining, light manufacturing, and to some extent as low-level civil servants, and due to the patriarchal attitudes of the white Rhodesian state, black men were likely to complete more years of schooling than their female counterparts. Under this system, then, black men were more likely to be taught to read, write, and speak English (Schmidt 1992). In those rare instances where black women could receive some formal education, they were at best able to receive about four years of instruction in the mission schools (Summers 1991; Osirim 1998). Needless to say, this education was highly gendered and included a rudimentary introduction to reading, writing, and basic computational skills, with the major emphasis on home economics, including sewing and in some cases knitting and crocheting. By and large, young black girls in Catholic and Protestant schools were being trained in domestic skills that enabled them to assist in the maintenance of the missions and later serve their households and families (Schmidt 1992). Some young, single women as well as junior co-wives did seek refuge at the mission schools as an escape from intolerable domestic situations (Phimister and van Onselen 1997). Overall, however, the emphasis on primary goods production, combined with race and gender-based systems of stratification, not only limited the development prospects for the future Zimbabwean state; such policies also significantly restricted the development of human capital, especially among black women.

Despite the fact that many women did not benefit from the formal education system, black women were still able to acquire some important domestic skills because female relatives frequently taught their kin to sew, knit, and/or crochet. In fact, this transmission of skills (although highly gendered) can be noted over several generations as a key vehicle of empowerment for poor and low-income women in the colonial and postcolonial state. Such skills enabled many Zimbabwean women to support their immediate families and to assist their extended kin.

In the sale of locally produced foodstuffs, such skills' transmission became vitally important for women as they "illegally" moved to the cities during the middle period of colonialism. These areas were officially off limits to women and were only open to those men who were legally (with the adequate papers and passes) working in the factories and mines. In addition to the need to pay taxes to the British authorities, by the 1940s in some cases, both women and men migrated to the cities after they lost their lands to larger and more successful cultivators (Phimister 1988). The women who migrated to the cities began to provide some of the indigenous foodstuffs that they grew in the countryside to the men who hungered for such products in the cities. Some of these women began the earliest markets in the high-density suburbs (the black sections of metropolitan areas) to provide food for the men before returning to these suburbs in the evenings (Seidman 1984; Schmidt 1992). Over time, the colonial authorities essentially ignored the women and allowed them to sell their goods in town. This satisfied the demand that black men had for these goods, while at the same time, black women began to develop commercial relations with white traders to purchase some of the food they did not grow (Horn 1994). Market trading and beer brewing thus became the first commercial niches that black women occupied in the towns.

By the 1940s, in some cases, the rate of population growth for black women migrants to the major cities exceeded that of men. In Bulawayo, for example, the population of black women grew three times as fast as that of black men from 1944 to 1949 (Phimister 1988). There were serious problems of overcrowding for blacks in major urban areas. During this period, it was not uncommon to find six to eight black residents living in accommodations originally designed for four. As a result, many of the earlier health problems that plagued black mine workers, particularly related to overcrowding and poverty, such as pneumonia and malnutrition, again surfaced as major problems from the 1940s into the postwar period (Phimister 1988; Phimister and van Onselen 1997; Raftopoulos 1997).

In addition to the poor quality of rural land that was the preserve of blacks and the need to meet their tax obligations to the state, blacks were attracted to the cities by the prospects of obtaining manufacturing jobs. Industrial development, however, was not new to Southern Rhodesia in the 1940s; it had begun in earnest in the early twentieth century. As demonstrated by world systems theory and feminist political economy, Zimbabwe (Southern Rhodesia) was restricted in its industrial development to light manufacturing, for the most part by Britain as the colonial power and to some extent by its close, regional ties to South Africa.[4] Nevertheless, industrialization in the colony began with manufacturing that supported mining, the major eco-

---

4. In many respects, the South African state held the upper hand in trade relations with Southern Rhodesia, with the former protecting many of its industries while flooding the Rhodesian market with imports. See Phimister (1988). The situation noted in the text here is demonstrated by feminist political economy because, at its core, feminist political economy builds on world systems theory and comparative political economy to explain the internal and external factors—such as colonialism and imperialism—that restricted the development of African and other Global South nations.

nomic activity in the region during early colonialism. In this regard, mine cyanide, water storage tanks, and light engineering firms were established to support mining (Phimister 1988). The success of tobacco as a primary product export also led to the manufacture of cigarettes. As was the case in several Latin American nations, the period between the two world wars in Southern Rhodesia witnessed the development of some import-substitution industrialization (Frank 1967). Light manufacturing was expanded in the areas of consumer goods for the local market: soap, candles, furniture, fertilizer, food processing (e.g., vegetable oil, bacon, and biscuits), and household utensils. Other light manufacturing endeavors included tools and small machinery, such as pumps, pipes, ladders, drills, and maize grinding mills (Phimister 1988). The postwar years brought significant growth in the industrial labor force. "In 1943, there were 327 manufacturing establishments employing 22, 549 people; by 1953, there were 648 employing 59,220" (Raftopoulos 1997, 57). Many labor migrants from the Southern African region also lived in Bulawayo and Salisbury (now Harare) at this time.

Life in the cities posed serious challenges and provided opportunities for some African women. The intersecting factors of gender, race, and class led to the expression of gender-based violence against women in urban Rhodesia (now Zimbabwe) during colonialism. This was particularly evident during the black nationalist struggles of the 1940s and 1950s, when urban African women were attacked during strikes in Salisbury in 1948 and, later, at the hostel called Carter House in 1956. For the most part, the women who lived in Carter House during this period were single, income-earning black women who worked as shop attendants and as domestic and factory workers in Salisbury. When some of these women ignored a bus boycott organized by the Radical City Youth League and chose to ride public transportation, the bus was stoned and the police fired tear gas (Barnes 1999). In the melee that followed, the hostel was attacked and several women were raped. During this period, some black women workers earned incomes surpassing those of their male peers (Barnes 1999). Living as single women in Carter House was viewed as flaunting one's independence and economic status. These women were challenging African patriarchy while their male counterparts were resisting the power of the state. Thus, these women had to be "put in their place," as noted by Barnes (1999, 145, 147):

Perhaps five or as many as sixteen were raped in the assault on the hostel. . . . The focus of male anger on these particular women illuminates some of the explosive undercurrents of urban gender relations in this period and the abandonment of the spirit of tolerance that prevailed briefly in the early 1950s.

In addition to the ways in which black single women working in the city and living in Carter House defied the conventions of British and African patriarchy as well as their internal colonial status, black women also challenged patriarchy and settler colonialism in other ways. Some women escaped the deprivation of the Tribal Trust Lands by engaging in sex work in the mining compounds and major cities. Although such work frequently entailed violence for many women, some were able to achieve greater equality with men in this process. As Phimister and van Onselen (1997, 46) state:

> Far from being degraded by the transformation of sexual relations into a sale of services, they held their own in "respectable society" with men. Indeed the most successful of these women climbed into the ranks of the petty bourgeoisie as houseowners, landladies and shebeen queens.

The agency of black women suggested by feminist political economy was further evidenced among black Zimbabwean women beer brewers or "shebeen queens." Along with their sisters, who sold food "illegally" in the makeshift urban markets during colonialism, shebeen queens were also engaged in activities that were outlawed by the British colonial state. These women were some of the earliest, most successful businesswomen in the microenterprise sector, selling their product to black men in cities and mining areas. In quoting from local leaders of the Industrial and Commercial Workers' Union (ICU), West (2002, 135) illustrates the illegal, illicit nature of these women's activities while demonstrating that they contributed to family maintenance:

> Thus Charles Mzingeli, the ICU leader . . . openly supported illicit beer brewing. As he told an audience of male workers: "The white people prohibit (beer brewing by the skokiaan queens). . . . They [the white people] are robbers. They arrest you and will not let the women make a few shillings. Similarly, James Mabena, an ICU stalwart in Bulawayo, . . ." considered it reasonable that women (brewers) should be allowed to earn a little money so as to buy necessities. To the Southern Rhodesian Native Association (SRNA) leaders, the skokiaan queens were seen as "veritable centres of vice."

There is no doubt, however, that these women challenged the British colonial state and patriarchy in the success they enjoyed as entrepreneurs. From the earliest years of the colonial state in the early twentieth century, beer brewing provided one of the very few opportunities that some black women had to financially empower themselves in the colonial period:

> Mine wages were so low and beer brewing so profitable that women selling beer to the miners frequently earned more than the miners themselves. According to a 1927 report of the Southern Rhodesian Investigation Department (CID), "It is well known that the sale of Kaffir Beer provides a large income for those who carry on this business. The profits range from any sum up to as much as 50 [pounds] during one weekend according to the population in the locality." The wife of a "police boy" from one mine "left for Nyasaland with over 900 [pounds] in her possession," the CID charged. Another woman had evidence to show she had deposited 800 [pounds] with a European. Practically the whole of these amounts had been obtained by the sale of kaffir beer. (Schmidt 1992, 60)

Despite the economic achievements of some sex workers and beer brewers, most black women experienced significant poverty and deprivation under British settler colonialism and remained outside the formal labor market. Some black men persisted in their resistance to the colonial state through union organization and strikes, such as the first nationwide strike by black workers in October 1945. This Railway Strike, which began with about 2,000 black railway workers and grew to about 8,000, was caused by the introduction of a new system of overtime pay, which benefited most but not the highest-paid black workers. Although the state appeared to lessen their control of black workers through such legislation as the Industrial Conciliation Amendment Act of 1959, which allowed for the formation of multiracial unions, white skilled workers still held a hegemonic role in controlling the unions. Registering a union remained extremely difficult, and general trade unions were not allowed, only skills-based ones (Raftopoulos 1997). Though black men still experienced the wrath of the white settler state, they, as opposed to their sisters, did gain some valuable national organizational experience in the Railway Strike, in the General Strike of 1948, and in the many other actions that followed, which gave them an advantage in the postindependence period.

Following these major strikes, the creation of the Central African Federation in 1953 (comprising Northern and Southern Rhodesia and Nyasaland) appeared to strengthen the power of the resident white population in the area. Despite growing black nationalism in the region, blacks were not consulted in any way about the decision to federate. As a result of the increasing opposition of black nationalists to white colonial domination and whites' opposition to black nationalism, the federation ended a decade after it began. In an attempt to stop all moves toward black majority rule, the Rhodesian government under the leadership of Ian Smith declared the Unilateral Declaration of Independence in 1965. This action resulted in the Liberation War.

On the national level in the decades that followed, however, Zimbabwe's economy began to decline during the liberation struggle against Smith's regime. As a result of Smith's proclamation, sanctions were imposed against Zimbabwe (Rhodesia), leading to substantial decreases in exports from the so-called independent country, as particularly evident in the middle to late 1970s. Zimbabwe (Rhodesia) also experienced major increases in the price of imports during the last decades of colonial rule. Sylvester (1991, 98) summarizes some of the major economic difficulties the nation faced during this period:

> The armed struggle then took its toll: Zambia closed its border with Rhodesia in 1973, and the new government of Mozambique followed suit, which led to higher transport costs, foreign exchange losses, and increased reliance on South Africa. In addition, the Rhodesian government funneled one-fourth of the total budget into defense in 1976 and imposed new restrictions on the use of dwindling foreign exchange. Between 1976 and 1979 imports dropped by about 40 percent, business expectations sank along with profits and there was little in the way of new fixed investment.

Black women again demonstrated their opposition to the colonial state in working alongside men in the liberation struggle. They fought in the Liberation War as well as supported the war effort through the provision of water, food, and clothing (Kazembe 1987; Batezat and Mwalo 1989). The critical roles of women's efforts during the war were particularly evident because the struggle was waged in rural areas and women were clearly the majority population in these regions (Cawthorne 1999). Unfortunately, not only were black women besieged by European-based patriarchy during this period, but they also suffered the patriarchy of African men, who put menstruating and pregnant women in separate training camps, sexually abused some women, and expected them to do the most menial chores (Cawthorne 1999). Such actions point to the linkages between colonialism and patriarchy that Schmidt (1992) and Barnes (1999) illustrate for both European and African men in Zimbabwe's (Rhodesia's) early colonial period (Osirim 2003c; McFadden 2001).

The perspective of feminist political economy provides the means to examine the exploitation of black women and men under colonialism and how this system limited the prospects for significant economic growth and development for the Zimbabwean state in the historical and contemporary periods. Conversely, this perspective also allows us to recognize and acknowledge women's authentic voices and agency in this period—the agency that is demonstrated in their actions against the state, such as their illegal migration to the cities, their work as "shebeen queens," and their taking up of arms against the colonial power. Such actions began to set the stage for women's entrepreneurial pursuits and empowerment in modern Zimbabwe.

## Women, the State, and Entrepreneurship in Contemporary Zimbabwe

Although black African women left the colonial period with some experience of urban entrepreneurship, specifically as market traders and beer brewers, and clearly illustrated their strength in the Liberation War, these women generally entered the postindependence period as the most disadvantaged group in the nation. They had lower levels of educational attainment than men, and due to their race and gender they had no access to formal-sector labor markets. They also experienced patriarchy at the hands of white and black men. The postindependence state under the leadership of Robert Mugabe, however, declared that his government would promote equality between women and men, especially because women had participated in the liberation struggle. He also planned to pursue an economic strategy that he and his party (the Zimbabwe African National Union, ZANU) believed would significantly improve the quality of life of black Africans.

In the first postindependence decade of the 1980s, the government frequently used rhetoric promoting the establishment of a socialist state, but such a polity and economy never materialized. In the early 1980s, Mugabe's government attempted a "growth with equity" strategy, which it hailed as a progressive means for economic development. In effect, the state hoped to increase economic performance, which had substantially declined during the Unilateral Declaration of Independence period and the war, by establishing a mixed economy where state and private investment would coexist in major sectors of the economy. At the same time, the state planned to substantially increase the provision of basic social services to the majority citizens, who were poor and low income. The Mugabe government was very successful in increasing the real rate of growth of gross domestic product (GDP) by 11 percent in 1980. Unfortunately, due to drought, falling prices for primary products, and frequent raids by South Africa, the GDP took a nosedive in 1983, to –3.4 percent. In 1986 and 1988, positive increases in these figures were again noted, with rates of 2.0 and 5.3 percent, respectively, (Stoneman and Cliffe 1989; Sylvester 1991).

In an attempt to further some of its equity goals, the state engaged in a few early efforts to encourage land redistribution. As had been the case during the ninety years of colonial rule, the vast majority of arable land in Zimbabwe was held by white farmers in large-scale plots. Due to the Lancaster House agreement, in which the British government funded part of the land reform during the first postindependence decade, it was clear that there would be no major land expropriation and redistribution in the early years of the new republic—most white farmers would be able to continue their cash crop farms. The provision that the government could only buy land at the market price under a "willing seller, willing buyer" scheme (in which the British government provided half the funding) essentially ensured that it was unlikely that the Mugabe regime would see major capital flight. Although the government had hoped to settle over 162,000 families in the first few years of the new regime, only slightly over 35,000 individuals were resettled on fertile lands by 1987 (Sylvester 1991). It appeared in the early postindependence period that Mugabe had learned from Samora Machel's experience in Mozambique that seizure of white commercial farms could have a devastating effect on the economy—because of both the direct production losses to the state in the absence of such large-scale farmers and the wrath such action would incur in the larger international financial community (Raftopoulos and Compagnon 2003). In keeping with its socialist goals, the postindependence state created several options, such as cooperatives and state farms, in addition to privately owned plots with communal grazing. The vast majority of all resettled families opted for the small, private plots during the period of resettlement in the 1980s. Land reform, however, had progressed all too slowly, and by 1996, only 71,000 families had been resettled (Raftopoulos and Compagnon 2003). The British government also removed its support for this initiative amid claims that, by the mid-1990s, it was primarily the black elite well connected to Mugabe who mainly benefited from the reforms.

The state furthered its efforts toward poor and low-income families through the expansion of basic social services, which they were denied under colonial, white-minority rule. The Mugabe government instituted free primary education for all, with major increases in state spending on education in the first two years after independence, and with smaller increases until 1986. Secondary education was heavily subsidized, and enrollments in the first form of secondary school multiplied nearly eight times, to 170,000 from 1986 to 1989. Total enrollments in educational institutions more than doubled in this period, from 1.3 million in 1980 to 2.8 million in 1986 (Osirim 1994). Free health services were introduced in this period for those earning less than $235 a month (Stoneman 1989). In rural areas, free primary health care and child care services were provided to the public.

In addition to the expansion of services of major benefit to women and children, the postindependence state engaged in two bold initiatives in the first two years after independence. First, it established the Ministry of Community and Cooperative Development and Women's Affairs in 1981 to eliminate all forms of discrimination against women and to ensure their meaningful participation in all spheres of national development. This agency specifically worked to improve women's access to basic social services along with providing greater access to and training for income-generating activities. The leaders of this ministry articulated specific socioeconomic and technical goals on behalf of Zimbabwe's women (Osirim 1994; Ministry of Community and Cooperative Development and Women's Affairs 1981):

1. To assist women to attain economic independence.
2. To ensure the availability and access of adequate social services to women. This included the adequate provision of health care, especially primary care facilities and the creation of day care and community centers.
3. To ensure the development of technology that will lead to reductions in women's work load and enhance their productivity.

With respect to improving income-earning opportunities for women, the government further assigned several tasks to the Ministry of National Resources and Tourism and the Ministry of Trade and Commerce. In the former case, assistance was to be given to women in the marketing of their crafts, particularly in proposed tourist centers. As would be expected, however, the Ministry of Trade and Commerce was responsible for the provision of vital support services for the establishment and maintenance of women's businesses, which, in addition to marketing, included creating favorable access to credit facilities, opening up new trade avenues in which women can easily participate, and keeping an up-to-date register of women's enterprises in the small and informal sectors (Osirim 1994; Ministry of Cooperative and Community Development and Women's Affairs 1981).

The state also provided women entrepreneurs with greater access to capital through Zimbank, in which the government was the major shareholder. Small loans were provided for women entrepreneurs with no collateral requirements. In addition, Zimbank cooperated with the Small Enterprises Development Corporation to provide training for women in business (interview with Dr. Mabokwa, Zimbabwe Ministry of Cooperative and Community Development and Women's Affairs, 1991). With the encouragement of the state and the Women's Ministry, local governments also provided a number of training programs for women interested in acquiring particular skills and/or in starting small enterprises and microenterprises.

After creating the Ministry of Community and Cooperative Development and Women's Affairs, the state improved the legal status of women through the passage of the Legal Age of Majority Act in 1982. This legislation ensured majority status for women and removed them from their position as minors in the state. It also recognized women's contributions to family wealth, providing them with a share of family property in the event of a divorce (Made and Whande 1989). Other national-level legislation prohibited discrimination in employment on the basis of gender, race, age, and creed. The Legal Age of Majority Act and related legislation made it theoretically possible for black women to join the formal labor force and to sign contracts in their own names. This was certainly an important first step in improving the prospects for women in the labor market and as entrepreneurs.

Although the Mugabe regime did improve the position of poor and low-income families, particularly women and children during the 1980s, it also solidified its power. In addition to the small attempts at land reform that, many argued, substantially benefited those close to Mugabe, attempts were also made to indigenize private firms by persuading companies owned by the British and by South Africans to sell their shares of local subsidiaries to the Zimbabwean government. Members of the Zimbabwe African National Union–Patriotic Front (ZANU-PF) and the civil service were significant beneficiaries of high-level positions in such enterprises as well as placement within parastatals. Some other major threats to ZANU-PF's control were removed by the elimination of the Patriotic Front–Zimbabwe African Peoples Union (PF-ZAPU), whose leaders were arrested and others forced to flee on charges of plotting Mugabe's demise. Further potential opposition was removed in this period through the massive killings of the residents of Matabeleland by the Zimbabwean Fifth Brigade between 1982 and 1985 (Raftopoulos and Compagnon 2003).[5]

By the end of the first independence decade, however, Zimbabwe found itself on the brink of economic crisis. The political and economic advances of the Mugabe regime were short-lived, and by 1989, the nation was facing an unemployment rate of approximately 1 million persons, or 50 percent of the potential labor force (Meldrum 1989). Decreasing prices for primary products on the world market, the continued destabilization of the region caused by South Africa, and frequent droughts seriously hampered the state's agenda for growth with equity. Decreasing state revenues combined with pressure from the multilateral agencies led Zimbabwe to establish an Economic Structural Adjustment Program (ESAP) in late 1990/early 1991 as its attempt to deal with the crisis. The acceptance of an IMF–World Bank structural adjustment program had been the path taken by many Southern nations in response to the global economic crisis of the 1980s as a necessary condition to obtain more loans from these institutions. Although the Zimbabwean government insisted that its program was "homegrown" and tailored to meet the nation's needs, the actual program included the same conditions that had been found in other structural adjustment programs throughout the South:

1. trade liberalization,
2. reductions in government expenditures,
3. devaluation,
4. reduction of controls over foreign currency, and
5. restrictions on trade unions.

Additional key targets that the IMF expected Zimbabwe to attain during this period of structural adjustment were (Kanyenze 2003):

1. Achieve GDP growth of 5 percent annually during the period 1991–95.
2. Raise the rate of savings to 25 percent of GDP.
3. Raise investment to 25 percent of GDP.

---

5. The Fifth Brigade was an elite military unit that was trained by the North Korean Army and was initially sent to Matabeleland to suppress about 500 dissidents who were followers of Joshua Nkomo. Estimates presented by the BBC News Service based on interviews with Ndebele residents of the area indicate that thousands were killed; see John Simpson, BBC News (http://news.bbc.co/uk/2/hi/africa/7388214.stm).

4. Achieve export growth of 9 percent a year.
5. Reduce the budget deficit from more than 10 percent of GDP to 5 percent by 1995.
6. Reduce inflation from 17 to 10 percent by 1995.

The paradigm of feminist political economy provides us with the tools to examine structural adjustment programs and their impact on women and men as part of the larger process of globalization. In this process, the international financial institutions and Northern hegemonic governments have encouraged the adoption of the neoliberal agenda (free market policies) and the shrinking of the state (DAWN 1995; Osirim 1998).

These structural adjustment programs are problematic for women and their microbusinesses for three main reasons. First, under these policies, many men lose their formal-sector positions and women are thus expected to increase the support of their families and households. More than 40,000 public-sector employees lost their jobs under this plan in Zimbabwe. Second, at the same time, women entrepreneurs are likely to experience more competition in the workplace from increased numbers of women and men who seek income-earning opportunities in the microenterprise sector as they face diminishing possibilities of earning a living from the formal economy. Third, in most areas of small enterprises and microenterprises, men are likely to be more successful than women because men have greater access to credit and, overall, more significant social capital. Despite the efforts of the Zimbabwean government and many nongovernmental organizations, this study will demonstrate that poor and low-income women entrepreneurs have not been the major beneficiaries of credit and training programs.

In general, structural adjustment programs have had their most deleterious effects on poor women and children. One year after the establishment of ESAP, 6.6 million of the 10.3 million residents in Zimbabwe were estimated to be living in absolute poverty (Kamidza 1994; Osirim 1998). Included among this population are many of the women in this study. The government's removal of subsidies and the institution of user fees for most basic social services meant that poor women and children have borne the major costs of structural adjustment. In the first three years after ESAP was put into effect, the shares of the total national budget allocated to health, transportation, and housing declined, respectively, by more than 20, 40, and 25 percent. The introduction of user fees in hospitals resulted in far fewer women and children seeking medical services. Although UNICEF ranked Zimbabwe as second in Sub-Saharan Africa for its immunization of children against measles at the start of the decade, it had become a killer disease in that country by 1993 because of the decline in the number of children receiving immunizations (UNICEF 1993; Kamidza 1994). Health care was further jeopardized by the major increases in the price of drugs and the exodus of many health professionals from the country (Nyambuya 1994). The reintroduction of school fees meant that many families had to make choices about which children to send to school. Under these dire economic circumstances, many families made the choice to remove their daughter(s) from school. Finally, unstable economic conditions combined with shifting gender roles for men have resulted in an escalation of violence against women (Green 1999; Osirim 2001, 2003c).

In addition to assuming an increased share of the household and family expenses (and for many women heading households, all the costs), some women have attempted to respond to the economic crisis by forming and/or seeking assistance from local associations and nongovernmental organizations. For many market women, for example, joining a rotating credit scheme or "round" has enabled them to keep their businesses afloat, maintain their families, and empower themselves.

Needless to say, ESAP failed in Zimbabwe. It worsened conditions for the poor, especially women and children, and if anything, it intensified the economic crisis. The state did not meet the IMF targets for several reasons, including recurrent droughts, dismal export performance, and high inflation resulting from excessive government borrowing to finance its even severely reduced operations. After the initial failure to meet IMF goals, the IMF suspended disbursement of funds to Zimbabwe under the Enhanced Structural Adjustment Facility in September 1995 and then moved Zimbabwe to a shorter program. By 1999, given continued poor economic performance and the impending political crisis, the IMF withdrew from Zimbabwe (Kanyenze 2003).

In the chapters that follow, this study examines the work and family lives of 157 women entrepreneurs through the lens of feminist political economy. Thus, particular attention will be paid to how the global economy, the state, and nongovernmental organizations—as well as the variables of race, class, and gender—have shaped these entrepreneurs' experiences at the end of the twentieth century. In turn, this study will also explore how these women entrepreneurs have responded to these structural conditions, demonstrated their agency, and empowered themselves.

# Chapter 3

# Crocheters as Dynamic Innovators and Producers of Material Culture

Of the various segments of the microenterprise sector discussed in this study,[1] crocheting is the one activity that is most unique to Zimbabwe and most directly tied to the colonial enterprise. Very little attention has been paid to the diversification of women's microenterprises and small-scale business activities in Zimbabwe, and crochet work is clearly an understudied area in the social science literature on this subject. Further, as compared with other handicrafts, crocheting is perhaps the most prominent woman's activity in the nation with a fairly long history (Barnes 1999). In the contemporary period, crocheting, combined with knitting,[2] is a subsector of microenterprises in which many women have demonstrated their business acumen and creativity and contributed to the development of material culture in their society. Over the past few decades, some crocheters and knitters have attempted to expand their "cultural production" in this area and the profitability of their enterprises by engaging in cross-border trade with South Africa and with other nations in the Southern Africa region.

During the colonial period, many black women learned how to crochet and knit from white women who taught this craft in women's clubs and to individuals. One example of this is the African Women's Club, founded in

---

1. Microenterprises in this study are defined as businesses with no more than five employees. Of course, many of the activities in this study contain only one person as owner-operator.

2. Although most women entrepreneurs in this field are engaged in both crocheting and knitting, crocheting is the activity that is more unique in Zimbabwe and the one with which Zimbabwean women are most closely identified. In this regard, the term "crocheting" will be used more often in this chapter.

1937, which taught knitting, sewing, and other crafts to its members. Though urban women's clubs became quite established in the 1950s, most of these clubs were begun by white women and had few women from black African townships as members (Barnes 1999). Black women also learned knitting and crocheting in their home economics classes in schools (along with cooking and sewing), where education was tailored toward race and gender to provide these women with the skills they would need for their house-holds, as well as for the homes in which they worked as domestics (Schmidt 1992). These realities demonstrate the central role that feminist political economy and intersectionality play in "making sense" of the lives of black Zimbabwean women. Unlike the situation today, women who were cro-cheters during the colonial period generally enjoyed somewhat higher levels of educational attainment (because many of them learned this craft in mission schools) than the majority of their sisters, and they were able to parlay their skills into economically successful enterprises. As noted by Barnes (1999, 32), this skill provided some women with a rare level of eco-nomic independence:

> In the 1950s, many people hadn't known about [crocheting]. I taught my niece how to hold a crochet [hook]. She is now in South Africa, selling doilies. I told her, "Use a crochet, there is life in it." People were not yet aware that crocheting has got money, has got life, so that you won't bother our husband [i.e., need to ask him for money].

From the colonial period to the present, crocheting has remained a craft that also points to the strength and importance of social capital and social networks, because women frequently transmit their crocheting skills within and across generations as well as among peers. An Ndebele woman in my study illustrated the important role that social networks played in encour-aging her to become an entrepreneur in this field:

> When I was a child, I wanted to be a doctor or a police officer, but I failed to do this. I finished primary school, attended secondary school, did my O-levels, and got four passes in Ndebele, commerce, geography, and math-ematics. I did not pass English, so I am now studying English and ac-counts in evening school. . . . What my mother taught me, crocheting, I am earning my living through this. I can manage to do any kind of jobs at home as well. I was encouraged by some of my friends to start the

crochet business. They were seeing that I was trying to see where to start my life. They suggested that I might be able to earn a living this way. (interview with Sharon Dube, a crocheter, Bulawayo, 1997)

Crocheting is also one of the very few segments of the microenterprise sector in Sub-Saharan Africa where subcontracting plays a major role in production, building on and expanding women's social networks.[3] Although they are very committed to providing higher education for their daughters and hope that they will pursue careers, crocheters today often teach their daughters how to crochet and knit as a type of insurance—a way of earning a living if all else fails. Though many of the crocheters in my sample have experienced financial difficulties in their firms, especially under the government's Economic Structural Adjustment Program (ESAP), their enterprises have enabled them to make substantial contributions to their immediate and extended families.

This chapter explores the business and family lives of women who began crochet firms in Harare and Bulawayo, Zimbabwe. Why did these women enter this occupation? How can we understand the gendered nature of the work that women do in this sector and their efforts to combine these activities with their domestic responsibilities? What particular challenges do they face as businesswomen in the microenterprise sector? To what extent did government policies and globalization in the 1990s affect the operation of their firms? What contributions have these women made to their families, their communities, and, in turn, to their nation?

## Demographic Profile of the Crocheters and the Decision to Start a Business

During fieldwork visits to Harare and Bulawayo, Zimbabwe, in 1991, 1994, and 1997, in-depth interviews were conducted with fifty-seven crocheters at their worksites located at or near various shopping centers. The ethnic distribution of this sample is very similar to the overall distribution of the major ethnic groups in the country. Seventy percent (forty) of the crocheters

---

3. Subcontracting has been an important activity associated with the informal/microenterprise sectors in East Asia and in Latin America. In many of these cases, large-scale firms subcontract with small enterprises and microenterprises in an effort to reduce their costs and increase the profitability of their firms. See Portes, Castells, and Benton (1989).

were Shona, the largest ethnic group in Zimbabwe, which makes up about 80 percent of the population, and 18 percent (ten) were Ndebele, the second-largest group in the country with about 16 percent of the population. As is the case among hairdressers, seamstresses, and market traders, some crocheters are members of ethnic groups based in other nations in Southern Africa, such as in Zambia and South Africa. Approximately 12 percent (seven) of this sample are members of non-Zimbabwean ethnic groups. This diversity points to the significant movement of goods, ideas, and populations throughout the Southern African region.[4]

The mean and median age of participants in this sample was thirty-eight years. Like their sisters in hairdressing and sewing, the vast majority of crocheters had received some formal education, with "some secondary schooling" constituting the largest single category of educational attainment. Approximately 35 percent (nineteen) of the respondents had received some secondary education, whereas another four crocheters had successfully completed their Ordinary Level (O-level) examinations and thus completed the first level of secondary school. One entrepreneur in this sample did receive some postsecondary education at a technical college, although she did not attain her O-level certificate. At the lower end of the educational spectrum, 30 percent (seventeen) of the businesswomen received less than six years of primary schooling, while 30 percent (seventeen) of the sample completed their primary education. Only one crocheter had not received any formal education.

During their childhood and adolescence, the vast majority of these entrepreneurs wanted to become nurses. Other businesswomen expressed desires to enter other gender-typed occupations, such as teaching or working as a flight attendant. Although two women mentioned that they had wanted to become seamstresses or crocheters since their childhoods, for the most part, these respondents were not interested in the world of microbusiness. A few women did differ from the norm of gender-typed occupations and mentioned that they wanted to become doctors or policewomen—the latter perhaps because of the power and authority that seemed to accompany such

---

4. Beginning in the early years of colonialism, black women from South Africa, Nyasaland (Malawi), and Northern Rhodesia (Zambia) had migrated to Southern Rhodesia (Zimbabwe). Women were absent from early studies of labor migration in Southern Africa, but Barnes and other feminist scholars have corrected this record in recent historical studies. Several of the early women migrants to Zimbabwe were prominent teachers, nurses, missionaries, and activists, and others were recorded by the police as prostitutes. See Barnes (2002).

a position.[5] Further, all these formal-sector positions were likely viewed as desirable because they were believed to provide a good, regular salary.

Although these businesswomen had high aspirations for more educational attainment and formal-sector positions in their youths, they were unable to realize these dreams for the same three main reasons that such occupations eluded market traders, hairdressers, and seamstresses. First, the vast majority of these women were blocked from entering formal-sector jobs because they lacked the requisite number of O-level passes that were the first criterion for obtaining professional, managerial, clerical, and sales positions in the formal sector. The fact that these women were largely from poor and low-income backgrounds and generally had many domestic and child care responsibilities throughout most of their youth left them little time for academic pursuits. Compared with their brothers of similar ages, young girls, especially those of secondary school age, would be saddled with many more daily responsibilities for the preparation of meals, dishwashing, laundry, and child care. Though young men did have household tasks assigned to them, these tended to be jobs such as car washing and making home repairs, which were not usually daily responsibilities.[6] Also, because they came from poor backgrounds, their families did not possess the resources to provide private tutoring, extra books, or supplies to facilitate their educational experience. Thus, it does not come as a surprise that many respondents in this sample did not pass five O-level examinations and thus did not receive their certificates for completing the first level of secondary school. Students who wished to retake the examinations had to reenroll in school and thus pay tuition and any additional costs associated with school attendance. Such possibilities were generally out of reach for poor families. Without this credential, these young women experienced structural blockage, which prevented them from obtaining formal-sector positions.

Second, many of these young women did not come from families that could afford to provide secondary education for all their children. In fact, when resources were so scarce, decisions were most often made to educate sons over daughters because the former remain a part of a father's family

5. It is also possible that several of the respondents mentioned "police officer" as a desired occupation because many of those interviewed at the Newlands Shopping Center were married to policemen and other officials in the nearby prison.

6. In her work on the division of labor among U.S. families, Arlie Hochschild (1989) discusses how women bear the major responsibilities for chores that have to be done on a daily basis, while most men have greater flexibility in their household tasks which most often do not require daily attention.

until death and continue to have obligations to support that family, whereas young women most often marry and join their husbands' families.

Third, female high school students who became pregnant while they were enrolled in school were forced to terminate their formal education. Many crocheters in this study experienced these problems and therefore, were unable to complete secondary school and obtain formal-sector jobs:

[I] was raised to work hard and not to borrow to pay for what I can't afford or don't need. I wanted to go to school and pass well, and learn to be a doctor or a nurse or even be an air hostess. I really wanted to be an air hostess, but there was no money for school. (interview with Maidei Mwambo, a crocheter, Harare, 1994)

Yes, I wanted to be a teacher, but I got pregnant and had to leave school. Later on, I became too ill to continue my education. (interview with Tsitsi, a crocheter, Harare, 1994)

I wanted to be a nurse. I did not have the qualifications and needed more O-level passes in order to go on. Shona Bible knowledge and human and social biology were what I passed. (interview with F. Tekenende, a crocheter, Harare, 1994)

Wanted to become a teacher. . . . Could not pursue this because my father had no money for me to go to school beyond standard four. (interview with Lisamiso, a crocheter, Bulawayo, 1997)

Although completing the first level of secondary school and receiving the O-level certificate was out of reach for the vast majority of participants in this study, many of the crocheters did gain additional knowledge and skills through training programs and other forms of informal education. Forty-six percent (twenty-six) of these entrepreneurs supplemented their primary or secondary school education with training in evening schools, community centers, churches, and local clubs. Five of these businesswomen enrolled in academic courses that they had initially failed in secondary school in an attempt to gain their secondary school certificates. Most of these respondents were either unsuccessful in their attempts or were still enrolled in these programs at the time of this study. A few businesswomen had pursued secretarial courses, which included instruction in typing, shorthand, and sometimes bookkeeping. Conversely, most women who continued to receive education beyond formal schooling were receiving instruction in home economics or domestic science. Among the skills they acquired were sewing, crocheting, knitting, and embroidery. Needless to say, these skills either directly benefited these women in their current enterprises and/or provided them with a few options for other types of work they might pursue in the microenterprise sector. In fact, during periods of economic crisis, it was not unusual to see women employing multiple skills or engaging in multiple occupations to maintain themselves and their families. Thus, crocheters involved in cross-border trade in South Africa also frequently sold dresses or other items of women's clothing that they or a friend had made.

In addition to the roles of formal schooling, evening schools, clubs, and other training programs, crocheting and knitting skills were mainly transmitted through women's networks. Though crocheting and knitting were sometimes part of primary school curricula and were also taught in community centers, churches, and clubs, most women learned these skills from female relatives, especially their mothers, sisters, and aunts. A few women in this study also learned how to crochet from female friends. In fact, women's social capital remains a very important factor in the emergence of subcontracting arrangements in crocheting enterprises, because women often rely on their relatives and close female friends and neighbors to assist them in making large crocheted items, such as tablecloths and bedspreads. Women who help with making these items are generally compensated on a piecework basis.

All in all, though women entrepreneurs experienced severe structural blockage with respect to educational attainment and acquiring formal-sector positions, they manifested a high level of commitment to education and skills development over the course of their lives. Unfortunately, the heavy demands of maintaining their households and their commitments to their extended families and enterprises, coupled with their lack of capital and the economic crisis, have made it extremely difficult for them to successfully complete a course of study that could lead to enhanced socioeconomic mobility. Their dedication and belief in the power of education to transform lives, however, remains quite strong and is a value they have fostered in their children.

Fifty-six percent (thirty-two) of these businesswomen held other positions before their current roles in crocheting. As would be expected, given their levels of educational attainment, most of their earlier work experience was also in the microenterprise sector. Many of these entrepreneurs were previously involved in sales as produce or clothing vendors or cashiers in small shops. Such sales experience is likely to serve as a valuable asset to these women in their current positions as entrepreneurs in the microenterprise sector. Some of the crocheters also had prior experience as domestic workers, laundresses, or farmers. Three of these entrepreneurs had worked as temporary teachers or teacher trainers before starting their current businesses.

About 40 percent (twenty-three) of the respondents were supplementing their earnings from crocheting and knitting with sales in other areas. Most of these women are selling stone carvings, the indigenous Shona art form that is widely associated with Zimbabwe. Though many entrepreneurs added the sale of soapstone carvings to their crocheting businesses by 1997, many women in this study noted that they had been selling such items on the side to supplement their earnings since at least 1991. The carving of stone figures remains within the purview of men, but as the economic crisis intensified, women were increasingly found selling these carvings, often alongside men.[7] Crocheters—particularly those located in some of the major tourist-oriented shopping centers, such as Newlands in Harare and the center at City Hall in Bulawayo—recognized the demand for such items among tourists and attempted to respond by providing items that Europeans and Americans generally identified as more "uniquely African" than most of the other crocheted and knitted items they made. Other businesswomen in this study tried to augment their earnings through the sale of produce or handmade women's clothing.

Therefore, women in this study began crocheting enterprises and engaged in other activities in the microenterprise sector to help support their families. Women in Zimbabwe view their responsibilities to their children and to their extended families as major dimensions of their identities (Bay 1982; Horn 1994; Osirim 1995). Due to the blocked opportunities that prevented them from entering formal-sector occupations, these women began crocheting businesses based on the skills they had acquired in school, clubs, and training programs and/or from their female relatives. These entrepreneurs were most often encouraged by relatives to establish crochet businesses:

> I had wanted to be a nurse, but I failed O-levels and didn't have the marks to continue. Don't think I learned anything in school, well, they taught me to sew, read, write, cook, and plow. Because it was dull at school,

---

7. The crossing of gendered occupational boundaries is also noted in other fields and regions during periods of economic crisis and adjustment. Though women historically were involved in fruit and vegetable vending, more men were participating in such activities during the time of these interviews in the major markets in Harare and Bulawayo. In her earlier work, Gracia Clark (1994) also noted that men were increasingly found trading in such commodities during the period of economic crisis and adjustment in Ghana.

I wanted to be a housewife. School was hard for me. I wanted to be a housewife because it's the only thing I thought I'd be able to do. My mother taught me how to knit. My mother-in-law later helped by giving the money and advice. She told me to start this business so I can have money. She found the space for me where I now sell. She is in the same type of business and has two ladies working for her. (interview with Joyce, a crocheter, Harare, 1997)

I went to school for seven years and passed grade seven. My parents didn't have enough money for secondary education. My aim was to go further in school, but I failed because my parents didn't have the money. My aunt taught me how to crochet doilies, and I learned to sew table-cloths in school. I wanted to be a teacher. I started this business because I know my only talent is crocheting. My aunt, because she also crocheted, encouraged me. (interview with Maube, a crocheter, Bulawayo, 1997)

Many women commented on the difficulties their husbands were experiencing in trying to provide for their families, and these women saw starting a business as a way to help. Feminist political economy provides us with the tools to analyze how globalization in the form of ESAP in Zimbabwe results in massive unemployment and underemployment, which leads women to seek new or additional avenues to help support their families. There is no doubt that material needs provided a major incentive for starting these enterprises and that these women had few viable options:

I saw that what my husband was earning was not enough to support us. . . . I would knit for the family, and they never paid me back, so I decided that if I did it professionally, I would get paid. (interview with Maidei Mwambo, a crocheter, Harare, 1994)

I would like to help my husband because his money was too little and short. To do something like dressmaking, I would have to go for training and I did not have enough money. (interview with Kusyedza, a crocheter, Harare, 1997)

I was looking for money. It is better to do this work because it pays more than domestic work and because I can get something everyday to eat. If I do some domestic work, I have to wait until the end of the month to get money. (interview with Ancilar Mee, a crocheter, Bulawayo, 1997)

In addition to providing crocheting and knitting instruction to these entrepreneurs, relatives played a major role in providing start-up capital to establish their businesses. The majority of these crocheters (61 percent, or thirty-five) received part or all of their initial capital from relatives. Compared with their sisters in sewing and hairdressing, crocheters were somewhat more likely to receive all their start-up capital from their husband or other relatives and somewhat less likely to start their businesses based on their personal savings. The fact that fewer crocheters compared with hairdressers and seamstresses began their businesses solely with their savings is to be expected, given crocheters' lower-status occupational histories. The entrepreneurs' siblings, as well as other female and male relatives, also contributed to establishing their enterprises.

Most crocheters in this study described themselves as lower class. Approximately 54 percent (thirty-one) of these entrepreneurs provided this self-assessment. The next largest group of businesswomen, 30 percent (seventeen) defined themselves as middle class. Three women mentioned that they were lower middle class, and one woman stated that she was upper middle class. A few women declined to answer this question. The entrepreneurs in this study largely based their responses on their perceptions of their occupational attainment in comparison with the broader population. Despite their class position, however, most of these women remained optimistic about the prospects for improving their socioeconomic status and that of their families in the future. They believed that their enterprises provided (and would continue to provide) opportunities for building human capital among their children and/or other relatives.

## Responsibilities for the Household and the Family: Understanding the Contemporary Division of Labor

Like market traders, hairdressers, and seamstresses, the majority of crocheters in this study were married. About 63 percent (thirty-six) of the crocheters were married at the time of the interviews, and three of these women stated that they were in polygamous marriages. Fourteen percent (eight) of the respondents were divorced, and 11 percent (six) were widowed. Two women stated that they were separated from their husbands at the time of the interview. Only 9 percent (five) of the businesswomen were single. Although the vast majority of adult women in Zimbabwe are married, the percentage of married crocheters in this study might be slightly higher than the norm among this population because this study oversampled the entrepreneurs at the Newlands Shopping Center site, the largest crochet market in Harare. This market was located immediately adjacent to a prison and a police barracks, and many of the women working there were married to guards and police officers employed at these facilities. Considering the convenience of this market's location, the structural blockage that the women working there generally experienced in the labor market, and the escalating costs of public transportation during the period of economic crisis and adjustment, their choice of this site as their workplace was an especially rational one.

When asked to describe their relationship with their current or former spouse, women generally responded that the relationship is "good, okay, or satisfactory." Very few entrepreneurs defined their relationships in glowing terms. Women who appeared pleased about their marriages generally mentioned that they were happy because they did not experience physical violence in their relationships and/or because their husbands provided financially for them and their children. Poor and low-income businesswomen in this study seemed especially concerned about material needs, which is certainly understandable given their socioeconomic status and the crisis in the nation. A crocheter in Bulawayo remarked:

> I'm happy because he does not hit me. I live nicely. He gives me money. (interview with Good Sucy, a crocheter, Bulawayo, 1997)

Another Bulawayo crocheter remarked:

> We were living nicely because if he gets money, he brings it to the house, even if the money was so small, we would just use it together for our children. (interview with Lisamiso, a crocheter, Bulawayo, 1997)

A crocheter in Harare similarly commented:

> We live fine. We don't argue or fight. I am okay with my responsibilities. (interview with Tsitsi, a crocheter, Harare, 1994)

Compared with the majority of her peers, another crocheter in Harare presented an unusual assessment of her marriage, although her comments also suggest her material concerns:

> We have a happy life. We love and care for each other. We used to have arguments, maybe there would be a small problem and an argument would

start in the past. Very few of these now, maybe if he misused the money, then an argument would start. (interview with Chipo, a crocheter, Harare, 1994)

In addition to the possibilities of physical violence, women discussed two other major problems that they experienced in their relationships: the possibility of their husbands taking another wife, a girlfriend(s), or an outside wife; and partners who did not provide financially for their families. These two problems are clearly related, because when Zimbabwean men become involved in additional relationships outside marriage or within the confines of polygamous marriages, some resources are most often diverted from the first to the other relationships. Because both customary and statutory law are recognized in Zimbabwe, polygamous marriages conducted under the guidelines of customary law are recognized. Although polygamous marriages are not as common in Zimbabwe as they are in West Africa, for example, many Zimbabwean men regard marriages as potentially polygamous. Though the women in this study acknowledged this possibility, they were generally not comfortable with such relationships and noted that they frequently led to the termination of the first marriage. Such polygamous relationships were especially problematic for poor and low-income women because of the loss (or potential loss) of scarce financial resources for their children. In studying marriage patterns in contemporary African societies, Collette Suda (2007, 66–67) observes that a new pattern of "formal monogamy" is practiced with essentially the same results as noted above:

Formal monogamy is often practiced alongside delocalized, clandestine, and informal polygamy involving "outside wives" and "outside children" who participate in a parallel programme and are usually condemned by the "inside wives" for messing up their lives. . . . For instance, family disintegration under conditions of extreme poverty have had undesirable effects on the well-being of women and children, some of whom have turned to street life in order to survive under some of the most difficult, deprived and deplorable circumstances in human experience.

In considering this issue, several entrepreneurs expressed sentiments similar to those noted by Suda:

Problems because he wants to take another wife. He is never at home. That is why it is better to sell things to help the children. Husband has another wife; he doesn't tell me, but I have seen the other wife. I think he has another child from that marriage. . . . Husband sometimes pays for school fees if I force him. He doesn't care for us. I pay for food, medicine, uniforms, books, and other clothing. (interview with Mary, a crocheter, Harare, 1991)

I am currently married. Life of people is very difficult. I stay with children at home. He [my husband] has another wife, so sometimes I am alone for two weeks. Not happy, because how can I be happy when my husband is not around? Last year, husband married another woman. I feel very cross, only because a woman cannot do anything. Don't talk to him about her, because just fight each other. No hitting, just yelling. (interview with Samantha, a crocheter, Harare, 1994)

We are still married but separated. Minor problems at home. We got along nicely, then he didn't want to buy clothes for the child and he left it up to me to pay for the child and to buy things for the house. He used his money on beer and girlfriends, and so on. . . . We talk now, separated though; . . . I feel now that it is not good. My child is from us both; she now depends just on me. If the father does not contribute, my child will feel like he is not her father in the future. Changes? Yes, I would like to see a change in the way that I am living. I would like to separate from my parents and go to my husband. The main problem is that where my husband is, the house is next to his parents, then he leaves everything to his parents. If he doesn't come home, his parents tell me what to do. My husband is the only son. (interview with F. Tekenende, a crocheter, Harare, 1994)

Although entrepreneurs in this study have very strong bonds with members of their extended families, relationships with their spouses' families were sometimes strained. Since women join their husbands' families upon marriage, the quality of such relationships is especially important in sustaining a marriage. As noted by a divorced crocheter:

My ex-husband and I used to get along, but the problem was that I had girl children only and my mother-in-law began influencing my husband to divorce me because he was the only boy in the family and they wanted to keep the family name going through the birth of a boy (grandson). (interview with Livinia, a crocheter, Harare, 1997)

The entrepreneurs in this sample had an average of four children. This compares favorably with the average fertility rate for women of child-bearing age in Zimbabwe, which was four in the mid-1990s (Chant and McIlwaine 1998). Only four of the respondents had no children; three of these women were single and one was divorced.

In attempting to understand the range of responsibilities that the entrepreneurs in this study had for their families and households, a consideration of their fertility rates only tells part of the story. The businesswomen in this study lived in very extended households and had responsibilities for other relatives far beyond their nuclear families. The mean and median number of persons who regularly spent the night in these crocheters' homes was six, with a range from two to eleven. Though this number generally included the entrepreneur, her spouse, and her children, in many cases it also included other extended family members, such as the nieces and nephews of the crocheter or her husband. These family members resided in very close quarters, with many homes containing only two or three rooms. Although most of these relatives did not provide financial assistance to the household, young girls or women most often helped with housework and child care and young men assumed some household duties. Adult daughters and sons who were working outside the home did financially contribute to the household. Like many of their Zimbabwean sisters, some of these entrepreneurs brought younger relatives from rural areas to live with them and assist with domestic duties and child care. In return, these relatives often received "in-kind" payments—room and board and/or opportunities to pursue formal education or enroll in other training programs. In some cases, these relatives were referred to as "house girls" or domestic workers. Some nieces, nephews, and cousins might have also resided in the businesswoman's home if their parents were deceased or unable to care for their children. There is a long-history of informal adoption in Sub-Saharan African societies, which has significantly increased with the HIV/AIDS pandemic. Occasionally, older relatives from rural areas also lived with the entrepreneurs in the study in an effort to obtain medical care in the city. As a crocheter stated:

> Some come because if they get sick, they can't see the doctors where they live so they'll see a doctor near me. I give money to those living with me. (interview with Barbara, a crocheter, Harare, 1991)

Twenty-two percent (thirteen) of these entrepreneurs employed a relative in their businesses. These workers might have crocheted or knitted some of the clothing, doilies, or other goods, crocheted part of a tablecloth or bed-spread, stitched together parts for one of the latter items, or washed the goods to be sold. In some cases, businesswomen provided housing for their workers:

> The worker helps with housework. In our customs, that is what we used to do—have the worker live with us. The worker does some housework and washes the crocheted goods. (interview with Rudo, a crocheter, Harare, 1991)

Such activities on the part of the entrepreneur helped build her social capital, which assisted in the operation and success of her business. These networks, however, were also important in providing child care and other assistance for crocheters, especially for those involved in long-distance trade.

The businesswomen in this study also had significant responsibilities for relatives and in-laws who did not live with them. Seventy-two percent (forty-one) of the sample provided money, food, and clothing to their relatives and in-laws who were not living with them. Though women join their husbands' families upon marriage and relationships with their in-laws remain important, the majority of crocheters provided some financial assistance first and foremost to their parents and other biological relatives. The majority of the sample (thirty-two) gave financial or in-kind support to their parents, siblings, or other relatives. Of these women, six entrepreneurs provided some support for both their in-laws and their blood relatives. Although some women did mention that they made regular cash payments to their parents—for example, Z\$30 to Z\$50[8] a month—most women stated that they did not give regularly scheduled payments to their parents and in-laws—they gave as often as they possibly could. They did view this support and the assistance that they provided for relatives living with them as focal parts of their web of responsibilities and important aspects of their identities as daughters, sisters, and aunts.

With respect to responsibilities within the household, crocheters, like their sisters in market trading, sewing, and hairdressing, were largely responsible for the housework and most of the child care in their homes. Given the number of extended family members living with these crocheters and the responsibilities accorded to their own children to assist with child care and housework, the burden for domestic responsibilities did not rest

---

8. At the beginning of this research in 1991, US\$1.00 = Z\$2.30. By 1999, US\$1.00 = Z\$37.00.

solely on these businesswomen. Conversely, Zimbabwean women, like their sisters throughout most of Sub-Saharan Africa, are viewed as responsible for the domestic sphere, even if it means supervising the work of other relatives or domestic workers. Though some of the women in this study did supervise domestic workers in household tasks, the majority of them still had many chores to perform, such as cooking, washing, and cleaning—largely tasks off limits to men. Their children, especially their daughters, performed many of the household chores, as explained by a crocheter in Bulawayo:

> Husband does not help out at home. No, you know, African men don't really work around the house. Kids help me with the housework. (interview with Rose, a crocheter, Bulawayo, 1991)

A very few crocheters noted that, unlike their peers, their husbands did assist with domestic duties:

> Husband had duties? Yes, he instructs the children on what to do. He sometimes buys the food, and so on. He does some of the cooking and cleaning. We help each other type thing. (interview with Rungano, a crocheter, Harare, 1994)

> My husband used to work for a company before. . . . He worked as a bricklayer from 1991 to 1993; now he is self-employed. . . . When I have someone who needs a jersey [sweater] quickly, my husband will help with the cooking; he also helps with the children. (interview with Chipo, a crocheter, 1994, Harare)

Most husbands who did work around the house generally confined their activities to gardening, household work, and making car repairs, and they were rarely engaged in the domestic and child care tasks that needed to be performed on a daily basis.

Compared with their peers in hairdressing and sewing, however, far fewer crocheters were able to officially hire domestic workers to assist them in their households. Twenty-three percent (thirteen) of these respondents hired women to help them in their domestic duties. Unlike relatives who performed such duties, these women received regular salaries for their work. Given that women and wives are largely viewed as responsible for the upkeep of the home, the entrepreneurs most often used their earnings to provide wages to the domestic workers. Yet even with the assistance of a domestic worker, businesswomen in this study still had many responsibilities for the maintenance of the household:

> I do the most I can. I make sure my children are well fed, whether my husband has clean clothes for work and whether the housemaid is doing her duties well. My husband does not really help out; only helps out when I am ill. . . . When we first married, he used to assist me more but when we hired a housemaid he stopped. I usually spend three to four hours per day doing chores—cooking, cleaning, and laundry. (interview with Petros, a crocheter, Harare, 1994)

With respect to financial resources for the household and family, women and men in this sample are increasingly sharing the expenses. Although, historically, men were expected to pay for the major household costs— including rent, utilities, food, and school fees—women have played a significant role in maintaining the family both financially and psychologically in the contemporary period. Given the fact that many men lost their positions in the formal sector during the economic crisis and the resulting ESAP, women have had to cover a growing share of family expenses:

> My responsibilities have changed. When he is unemployed, things became more difficult. [I] have more responsibility with fees, food, rent, and school fees. My husband is currently unemployed. (interview with Sipiwe Sithole, a crocheter, Bulawayo, 1994)

At the very least, in these families, crocheters paid for clothing for themselves and their children as well as all or part of the food bill. In addition, these businesswomen were increasingly paying for school fees and the indirect costs associated with attending school, such as uniforms, books, and transportation. A married crocheter whose husband had taken another wife commented:

> Husband sometimes pays for school fees if [I] force him. He doesn't care for us. I pay for food, medicine, uniforms, books, and other clothing. Sometimes husband gives us Z$50 but doesn't help much. It's very expensive to be a wife because children cry to me for things—not father. (interview with Mary, a crocheter, Harare, 1991)

A more common response, which reveals the shared pattern of paying for household expenses among crocheters, was the following:

[I] pay for school fees. My husband pays the food, medicine, books, and other clothing. We both pay for uniforms. . . . [My] husband pays for housing, and we both pay for utilities and clothing. (interview with Love More, a crocheter, Bulawayo, 1997)

When compared with their peers in sewing and hairdressing, crocheters were sharing more of the overall costs of maintaining their households with their spouses. Significant sharing of responsibilities between the entrepreneurs and their husbands was even noted with respect to decisionmaking about the use of money. There are at least two major explanations for the more equal roles noted between women and men in this regard. In Zimbabwean families, as well as in many other Sub-Saharan African families, women's and men's finances are generally kept separately, and as the crocheters in this study assumed a role more equal with their husbands' in financially maintaining the family, women's decision-making power concerning the use of money increased. With respect to the former, although women are either completely or partially paying for many more household expenses than in the past, women and men rarely have joint accounts. Therefore, after possibly giving their husbands some money toward the payment of rent and/or utilities, women are generally paying for several expenses from their own revenues. This includes payment of school fees, books, uniforms, other clothing, and food for their families. As noted above, women have their separate accounts; and for the most part, they try to maintain secrecy about their earnings and savings from their husbands, lest the latter reduce their contributions to family maintenance. Downing (1995) noted similar findings in her work on women's microenterprise development in several African and Caribbean countries. In such cases, then, the Zimbabwean crocheters were exerting control over their own financial resources. Further, there is generally a positive correlation between financial contributions to the household and the level of decision-making power held by a woman or a man as the head of a household (Blood and Wolfe 1960; Pyke 1994; Andersen 1997; Lips 2005). Thus, as women have assumed greater responsibility for the financial maintenance of the family, their influence on decision making in the household has increased. In a very few cases in this sample, however, husbands still made more of the major decisions about how money would be used. As noted by crocheters in Bulawayo:

I give money to my husband so we can both use money. [My] money is too little so he [has] always been the husband. He makes the money decisions because he's the man and must do that. (interview with Amanda, a crocheter, Bulawayo, 1994)

I pay for all the kids' school fees, except me and my husband split uniforms. . . . My husband decides how money is saved or spent; I decide what to buy, what schools the kids attend; and we both decide what bills to pay and how to discipline the kids. (interview with Sibongile, a crocheter, Bulawayo, 1997)

Mothers who were divorced from their husbands in this study remarked that they were largely responsible for all the household expenses. Ex-husbands were not observed contributing to the support of their children. Sometimes, the mothers received assistance from their relatives. Responses such as the following were quite common among these crocheters:

I pay for all of the children's expenses. When I was married to my husband, [he] used to do most of the things, though I was also employed and we would assist each other. . . . I am staying in my parent's home. I get a little help from my brother for food, and he helps me pay for utilities. I pay for medical, repairs, and clothing, in addition to the costs of sending my children to school. (interview with Livinia, a crocheter, Harare, 1997)

During the time I was married, husband helped, but now he gives nothing. . . . I provide all the financial support. It is better now that I am not married, but I do more . . . [I wake up] between 5:30 and 7 AM and wash the clothes. At 6 PM, when I return, I iron. I make all the decisions regarding the family. (interview with Ruth Nyamayabo, a crocheter, Bulawayo, 1997)

Under Shona and Ndebele customary law, children belong to their fathers' family. With economic crisis and adjustment, however, fewer men are seeking custody of their children in the case of divorce. More and more children are remaining with their mothers, and the tasks of both financial support and childrearing are resting mainly on their shoulders. This was especially noted among the crocheters in this study, who reported that they very seldom, if ever, received support from their children's fathers. Thus, several separated or divorced businesswomen in this study were bearing increased financial, social, and emotional responsibilities in their families as heads of households. This closely parallels developments in the larger society, where the percentage of female-headed households has been increasing in the nation and in the region, and at the time of this study was about 30 percent of all households in Zimbabwe (Neft and Levine 1997).

One exception to the absence of a father's support was noted by a crocheter who is separated from her husband and did receive some financial support from her children's father (when ordered by the court), although this stopped after a few years:

> I pay for all the kids' expenses. When my husband lived with me, he paid the expenses. After we separated, the community court attached his wages and made him pay support for two years. After that, he changed jobs and the money stopped. (interview with Rose, a crocheter, Harare, 1997)

Another important consideration with respect to the division of labor based on gender is who holds greater decision-making power with respect to household matters. In addition to making decisions about financial matters in their households, married crocheters played key roles in overall decision making for their families. As would be the case throughout the country, the vast majority of these businesswomen were the sole decision makers about how, when, and by whom housework would be done. Surprisingly, they also made most of the major decisions about the raising of their children and the schools that they would attend, although somewhat more sharing of duties between mothers and fathers was noted in the discipline of children.

All in all, women's decision-making roles about child care and housework point to their major responsibilities for these tasks in their families and households, which, on a daily basis, substantially exceed those of men. These duties—coupled with the financial assistance that they provided to their extended family members and to their own households—add up to substantially heavy domestic burdens. The businesswomen in this study viewed these responsibilities as focal parts of their identities, and in this respect, the operation, maintenance, and growth of their enterprises were major concerns in helping them meet their obligations. As some crocheters stated in discussing the relationship between their sense of self and their domestic responsibilities:

> I am happy. I wouldn't like to see anything changed. No, it should stay the same. It's a matter of custom. (interview with Rose, a crocheter, Bulawayo, 1991)

I feel very happy because I am used to doing them. The responsibilities I have at home vary somewhat from day to day. A lot of work in the house, seeing to children, washing, crocheting goods, cooking. I can't change these things. (interview with Rudo, a crocheter, Harare, 1991)

It is my responsibility as a wife and a woman. I enjoy looking after my home. (interview with Ndaizioeyi, a crocheter, Harare, 1994)

I feel good because I manage to supply my children with their needs. I don't want to see anything change. . . . I have to take responsibility for my children. It is alright. (interview with Nlil, Harare, a crocheter, 1997)

In the process of fulfilling their responsibilities to home and family, these entrepreneurs, in turn, contributed to community and national development.

## The Operation of the Firm

The women who own crocheting businesses are clearly entrepreneurs—first and foremost, because they established and are responsible for the operation of their firms. In addition, they are clearly engaged in innovation and in the production of material culture, they reinvest profits in their firms and in the development of human capital, and they diversify production to meet market demands. These businesswomen are committed to maintaining their businesses not just for short-term profits but also for the contributions they can make to their families and to their communities in the long run. These enterprises also provide these women with opportunities to express and further develop their creativity.

The remainder of this chapter discusses how entrepreneurs in crocheting established and operated their firms and how these women engaged in sales and production techniques that resulted in innovation in their enterprises. It also explores the relationship of these firms to the state and to state policy and the aspirations of these businesswomen for the future of their businesses. Their business activities and commitments to the future development of their families and their enterprises demonstrate that they have moved beyond the level of simple survival in their firms. They are actively working toward the growth and expansion of their businesses, and in the process they are contributing to their families, to their communities, and to national development.

The crocheting enterprises in this sample had a mean and median age of eight years and thus were about a year older than sewing, hairdressing, and market-vending establishments. As with their sisters in trading, hairdressing, and sewing, the largest single source of start-up capital for crocheters was their personal savings. Thirty-nine percent (twenty-two) had saved money from their previous occupations and/or from their household money to begin their firms. As is the case for most women in this study, the crocheters had previously held positions in the microenterprise sector. Before they established their current activities, they worked as traders selling food or clothing, engaged in home-based knitting and crocheting ventures, or were domestic workers or casual laborers in hospitals or stores. Two women were previously employed as teachers—one in a primary school and another as a trainer of teachers in home economics. Teaching at these levels in the educational system did not require a university degree, and, in fact, women were sometimes qualified to teach in these capacities with only a primary school certificate. In other cases, O-level certificates and/or certificates from teacher training colleges were required to teach in primary, secondary, and vocational schools.

Husbands were the second-largest single source of start-up capital for crocheting establishments. Approximately 26 percent (fifteen) of crocheters obtained all their funding from their husbands. Female relatives were twice as likely as their male counterparts to provide the initial capital for crocheters. About 21 percent (twelve) businesswomen received their funding mainly from their mothers and sisters, compared with 11 percent (six) of the crocheters who received money from their fathers and brothers. As stated above, mothers and sisters were also very salient in teaching the respondents how to crochet and knit. They also encouraged these entrepreneurs to begin these enterprises and frequently gave them advice on how to sell their goods. Finally, about 3 percent (two) of the sample obtained their initial investments from a combination of sources, which most often involved the crocheters pooling contributions from several relatives. These cash outlays are largely a combination of gifts and loans from relatives. Table 3.1 outlines these sources.

Employment creation is one lens through which the contributions of crocheters to community and national development can be assessed. While individual small enterprises and microenterprises in the North and the South have historically provided small numbers of jobs, they are collectively most important in both hemispheres for creating the largest number of overall positions. Social scientists who study small enterprise and microenterprise

*Table 3.1. Sources of start-up capital among crocheters*

| Source of capital | Number of respondents | Percent |
|---|---|---|
| Personal savings | 22 | 39 |
| Husband | 15 | 26 |
| Female relatives | 12 | 21 |
| Other male relatives | 6 | 11 |
| Bank or finance agency | | |
| Multiple sources | 2 | 3 |
| Total | 57 | 100 |

*Note:* The blank cells indicate that banks or finance agencies were not a source of start-up capital for crocheters in this study.
*Source:* Author's study data.

development have frequently argued that employment generation is a major indicator of success (growth) for these firms and one factor that separates successful firms from survival activities (Mead 1999). Crocheters did provide employment in their firms. In fact, unlike hairdressers, seamstresses, and traders, crocheters most often provided income-earning opportunities to other women through subcontracting arrangements. In the few cases where women were employed on a regular, full-time basis to crochet or knit goods, entrepreneurs generally paid these workers Z$120 to Z$400. Unlike the development of the microenterprise sector in other regions of the world—such as East Asia, where subcontracting arrangements have been significant as large local and multinational firms outsourced work to smaller establishments in an effort to increase profits—subcontracting has been very rare in Sub-Saharan Africa (Portes, Castells, and Benton 1989). Because foreign investment and the rate of establishing global assembly production facilities have been relatively low in Sub-Saharan Africa, it stands to reason that subcontracting as a result of downsizing on the part of large corporations would be relatively rare.

The crocheters in this study, however, engaged in subcontracting arrangements within the microenterprise sector of the economy. Fifty-three percent (thirty) of these businesswomen provided an average of two positions per firm, mainly through subcontracting arrangements with other women who did not work outside the home or who held other jobs in the sector. Businesswomen in this study sought to increase the efficiency of their enterprises by subdividing large tasks to several women. For example, the task of crocheting large tablecloths and bedspreads was largely given out to a few women who would each crochet dozens of squares (of possibly 3-by-3 inches), which were later stitched together by the entrepreneur to make a finished product. Women who crocheted the individual squares were paid on a piecework basis, sometimes averaging about Z$0.50 per square in 1994. Businesswomen were most likely to subcontract out all or part of their work in crocheting and knitting during the busiest seasons of the year—during the winter and the Christmas holiday season. During the busy season, crocheters would often subcontract out the knitting of sweaters, paying women approximately Z$30 per sweater. Such subcontracting of sweaters contributed to the innovation noted in firms, because each knitter created her own designs and, coupled with the sweaters made by the entrepreneur, this ensured that each sweater had a unique pattern. Truly no two sweaters were alike. Such distinctive, handmade goods were very appealing to tourists and South African dealers.

Subcontracting not only demonstrated an entrepreneur's attempts to increase efficiency in her firm, but this form of employment also increased a businesswoman's social capital (and that of her employees). Crocheters often subcontracted some of their work to other female relatives, neighbors, and friends, who could be relied upon to take on such assignments on relatively short notice. The women on both sides of these arrangements extended their social networks and their camaraderie with other women, which could serve as important sources of support in business and personal matters. Such arrangements also enabled these businesswomen and their employees alike to share designs and techniques for knitting and crocheting with each other.

Through subcontracting, the businesswomen in this sample created temporary positions, which did provide income-generating opportunities to other mostly poor and low-income women in Harare and Bulawayo. In addition to assisting in the development of these enterprises, such actions contributed to the growth of human capital as well as poverty alleviation in poor urban communities.[9]

Innovation was another important factor in this study and one that further demonstrates not only the commitment of entrepreneurs to the development and growth of their firms but also their creativity and their understanding of

9. This is not to suggest that crocheters' subcontracting arrangements were never exploitative of the poor women whom they mainly employed. Certainly entrepreneurs intended to increase their profits through such practices, paying these women on a piecework basis averaging a few cents per crocheted square (or a few dollars per sweater). The finished goods clearly sold for more than the price of the labor that produced them.

Figure 3.1. Crocheters at the City Hall Crochet Market, Bulawayo, Zimbabwe, July 1994

the market, and, in some cases, illustrates their contributions to the development of material culture. Crocheters had significant business acumen and in many respects, they exhibited perhaps the most interesting examples of innovation in this study. Since the beginning of their enterprises, 68 percent (thirty-nine) of these businesswomen have used new materials and/or introduced new products into their businesses.

The crocheters make a wide range of clothing and other decorative goods for the household. They make sweaters, women's and children's tops, dresses, doilies, tablemats, tablecloths, and bedspreads—among other items. Many women began by only making doilies and then expanded their production to include several of these other items. Most of the goods they make are Western in orientation and are meant to appeal largely to expatriates in Southern Africa and to tourists (see figures 3.1 and 3.2).

The majority of crocheters changed the colors and patterns of the goods that they made. This was particularly evident in my fieldwork visits after 1991, when goods had been made mainly in beige cotton. When I later returned to the crocheters' sites in 1994 and 1997, tablemats and doilies were

Figure 3.2.  A crocheter at the Kamfinsa Crochet Market, Harare, July 1994

increasingly being made in white cotton and in other bright colors, such as magenta and turquoise. As illustrated by a crocheter in Bulawayo:

> I started with doilies and small things. Got more money and expanded to other goods. It is a way of living; now things are a bit better—$45 for spools of white, $22.50 for cream. Used beige at the beginning and then able to use white. (interview with Sipiwe Sinole, crocheter, Bulawayo, 1994)

In some ways, it was surprising to find this innovation, considering that many businesswomen had been complaining about the exorbitant prices of white and brightly colored yarn. These women noted, however, that white and brightly colored items greatly appealed to tourist and expatriate customers. These entrepreneurs also frequently changed the styles of the clothing they made, with different designs appearing in each hand-knitted sweater.

The most exciting examples of innovation among crocheters, however, were noted in the new items that they began making and/or selling in the mid-1990s. In an effort to increase their sales and to appeal to the tourist market, which appeared to have significant potential for growth with the coming of majority rule to South Africa, crocheters began to make and sell batiks and to sell Shona carvings in addition to the other knitted and crocheted items.[10] Batiks were again made in very vivid colors, with designs that appeared uniquely African, and in many cases, Southern African, often including symbols from the region such as the Zimbabwe bird. These bright and appealing objects, which can be used as wall hangings, bedspreads, and/or tablecloths, were hung on clotheslines in the crochet markets immediately adjacent to the hand-knitted sweaters and crocheted tablecloths.

In addition, in the first few years after the inception of ESAP, the crocheters began to sell Shona soapstone carvings, an art form widely recognized internationally. Shona sculpture from the region consists of carvings of women, men, and children, generally depicted as families, as well as figures of animals. Such sculptures are usually made by men and until the early to middle 1990s, street corner artists and other men in the microenterprise sector most often sold these works. Beginning with my second fieldwork visit in 1994, I began to notice that the crocheters were increasingly selling soapstone carvings in addition to their handmade goods. In recent years, businesswomen in crocheting have identified these items as in high demand among tourists and have added them to their roster of goods for sale. Such examples of the crossing of gender boundaries with respect to sales in the microenterprise sector have become far more evident as Zimbabwe's economic crisis has deepened. Shifts in the gender-based division of labor have also been noted in areas traditionally dominated by women, such as market trade, in periods of deepening economic crisis.[11] Several crocheters in this study discussed innovation in their firms in terms of adding Shona stone carvings and batiks to the roster of items that they sold:

10. Batiks made by black Zimbabwean women in the contemporary period can be considered ethnic or tourist art (*turistica*). E.g., as noted among scholars studying the tourist market for local crafts in Mexico and Nepal, ethnic arts such as Zimbabwean batiks are generally made for tourists from Europe and North America. Such objects are distinct from goods that the local populations use, but are still culturally important to the Zimbabweans who produce them. This is especially evident in their incorporation of local symbols in the batiks. See Hitchcock and Teague (2000).

11. Clark (1994) has noted the increased presence of men in Kumasi Market in Ghana selling products historically sold by women in periods of economic crisis and adjustment in that nation. I have also made similar observations with respect to more men engaged in fruit and vegetable vending in the Mbare and Manwele markets in this study.

I sell stone carvings, hand-knit sweaters, crochet tablecloths, clothes, bed-spreads, and doily sets. I started knitting jerseys [sweaters] in 1992 so that I could earn more money. Started selling carvings in 1993 as a backup when the other things weren't selling so well. The cotton wool is far more expensive now compared to the cost in 1981. In 1985, a ball of cotton cost $15; now it is $35. (interview with Kunaka, a crocheter, Harare, 1994)

Started with crocheting only but realized white foreigners wanted more items and so started selling jerseys and other carving items. Now, I sell wood carvings, stone carvings, jerseys, all crochet work, bedspreads, tops, tablecloths. (interview with Maud, a crocheter, Harare, 1997)

In 1983, making crochet dresses only. Added batiks in 1995; five years ago with money, I added carvings. Sell batiks, jerseys, tops, sets, dresses, carvings, necklaces, wood carvings. Yes, I also change the patterns and colors. (interview with Kisyedza, a crocheter, Harare, 1997)

One crocheter from the Newlands Shopping Center, again, the largest cro-chet market in Harare and a major tourist venue, has significantly diversi-fied her production and sales not only by selling Shona carvings but also by making and selling items appealing to customers with pets. In this regard, when compared with her peers at Newlands, she has certainly made her site in the market more distinctive:

I sell tablecloths, jerseys, stone carvings, dog and cat mattresses, wooden carvings, and bowls. I started in 1990 with jerseys and tablecloths only. This year we began to sell wooden goods. I began selling the stones about three years ago. I began selling the dog mattresses last year. I made these. (interview with Rose, a crocheter, Harare, 1997)

These examples of innovation demonstrate that the crocheters were very conscious of the tastes and demands of their white Zimbabwean customers, South African buyers, and tourists visiting the area largely from Europe and the United States, as well as their black Zimbabwean clients. At the four crochet markets visited in Zimbabwe, two sites were very popular with tourists: the Newlands Shopping Center in Harare and City Hall in Bul-awayo. These were the largest sites for crocheters in these cities, and though black Zimbabweans did purchase goods from these businesswomen, whites from Zimbabwe, the Southern African region in general, and tourists were the more frequent customers. The crocheters based at City Hall and especially those at Newlands exhibited high levels of innovation, particularly marked by the addition of batiks and Shona carvings to their roster of goods for sale. These changes made in the operation of their firms further illustrates that these entrepreneurs aimed to increase their profitability and were committed to the growth of their enterprises. As demonstrated in the framework of feminist political economy, these businesswomen were active agents in their lives and were operating their firms beyond the level of simple survival.

## Responsibilities as an Entrepreneur

The crocheters have a variety of tasks to perform in their enterprises, and because few of them employ regular, full-time workers, most of the responsibilities rest with them. The vast majority of businesswomen in this sample crochet and knit; although slightly more than half these women (53 percent) do employ workers, largely through subcontracting arrangements to assist with these tasks. These entrepreneurs knit and crochet goods at their worksites while sitting on the bare ground, on an old can or crate, or on a mat that they brought from home. After arriving at their worksites at approximately 8 AM, they display their items and usually begin crocheting or knitting new articles of clothing or household accessories. They stop their knitting or crocheting periodically to attend to customers who stop at their worksite or whom they are trying to lure from the sidewalk or from the site of another crocheter. After the brief interruptions for sales, they return to their knitting or crocheting, which they generally continue until sometime between 4:30 and 6:00 PM, at which time they generally leave the market. Many entrepreneurs do take their work home with them and continue their crocheting and knitting in the evenings. Businesswomen were very astute and thorough in describing their duties and generally expressed pleasure in their work if it resulted in sales. They discussed the benefits of their work in very material terms:

> I come here at 8:00 AM. I display my things, I start crocheting some of the things I sell. I can store my things here at night. I do not have to carry them back each day. I leave them here at 4:30 PM. I also do crocheting at home in the evenings. I'm impressed by what I am doing, because [I] hear most people admiring what I am doing. I am managing to get what

will be benefiting my living. (interview with Sharon Dube, a crocheter, Bulawayo, 1997)

I start at 8 AM and end at 5:30 or 6:00 PM. I start opening my bags and displaying my goods and clean and polish the carvings and then we start crocheting. At night we leave our goods here, we wrap the batiks in bags and store them here. I keep a record book [and] at month's end, I order batiks and carvings. I get the batiks from Murewa and Mutare. Men make these and sell them—guys from Chitinguwiza come and sell the carvings to us. The artists come to sell them to us. (interview with Kuseydza, a crocheter, Harare, 1997)

I get here at 9:00 or 10:00 AM since I have a child I come late. I display my things and sit down and wait for customers. I crochet here as well. I can make a set of doilies in three days. Some of the workers take two months to finish five sets. I leave here at 4:30 PM. Sometimes I crochet in the evening; sometimes I don't. I store my goods here. I wash, starch, and iron the goods when I am finished. I feel okay just because I get money for food, clothing, so it makes my life better. (interview with Salschide, a crocheter, Bulawayo, 1997)

The perspective of feminist political economy, with particular emphasis on intersectionality, enables us to see why concerns about money and the extent to which they were able to realize profits from their activities are particularly important to these businesswomen. Because these black Zimbabwean women come from mainly poor and low-income backgrounds with low levels of educational attainment, they are blocked from entering the formal sector. As stated above, they have major responsibilities for their families, which became even more acute under conditions of economic crisis and adjustment. In addition to relatives in their households, they were also major sources of support for their extended family members not living with them, especially parents and in-laws. In an immediate sense, the financial viability of their activities was so important to these entrepreneurs because it enabled them to educate their children. As noted in the remarks of some crocheters:

I have achieved success because my children are at nice schools. We get money to buy food and clothes. Success means to have money. (interview with Rudo, a crocheter, Harare, 1991)

[Crocheting] is better than staying at home. I have money to look after children. It is easy; like it a lot. . . . Children can go to school with the money I get, but it isn't much. (interview with Mary, a crocheter, Harare, 1991)

In discussing their responsibilities, the crocheters also commented on the difficulties they experienced in this business and at the particular sites where they worked:

It is a good enough job, but being open to the elements is not good. What can I say if I am not qualified to do anything else. It is better than nothing but it is not much. (interview with Francisco, a crocheter, Bulawayo, 1994)

Must have enough wool because if not, no business. If sell items, make sure to buy wool right away. If any items sell, also make sure [to] pay women. Cheerful with customers; mustn't be rough, must understand each other and customers' needs. Sometimes so tiring, especially if things not bought. Feel like retiring. Sometimes even feel like getting out when not doing well, like when it's cold. Like work because it's cash. (interview with Amanda, a crocheter, Bulawayo, 1994)

I don't like being out in the open and getting rained on. Furthermore, the only source of water is the toilet [unpleasant] and so you can spend a whole day very thirsty. . . . It is like the City Council just wants to get the money from us for nothing. This is a very crowded space with as many as fifty people. (interview with Mwambo, a crocheter, Harare, 1994)

When it is cold and rainy, I do not have a proper place to sit. . . . I just want a nice place like a room and I can pay for this per month to stay and work and display the goods. The problem is accommodation. (interview with Ancilar Mee, a crocheter, Bulawayo, 1997)

The conditions of work for the crocheters in Harare and Bulawayo posed many health risks for these women. As stated above, the women at the four sites investigated sat on the bare ground or on a crate, a can, a large drum, or a mat that they brought with them for their entire day at the crochet market. They had no protection from the elements and sat on this land designated by the two cities' councils in summer as well as in winter. These parcels of bare land also had no toilet facilities or storage places for their goods or any meals that they might have brought with them. In the interviews, several women mentioned that the city councils promised to improve these facilities, but as of my last fieldwork visit in 1999, nothing had been done. The severity of the current economic and political crises suggests that these sites will not be improved in the foreseeable future.

Despite the neglect of these markets by the municipal governments, these entrepreneurs took great pride in their duties and in their places of work. One would frequently see crocheters sweeping their spaces and dusting off their stone or wooden artwork for sale soon after reaching their worksites. One crocheter expressed her belief that the Harare City Council should improve their worksite, but she also mentioned her willingness to assist, despite her meager resources:

> Like to make Newlands a nice place—put something to help water run off; [create] shelter. Want City Council to do some of it, and we were promised it would happen. (interview with Rudo, a crocheter, Harare, 1994)

## Economic Indicators of Firm Performance

Although the majority of crocheters did not keep precise records of the economic transactions of their enterprises, they did express a clear sense of the sales trends and the profitability of their activities. From the establishment of their businesses to the time of the interviews, nearly half (47 percent) of the entrepreneurs reported that sales had increased in their firms. Annual sales ranged from about Z$37 to Z$18,000, with most crocheters selling a few hundred dollars worth of goods each month. Some of the businesswomen who experienced growth in sales explained this in terms of their increased efficiency in making crocheted and knitted items and the overall inflation in the price of goods in Zimbabwe. As June, a crocheter from Bulawayo stated: "Prices higher so people pay more and I can make things faster now than before" (interview with June, 1991). Another crocheter attributed sales increases to having more goods to sell and to improved business performance:

> I knew how to manage the business better last year as opposed to when I began. I knew how to do more things to encourage people to come and

buy. I also have more jerseys [sweaters] available to sell than I did in the beginning. (interview with Simba, a crocheter, Harare, 1994)

Still another crocheter had a similar response in 1997:

Now I sell more because I think I am a good saleslady and I have more goods on display. (interview with Violet, a crocheter, Harare, 1997)

These businesswomen also attributed the growth in sales to increased tourism in the region and to weather conditions. With the coming of majority rule to South Africa, tourism to Zimbabwe and the Southern Africa region more generally were expected to increase. Crocheters did benefit from this development at least somewhat in the early period, not only because of Zimbabwe's proximity to South Africa but also due to Zimbabwe's own tourist attractions, such as Victoria Falls. Further, handmade crocheted and knitted items were in high demand among both black and white South Africans, who had few of these goods available to them locally. Most clothing available for sale in South Africa was machine made. Not only were many of the handmade Zimbabwean items more appealing, but in most cases, they were also cheaper. Further, poor and low-income black South Africans often bargained with black Zimbabwean crocheters for a "good" price, or bartered secondhand clothes for new knitted sweaters. Therefore, crocheted and knitted goods were accessible for black poor and low-income populations. In addition, the demand for these items increased, particularly due to the abnormally cold winter of 1994. This was the coldest winter in recent memory in Zimbabwe and South Africa, with temperatures dipping into the low 30s on the Fahrenheit scale in the former and with snow falling in Johannesburg. In nations with no central heating, crocheted and knitted bedspreads and sweaters were clearly in high demand. Several crocheters cited these explanations in their interviews:

[Sales have] increased. People buy more because now being sold in South Africa. Didn't sell in South Africa before. (interview with Samantha, a crocheter, Harare, 1994)

Prices are higher, more customers. Some people come and order jerseys for South Africa, so selling more. (interview with Ms. Margaret, a crocheter, Harare, 1994)

This business is up. More customers are coming. More of these customers are foreigners than in 1990. (interview with Chipo, a crocheter, Harare, 1994)

This year, more customers than last year. More customers because it's colder this year. (interview with Ailzi, a crocheter, Harare, 1994)

Many businesswomen in this sample, however, told a different story. They reported declining (24 percent), fluctuating (11 percent), or unchanging sales (7 percent) from the beginning of their enterprises to the time of the interviews. Decreasing and fluctuating sales are particularly understandable, given the economic crisis and ESAP. Escalating unemployment, greater competition from more crocheters entering the microenterprise sector, and the removal of price controls from staple products, coupled with escalating inflation on all goods, resulted in decreased demand for crocheted and knitted goods among many segments of the population. As one businesswoman stated: "ESAP—there is no money" (interview with Sibusiso, a crocheter, Bulawayo, 1994). Some crocheters also noted that the increased cost for raw materials led to a decrease in the numbers of items that they made, and thus they had fewer items to sell. Overall, rising unemployment and the increasing prices of most goods kept many potential customers away from the crochet markets. These factors were noted in the explanations given by crocheters for decreasing or fluctuating sales:

Things have gone up in price, especially the cotton we crochet with. So I no longer get enough buyers and I can run at a loss. (interview with Francisco, a crocheter, Bulawayo, 1994)

Things are getting tougher as time goes on because of the increasing cost of the materials. (interview with Ndaizioeyi, a crocheter, Harare, 1994)

Now we have less sales. This is because the market is flooded with traders, as you can see. Therefore, the probability of me selling anything is through the grace of God and nothing else. (interview with Chinanisa, a crocheter, Harare, 1994)

Yes, business has decreased because now there are so many of us in this trade, and this makes it difficult to sell the stuff. (interview with Livinia, a crocheter, Harare, 1997)

In 1992, there were more customers. I think I sold more. In 1992, people used to come and order our doilies to take these to sell in South Africa. Could order ten to fifteen sets. Black Zimbabweans were also selling these goods in South Africa. (interview with Lisamiso, a crocheter, Bulawayo, 1997)

Perhaps more than the other categories of economic indicators that crocheters were questioned about, assessing the value of assets and their changes over time appeared to be the most difficult to estimate. Most businesswomen stated that their assets had increased. Several entrepreneurs, however, did not provide a figure for assets and replied that they simply did not know the value of their businesses. Because these crocheters did not own shops or any other official space for their enterprises and few of them owned machinery, with the exception of a few knitting machines, one would expect the overall value of their assets to be low. Those who did respond estimated that the value of their assets ranged from Z$60 to Z$30,000, with the approximate worth of most firms ranging from Z$500 to Z$2000. The entrepreneurs in this sector estimated these figures based on the value of all the goods and machinery that they owned for the business at the time of the interview and all the cash and savings that they had available for the enterprise. A few crocheters did assess the value of their businesses as exceeding Z$10,000, with a significant portion of this value including business savings. In general, however, a strict separation between business and personal capital did not exist for these businesswomen, and so one is cautioned not to consider the somewhat "higher" amounts to belong solely to these establishments. These women explained their increased assets as stemming from improved business performance, increased inventories, the diversification of production and sales, and higher prices for their goods:

Value of the business equals Z$500. Worth more because cotton is more now than before. (interview with June, a crocheter, Bulawayo, 1991)

The business is worth Z$8,000, including wool and unsold products. Just started in May; when started the business was worth Z$450. (interview with Amanda, a crocheter, Bulawayo, 1994)

As I gain experience, I learn from others. Learn from others and changes colors to what sells. Value of business equals Z$1,500. In 1993, value was less than now because of my experience and more products. (interview with Tennyson, a crocheter, Harare, 1994)

Business is up. More customers are coming, and more of these customers are foreigners than in 1990. Value of assets about Z$5,000. Any changes? Yes, the numbers of customers are up. Each customer is buying more than in 1990. (interview with Chipo, a crocheter, Harare, 1994)

Value of assets is Z$10,000. Yes, I used to sell crochet work only, but now I also sell carvings. (interview with Chinanisa, a crocheter, Harare, 1997)

Eighty-six percent (forty-nine) of the crocheters stated that they had earned profits since the establishment of their enterprises. The majority of participants did give some estimates of the profitability of their firms at the time of the interviews, although six women in the sample did not provide any figures. Profits ranged from Z$10 to Z$5,000 a month, with most crocheters estimating that they earned a few hundred dollars profit each month. Only two women stated that they earned more than Z$2,000. Many entrepreneurs remarked, however, that whereas they had earned profits since the start of their businesses, profits had not been rising steadily over the years. In fact, several claimed that due to the problems created by the economic crisis and ESAP, they had witnessed decreasing profits in recent years:

Profits—a little. Around Z$40 for savings and at times nothing. Sometimes borrow from younger sisters if not enough. Actually no profit because of high cost of living. (interview with Sipiwe Sinole, a crocheter, Bulawayo, 1994)

Plus or minus 200 per year. But I don't think I will have any profit this year. Everyone looks; no one buys. (interview with Caroline, a crocheter, Bulawayo, 1994)

ESAP is here to make people suffer. Profits in 1992 were Z$600; in 1993, they were Z$200, in 1994, I estimate that they are Z$100. (interview with Sibusiso, a crocheter, Bulawayo, 1994)

Earned any profits? Yes, there was a time when I could save Z$200 per year, but since 1990, there is no more money and I spend what I earn. (interview with Francisco, a crocheter, Bulawayo, 1994)

Business has decreased because now there are many of us in this trade and this makes it difficult to sell the stuff. (interview with Livinia, a crocheter, Harare, 1997)

Seventy-two percent (forty-one) of the crocheters stated that they alone made the decisions about how profits would be used in their businesses. Nine percent (five) of the entrepreneurs stated that decisions about the use of profits were jointly made by them and their husbands. In two cases, husbands were the sole decision makers about the use of profits. Two crocheters remarked that other female relatives made the decisions about investing profits, and one businesswoman noted that she sought the advice of her workers on this matter. The fact that decision making rested primarily in the hands of the entrepreneurs in this study is an important finding regarding the autonomy of women in managing their own businesses. The feminist political economy paradigm draws our attention to how women in this sector have exhibited their agency and empowered themselves by controlling the use of capital from their establishments, even if the amounts of capital that they control are small. Despite the fact that there is not a strict separation between business and personal capital for these entrepreneurs, their investment choices regarding the use of their profits have enabled them to enhance their contributions to the development of their families, their communities, and the nation.

How have these businesswomen contributed to the overall process of development? Fifty-one percent (twenty-nine) of the crocheters commented that they reinvested profits directly in their businesses. When they earned profits, they increased their stock of cotton and wool for making sweaters as well as purchased knitting machines in a few cases. Some crocheters also used their profits to invest in the more expensive cotton made in such vibrant colors as magenta, turquoise, and emerald, which were especially appealing to tourists. As stated above, slightly more than half these entrepreneurs provided employment for women, mainly through subcontracting arrangements. Although most crocheters in this study have encountered financial setbacks due to the economic crisis and ESAP, the reinvestment of their profits, improved performance, and employment generation in their businesses have enabled them to contribute to local and national development.

Profits, however, were put to other good uses beyond the operation of their firms. For the most part, the crocheters in this study did not allocate themselves regular salaries. Thus, they drew from what they termed "profits" to meet their families' basic needs for food and clothing. Beyond these essentials and reinvesting in their businesses, the women in this study were most committed to three additional areas: investments in education for themselves and their children, providing household durables and home improvements, and supporting their extended families. Sixty-one percent (thirty-five) of the entrepreneurs stated that they paid school fees for their children and/or for other relatives, for example, their nieces. Providing education for their children was their uppermost concern, certainly on a par with their decision to reinvest in their enterprises. A few women in this sample were enrolled in continuing education programs, in which they were striving to attain their lower-level secondary school certificates, and thus they were paying the fees for these programs.

In these activities, the crocheters were contributing to the development of human capital, an essential component in building local communities and in developing societies. Feminist political economy shows us that despite the difficult conditions caused by the economic crisis, these women were determined to maintain their families and their homes. This theory illustrates the gendered effects of this crisis and how these astute entrepreneurs empowered themselves and crossed gender lines to maintain their families and communities. Because many men had lost positions in the formal sector and were increasingly dependent on part-time or irregular employment, as well as work in the microenterprise sector, 51 percent (twenty-nine) of the women in this study invested in the upkeep of their homes by paying for repairs and purchasing needed household appliances and furniture. In this sense, these businesswomen crossed established gender boundaries and assumed roles that were the purview of men, and in this process, the former contributed to family wealth. Finally, the crocheters were very dedicated to their extended families, particularly in this period of economic crisis. Forty-nine percent (twenty-eight) of these women used some of their profits to provide money, food, and/or clothing for their parents and in-laws. Their efforts helped to reduce the further decline of more families into the depths of poverty.

Although many of these enterprises might not be considered successful in a strict economic sense—in other words, by demonstrating significant growth in profits and/or employment over the years—they have contributed to local and national development (Mead 1999). These businesswomen have accomplished this by reinvesting their small profits in their enterprises, by developing human capital through employment generation (albeit occasional employment), by educating their children, and by supporting their extended families. One crocheter aptly described the frequent juggling act of these entrepreneurs with regard to investments in their firms versus their families:

> Sometimes you feel you want to buy wool, but my sister might need shoes, so I use the money to help my sister as opposed to buying things [wool]

for the business. I have to balance the responsibility to the family with the business. (interview with F. Tekenende, a crocheter, Harare, 1994)

## Government Policies, the Economic Structural Adjustment Program, and Globalization

Like many of their sisters in the Global South, the crocheters in the micro-enterprise sector have been affected by globalization, in the form of ESAP, established by the Zimbabwean government at the behest of the International Monetary Fund and the World Bank in late 1990/early 1991. Feminist political economy illustrates the role of international actors and the state in creating the crisis and particularly its gendered consequences, while demonstrating the active responses of women entrepreneurs to the challenges. Although ESAP was designed to stem the tide of the economic crisis that gripped the nation beginning in 1990, the program intensified the crisis, most especially for poor women and children in Zimbabwe. As poor and low-income women, the majority of entrepreneurs in this sample were negatively affected by ESAP. They were astute and could identify as well as understand how this program had negatively affected their firms. They experienced the consequences of this program in both their business and personal lives—in the form of increased unemployment in their families; increased costs of raw materials and basic commodities, licenses, and customs duties for their firms; increased competition from more crocheters entering the market selling the same goods; and increased costs for education, housing, health care and transportation (Horn 1994; Osirim 1995, 1998; Darkwah 2002).

Many businesswomen began by discussing how escalating unemployment in Zimbabwe under ESAP was responsible for reduced sales and profits in their establishments and changes in their quality of life:

Unemployment: . . . When more people are working, more people will buy my work. (interview with Barbara, a crocheter, Harare, 1991)

Yes, if people lose their jobs, it affects the business. If people lose their jobs, they will not buy goods to send overseas and if people lose jobs, we can't get cooking oil, we won't get flour and we can't cook vegetables without oil. Yes, ESAP does have to do with employment. (interview with Kusyedza, a crocheter, Harare, 1997)

Yes, if people lose jobs in Harare, this is why we get security. If people don't get jobs, they are the ones who will steal. These robbers will sell to someone to get money. (interview with Rose, a crocheter, Harare, 1997)

Another businesswomen noted how "illegal," unlicensed sellers, in this case selling Shona carvings, negatively affected her sale of crocheted goods:

Yes, unemployment in Zimbabwe does affect the business because too many unemployed people come here running after the customers selling their things without permission. For example, carvings and then the people won't buy the crochet goods. (interview with Lisamiso, a crocheter, Bulawayo, 1997)

Higher customs duties and fees for import licenses often led to shortages of needed raw materials for these entrepreneurs and problems in exporting their goods. In addition, high rates of inflation in Zimbabwe, coupled in some cases with scarcity in the market, led to increased costs for raw materials:

If we want to sell our things out of the country, we are charged a lot of money in customs duty. (interview with Tsitsi, a crocheter, Harare, 1991)

Time when making [my goods] with beads. All plastic—white people don't like plastic ones. Economy made beads not available. (interview with Sipiwe Sinole, a crocheter, Bulawayo, 1994)

The municipal authorities are the ones who regulate our activities, making us pay rent here in the open. ESAP has caused the cost of wool/cotton to rise. Even when we increase the prices of our goods, it doesn't help because all other things are more expensive, and our money buys less. No one wants to buy expensive things either. (interview with Ndaizioeyi, a crocheter, Harare, 1994)

Perhaps one of the most frequently heard problems associated with ESAP was the increased competition in the market from the growth in the number of women selling crocheted and knitted clothing and household goods. The feminist political economy paradigm leads us to consider not only how the capitalist global economy creates a gender-based division of labor internationally but also how this is manifest at the level of the nation-state. As many Zimbabweans, most especially men, lost their positions in the formal sector, more women attempted to support their families or supplement their partners' or other family members wages (if the latter were employed) through income-generating activities in the microenterprise sector. Crocheting and knitting businesses provided opportunities for some women who had these skills, and in this period of economic crisis, more women were acquiring these skills with the help of their female relatives. The major growth in the number of crocheters can be noted through observing their site at the Newlands Shopping Center in Harare. The number of traders there increased from about forty in 1991 to more than eighty in 1997. These businesswomen expressed their frustration with the influx of crocheters in the marketplace:

> Things are too expensive, so too many people are crocheting to sell the same goods, like doilies. There is something wrong. Everything is going up. My husband earns little money, people don't have much money. (interview with Priscilla, a crocheter, Bulawayo, 1994)

> If too many vendors, then less customers will come. Think there are too many vendors, so there are fewer customers. (interview with Ms. Margaret, a crocheter, Harare, 1994)

The removal of government subsidies from social services and the end of price controls on staple products led to significant growth in the rate of inflation. These problems were compounded by the massive unemployment and devaluation of the currency that were part of ESAP. Thus, local residents found it exceedingly difficult to buy crocheted and knitted goods, which were increasingly viewed as luxury items. In a period when many families were struggling to provide the basic necessities, handmade clothing and household items became unattainable:

> Inflation—everything is costing more and more and people have less money since ESAP in 1990. (interview with Sibusiso, a crocheter, Bulawayo, 1994)

> Prices at other places affect our prices, what people expect to buy my goods at. They have to understand that with transport costs and material costs, my prices are as they are so that I can make a margin of profit. (interview with Tennyson, a crocheter, Harare, 1994)

The Economic Structural Adjustment Program affects our business because our customers are now few because they can't spend money on our goods. (interview with Maud, a crocheter, Harare, 1997)

Because of ESAP, most companies are closed. So most people are not working, which means that they don't buy as they used to. (interview with Rhoda, a crocheter, Bulawayo, 1997)

Globalization, particularly as manifested in ESAP, took a negative toll on these entrepreneurs, their businesses, and by extension their families. Though most crocheters had certainly realized some growth in profits since the startup phase, many women had witnessed declines in sales and profits in the middle to late 1990s. Despite these downturns in the economic performance of their firms, these businesswomen had achieved some success in their enterprises, had developed coping strategies for the most difficult times (which will be discussed in chapter 6), and were generally optimistic about the future.

## Views of Success and Aspirations for the Future

Despite the difficulties caused by the economic crisis and ESAP, 61 percent (thirty-five) of the crocheters stated that they had experienced more overall successes than failures in their businesses over the years. Those businesswomen who had witnessed more problems in their businesses (18 percent) were almost evenly split with those who believed that they had experienced successes and failures just about equally (14 percent). As discussed above, many of the problems that crocheters experienced were related to ESAP and the lack of adequate, safe worksites. Some crocheters further commented:

There was more success, but now, you buy cotton today and it is one price; you buy cotton tomorrow and the price has gone up. But over the entire twelve-year period, there has been more success than problems. (interview with Faith Dhliwayo, a crocheter, Bulawayo, 1991)

Some years there were success, but no longer. Ever since ESAP began, people were retrenched. . . . More failure, especially now since ESAP. No one has bought anything in all the time you've been here. (interview with Francisco, a crocheter, Bulawayo, 1994)

I don't like being out in the open and getting rained on. (interview with Maidei, a crocheter, Harare, 1994)

The majority of the respondents who achieved success did not limit their descriptions to their enterprises. In fact, their definitions of success again demonstrated the multifaceted nature of their lives, where business and family matters were intersecting areas of concern. They defined success largely in terms of material achievements for their businesses, their families, and their homes, with providing education for their children highly ranked among these priorities:

My children have finished school, and I am able to buy property for my home and cattle for my fields. (interview with Kunaka, a crocheter, Harare, 1994)

I have had mainly success because I can pay school fees for my children. My husband and I help each other pay for these. (interview with Simba, a crocheter, Harare, 1994)

My children completed their education and are now self-reliant. I can look after myself. I am in the process of electrifying my home. I was able to drill a borehole myself. (interview with Chinanisa, a crocheter, Harare, 1997)

Initially, I was embarrassed with this job, but now I am proud of it because I have raised my children through this work. . . . I managed to take my children to boarding school and buy them clothes. I can even afford to have a good life. (interview with Livinia, a crocheter, Harare, 1997)

I had success because I expanded the business as I bought new goods, for example, the carvings. (interview with Dorothy Mhonda, a crocheter, Harare, 1997)

In their responses, some businesswomen further described the interconnected nature of their business and family lives and the success that they realized in these overlapping spheres:

Because of the business, I have managed to get so many things. I have a sewing machine now through the sale of jerseys [sweaters]. I know that next year my daughter will be able to go to crèche because of the money that I have gotten from this business. (interview with Chipo, a crocheter, Harare, 1994)

The years 1992 and 1993 were successful because I extended the house and all the children were going to school. [I received] lots of goods after ordering from Kadoma for the business. (interview with Maud, a crocheter, Harare, 1997)

Finally, a few women described success in terms of the independence their enterprises afforded them. The autonomy they realized as a result of their business endeavors laid the foundation for greater self-confidence and empowerment in the broader society:

I am successful because I am self-employed. If I don't feel like coming to work, I don't have to. I decide on my own styles, and so on. No one tells me what to do. (interview with Faith Dhiliwayo, a crocheter, Bulawayo, 1991)

Yes, at first I did not have anything from my own benefit. I was a dependent on my brothers and sisters. Now, I can stand by myself. . . . At first, I felt shy to be in the city selling something and the public in such a crowd like this, because I was the youngest in the market. I felt so shy to try and call customers. . . . I've gained courage to speak to different kinds of people, and I've learned to be social with other people. (interview with Sharon Dube, a crocheter, Bulawayo, 1997)

Entrepreneurs in this sample further demonstrated that they had moved beyond the level of "simple survival" in these firms in their aspirations for the future. The respondents in this study were largely committed to expansion and growth in their activities over the long term; they did not begin these businesses as temporary ventures just to get them through a difficult economic period. Several crocheters wanted to own shops for their operations, while others wanted to establish export markets. Some women hoped to expand their inventories and the range of goods that they sold, sometimes by diversifying into related activities, such as sewing. Others hoped to acquire new ideas for their businesses by investigating how women operated businesses in other countries. They expressed these desires as:

Would like to do plenty. Go outside of the country to see what other [business]women are doing. (interview with M. E. Zhiraazago, a crocheter, Bulawayo, 1991)

Add sewing to my business and make it big. (interview with Micky, a crocheter, Bulawayo, 1991)

Having my own shop of crochet work. If I cooperate with others, I think we can have one. I think we'll do it in the future. (interview with Amanda, a crocheter, Bulawayo, 1994)

Want to open a factory and take jerseys to sell in South Africa. If I save a lot of money, I can open a factory. Don't have passport to take jerseys yet. Passport in process now. Will start as soon as I can. Rent houses there and sell. (interview with Ms. Margaret, a crocheter, Harare, 1994)

If I had enough money, I would like to get more things to sell—carvings and handmade goods—and maybe even open a shop. (interview with Kunaka, a crocheter, Harare, 1994)

I would like to keep working to improve my business and maybe be able to export to other countries sometime. (interview with Tsitsi, a crocheter, Harare, 1994)

One woman discussed the need to improve the physical environment where she worked in the largest crochet market in Harare. Unfortunately, the economic and political crises gripping the country have meant that such projects are unlikely to begin anytime in the near future:

Like to make Newlands a nice place. Put something to help water run off, shelter. Want City Council to do it, and we were promised it would happen. Hopefully, in October—I think it will happen. (interview with Rudo, a crocheter, Harare, 1994)

As was the case in discussing "success," concerns for the development of their businesses were often stated by these entrepreneurs in conjunction with their hopes for their families. Again, among family issues, the desire to educate their children was uppermost in their minds:

Want my children to be a mechanic or doctor, so if they are working, I will be free. (interview with Scholastic, a crocheter, Harare, 1991)

Want my children to have a good life. Want my youngest daughter to be a doctor because she is good in school. . . . My goal is to make money so that I can give children something. (interview with Mary, a crocheter, Harare, 1991)

I have been very strong so far raising my girls alone. I hope I can complete the task successfully. As it is, two of my daughters are acquiring diplomas in various fields, and I hope the other two will follow suit. (interview with Livinia, a crocheter, Harare, 1997)

Many women also discussed their dreams to purchase or build a house for their families. Though material concerns were very important to crocheters, these were discussed in the context of fulfilling their immediate and extended family needs for education, food, and shelter. For the most part, these businesswomen did not express a desire for personal material goods that only they would enjoy but rather discussed those items that would enhance the overall well-being of their families, especially their children.

All in all, the crocheters in this study illustrated that they were committed to the growth and development of their firms in order to surpass the level of survival. They were critically engaged in business practices to achieve these ends—namely, they were dynamic innovators who diversified production and sales, they introduced subcontracting in their firms to enhance efficiency and thereby generated temporary employment, and they reinvested profits in their businesses. They experienced setbacks in their business and personal lives as a result of the economic crisis, ESAP, and other structural conditions, but they reported that over the course of their business operations, they had achieved more successes than failures. Moreover, they had aspirations for the future that further demonstrated their commitment to the growth of their activities, and they remained optimistic about the prospects for achieving these goals, even in the face of economic crisis. Rather than subscribing to some false notion of two dichotomous roles in their lives—as entrepreneurs versus mothers or wives—they acknowledged and accepted the intersections of the professional and the personal, even though they realized that they were performing a very difficult juggling act. Unfortunately, the intensification of the economic and now political crisis, coupled with the HIV/AIDS pandemic, has pushed the realization of their goals into the more distant future.

# Chapter 4

# "The Market Sustains Me": Traders Persisting under Difficult Odds

In considering the various activities in which women are engaged in the microenterprise sector in Africa, trading has been the area most widely researched by social scientists, particularly during the past two decades (Clark 1994; Robertson 1984, 1997; Horn 1994; House-Midamba and Ekechi 1995; Osirim 1995, 1996, Darkwah 2002; MacGaffey and Bazenguissa-Ganza 2000; Snyder 2000). Market traders occupy a very significant niche in social and economic history as well as in the economic development of contemporary Sub-Saharan Africa. West African women have a long history in local and some long-distance trade, which has been documented dating back to at least the eighteenth century. These activities have enabled women in West Africa to become major contributors to family maintenance and to the education of their children and, in some cases, have enabled them to attain economic independence.

Although both women and men are involved in trade throughout the continent, a gender-based division of labor generally exists in market vending. The paradigm of feminist political economy sheds light on the gendered aspects of trade, where the combined effects of patriarchy, colonialism, and globalization are revealed in the goods sold by women and men. More and more women have been forced into trade by patriarchy, as expressed by Africans and British colonials; by structural blockages in education and employment; and by the vagaries of contemporary economic crises and structural adjustment. Women's activities in this field have been most often associated with the sale of food, clothing, and other domestic items, whereas men have generally participated more often in the sale of manufactured goods, electronics, and more recently high-technology goods. These distinctions in what women and men sell have generally meant that women are in the low-status, low-return end of market vending, while men usually sell more prestigious goods, from which they earn higher incomes (Horn 1994; Downing 1995; Osirim 1995; Robertson 1997). One slight exception to this model was illustrated among Ghanaian traders who engaged in lucrative trade in global consumer items, most often in East Asia. Although they sell "gendered" goods such as cosmetics and hair care products, these items are in high demand among Ghanaian women (Darkwah 2002, 2007).

Women in urban Zimbabwe do not share the long history in market trading enjoyed by their West African sisters. In fact, as stated above, under the race-based system of stratification that existed in Zimbabwe during colonialism, living and working in cities were largely off limits to the majority of black women. Unlike their male counterparts—who were expected to find work in cash crop farming, mining, and manufacturing—black women were expected to remain in the Tribal Trust Lands (black rural areas) and eke out a living in subsistence agriculture. At the beginning of colonialism in the 1890s, however, a few black women began trading in Harare, where there was a marked increase in the number of women selling fresh produce in the 1930s (Horn 1994). In the early years, many vendors hawked their vegetables along the city streets, as well as selling some goods door-to-door in the low-density suburbs (white areas). In the early 1940s, official market stalls were established in the black townships of Highfield and were later relocated to Mbare (Horn 1994). During the colonial period, black women vendors were particularly able to provide black male workers who lived in the barracks-like dormitories in Harare with the green, leafy vegetables and other products traditionally used in Shona and Ndebele cooking.

Today, black women traders continue to sell their fresh and dried produce in both Mbare Market, the largest market in Harare with more than 1,000 traders, and also in markets throughout the high-density suburbs of Harare and other major cities. In the large markets, women tend to sell their goods in stalls, which they rent from the City Council. The economic crisis, however, has led to an increase in the number of women vendors, so this study found larger numbers of women trading goods in makeshift markets, which they had constructed next to some of the established markets in the major cities. For example, at Manwele Market in Bulawayo, the second major field site for interviewing traders in this study, though some women sold their goods from their individually rented stalls, others traded from the stands and tables they constructed adjacent to the market. The economic crisis and the Economic Structural Adjustment Program (ESAP) have also led to greater numbers of women hawking their goods along the downtown streets.

Many traders in this study often complained about the growth in the number of women "illegally" selling their goods in business districts frequented by white and black Zimbabweans, as well as hawking their goods at bus stations and other locations. The traders remarked that such hawkers made it difficult for them, as established vendors, to do business in the designated markets, because the hawkers did not undergo health inspections and sometimes sold spoiled food. The traders noted that their occupation would be blamed collectively whenever there was an outbreak of a food-borne disease. They also discussed the increased competition they experienced from the hawkers during the economic crisis and structural adjustment, but they appeared more incensed by the health problems that they believed the hawkers had created in the cities. In the early 1990s, the illegal hawkers were often subject to harassment by the police. Their goods would be confiscated and the women fined. Even when the women paid the fines to the authorities, they seldom received their goods back. By the late 1990s, however, the intensified economic crisis meant that the police and the state were increasingly turning a blind eye to the growing number of women selling on the streets. By then, it had become absolutely clear that these women were desperately trying to sustain themselves and their families. Thus, in the contemporary period, not only have the numbers of women traders multiplied but they have also become more dispersed over a wider range of areas within the cities studied. In other words, "hawking," or selling one's goods outside the confines of a market, has become even more commonplace in Zimbabwe's major cities.

This chapter explores the personal backgrounds as well as the business and family lives of women who worked in the Mbare and Manwele markets in, respectively, Harare and Bulawayo, Zimbabwe. Intensive interviews were conducted with market traders in these locations, as well as participant-observation, in 1991, 1994, and 1997. After describing the personal backgrounds of the entrepreneurs in this sector, the chapter examines the composition of their households and the division of labor in their families. A comprehensive investigation of their business practices, the financial profiles of their firms, and the impact of government regulations and globalization on their enterprises will be undertaken. Though these women are facing extremely difficult circumstances under the economic crisis and structural adjustment, their commitments to their businesses and their families have enabled many of them to move their firms beyond the level of simple survival.

## Who Are the Market Traders? Demographic Profiles

The market traders were the largest category sampled in my study, with sixty-one entrepreneurs intensively interviewed. These vendors were an average of forty-one years old and were from ethnically diverse backgrounds. More than half the sample—57 percent (thirty-five traders)—were Shona, the largest ethnic group in the country, followed by the Ndebele, who constituted 21 percent (thirteen) of the sample. The Tonga and Venda groups—very small ethnic groups in Zimbabwe, representing about 1 percent of the national population—were also included in the sample, with one vendor from each group. Women from Zambia, Malawi, and South Africa were also in the study and made up about 16 percent (ten) of the sample.

As was the case among other categories of businesswomen in this study, the transnational character of the sample illustrates the fluidity of the borders and the increasingly important role of migration within the Southern African region, particularly in periods of economic crisis. The perspective of feminist political economy illuminates the terms and processes of Southern African nations' incorporation into the world capitalist system and elucidates why Zimbabwe, which at this time had a highly developed economy, served as a powerful magnet for labor migrants to the region. During the 1980s, Zimbabwe was clearly the second most developed economy in Sub-Saharan Africa after South Africa.[1]

In assessing their social position in contemporary Zimbabwe, nearly two-thirds (thirty-eight) of market traders defined themselves as lower class. Twenty-two reported that they were middle class, with fifteen describing themselves as solidly middle class (as opposed to lower middle class). Yet despite their self-reported class positions, these vendors were concentrated on the lowest rungs of the nation's socioeconomic ladder and were generally poorer than their counterparts in crocheting, sewing, and hairdressing.

When compared with their sisters in these other fields, the market traders also had the lowest levels of educational attainment in the study. At the extreme ends of the distribution, four vendors had never attended school, and one woman did earn her Ordinary Level (O-level) certificate. Nearly half the sample (49 percent, thirty women), had only completed a few years of

---

1. Since the beginning of the new millennium and the intensification of the economic and political crises, many Zimbabweans have left the nation and settled in other Southern African nations, such as South Africa and Botswana. In addition, many migrants have also settled in Europe, Australia, and the United States.

primary school, and 23 percent (fourteen) had completed this level of schooling. Ten traders (16 percent) had attended some secondary school, and two additional vendors had also achieved some postsecondary education, even though they did not successfully pass five O-level examinations.

As discussed above, the inability to successfully complete lower secondary school (i.e., passing the required O-level examinations) means that individuals cannot obtain positions in the formal sector of the economy. Passing the five O-level exams in the basic subjects, including the English language, is quite a difficult feat for young women from poor and low-income backgrounds, due to their heavy responsibilities for housework and child care. Although young men also have responsibilities in the domestic sphere, they have far fewer daily demands on their time (e.g., household repairs, car washing, trash collection, grass cutting) than young women, and thus the men can devote more time to their studies.[2]

Moreover, young men enjoy a more privileged position in terms of educational attainment in their families and in the society at large, because they assume roles as household heads as adults and are also expected to support their families, including their elderly relatives. Once they marry, women leave their natal families and join their husbands' households. Therefore, in many cases, fathers in poor and low-income households believe that educating daughters is a waste of valuable, scarce resources. The economic crisis and structural adjustment have placed greater pressures on low-income families, and this has frequently meant that many parents have removed their daughters from school. The intersectionality paradigm, as a key feature of feminist political economy, demonstrates how, historically, African patriarchy combined with colonialism restricted the mobility of black African women to the lowest level of society. Today, this system's legacy, combined with the contemporary economic crisis, has led to low levels of educational attainment among black women and further positioned them at the bottom of the Zimbabwean socioeconomic hierarchy. A trader in Bulawayo summed up these problems:

> I like trading. I chose this because I did not go to school for it to satisfy me. I wanted to go for more schooling, but because of money, I had to stop school. I had to do trading because of my grade. (interview with Jessica, a trader, Bulawayo, 1994)

---

2. As discussed above, Arlie Hochschild (1989) earlier noted this distinction in the nature of women's and men's household labors in the United States.

Due to the structural blockage that traders experienced in the labor market, they were determined to provide as much education as possible for their children, especially their daughters. Throughout the interviews for this study, women continued to express the need to educate their children as a goal that their businesses would hopefully enable them to achieve.

Although their experiences with formal education were more limited than their peers in crocheting, hairdressing, and sewing, the traders did enroll in many other programs to expand their knowledge and skills. Apart from learning how to trade, these women had many other skills that could and did enable them to increase their incomes in the microenterprise sector as well as aid them in meeting their domestic responsibilities. Women's clubs, Red Cross training, Mothers' clubs, training institutes, and microfinance clubs had provided them with a wide range of short courses in marketable skills—including dressmaking, crocheting and knitting, typing and secretarial training, fashion design, pattern making, cooking, adult literacy, accounting, teacher training, and poultry farming. Some of them enrolled in these courses after they left secondary school, and others enrolled as adults. In all sectors of this study, women were committed to education for themselves and their families, and they viewed education as a process that should continue throughout one's life.

More than three-quarters of the sample had held positions prior to their current market trading venture. Most of these earlier positions were in the microenterprise sector, which is understandable given their lack of O-level qualifications. The most widely held prior position was domestic worker (25 percent of the sample, fifteen women). In addition to the lack of sufficient educational credentials to enter the formal sector, this position also reminds us of the race-based system of stratification that characterized British colonialism in Zimbabwe. Poor, black African women in this system experienced the intersection of multiple forms of oppression in their daily lives—that of being lower class, black, and a woman. A list of these women's previous positions—factory workers in small-scale plants, nursery and primary schoolteachers, cooks, salespersons and cashiers, and homework as seamstresses and knitters, among others—also demonstrates that they did occupy jobs utilizing many skills learned in training programs.[3] Some women held previous positions as traders in areas other than their current sales of

---

3. In the past, primary school teachers did not have to be university graduates to hold such positions. In some instances, completion of primary school was considered sufficient to teach this level of education.

fruits and vegetables, such as cloth, clothing, and linen sales. As is the case for most women in Zimbabwe and in Sub-Saharan Africa, a few women in this study had been subsistence farmers or agricultural workers.

Like their counterparts in the other subsectors of this study, many traders had aspired to become teachers or nurses as adults. About 32 percent of the respondents reported that they wanted to enter one of these professions, but for the most part they could not pursue their dreams because they had not successfully completed lower secondary school, as noted by a few traders:

Teacher—[wanted to become this] when I was young. I haven't thought about anything else. Couldn't pursue teaching; not enough money to continue in school. (interview with Gelly Marsuku, a trader, Bulawayo, 1991)

As a child, [wanted to become] a nurse or a teacher. Didn't pursue these because not enough money to stay in school. I would like to do knitting full time. I am not fully skilled to do the knitting. (interview with Shira, a trader, Harare, 1994)

Teacher. I did not pursue this because I did not pass all my O-levels and there was no money for me to return to school. I tried to get a job helping the patients with the Red Cross, but I did not get the job because I did not have enough O-level passes. You need five O-level passes to get that job. I have not thought about pursuing any other job now. (interview with Donorvin, a trader, Harare, 1994)

These dreams are still alive among some traders, who are continuing in their pursuit of their occupational goals. In this regard, they further demonstrate their commitment to education over the course of their lives:

Teacher—I want to be a teacher, yes. I am trying to go to the night school classes. I will take the O-level exam again in November, then, if I pass, go to a college [A-levels] and university. (interview with Molly, a trader, Harare, 1994)

A few traders also aspired to become a dressmaker, a computer programmer, or a police officer. Approximately 38 percent (twenty-three) of the sample stated that becoming a market trader had been a desire since childhood.

The businesswomen in this sample had largely acquired their skills as traders from other women, most often other female relatives. Mothers, grandmothers, and aunts were most important in teaching these women how to trade. Nearly half (42 percent) of all the women entrepreneurs who responded to this question mentioned at least one of these relatives. Sometimes young women learned this work on the job, for example, by assisting their mothers or other female relatives in operating their stall and purchasing goods. Male relatives—such as fathers, brothers, uncles, and husbands—played a more limited role in transmitting skills to traders. These findings are very similar to those discussed by Clark (1994) with reference to traders in Kumasi, Ghana, and by Robertson (1997) with respect to traders in Nairobi. Clark noted how observation and practice were the main methods for learning the trade. Her work in Ghana further illustrated the gendered nature of trading—young women often worked with their female relatives (mothers and aunts), especially in learning how to trade. Robertson's study indicated that not only was there a gendered aspect to how women acquired skills in market vending but there was also a historical dimension. Only since the 1940s had female relatives generally taught young women how to trade. Before then, mainly agricultural skills were passed on from mothers to their daughters.

Given their limited educational credentials, their subsequent blockage from many areas of the labor market, and the poverty they experienced in the broader society, women perceived market trading as one of the only available avenues in which they could generate an income. Compared with the other areas of the microenterprise sector studied here, market trading offered even fewer barriers to entry, particularly because it did not require the technical skills (e.g., the ability to knit, sew, and braid or straighten hair) needed in the other areas. Trading did not require large amounts of start-up capital, machinery, or employees. It was an occupation that offered flexibility. In a fashion similar to that of the traders in Kumasi Central Market in Ghana, the Zimbabwean vendors went into trading in part because they had very limited access to capital and the occupation offered flexibility (Clark 1994). As stated by the traders from the Manwele and Mbare markets:

This was one of the easier things to do that you didn't need a lot of money to start off with. I could watch my child and do the business. When the child gets older, I want to go back to nursing work. (interview with Beauty Ncube, a trader, Bulawayo, 1991)

To keep my children, . . . this business I could start with little money. For other business like dressmaking, I have to have more learning and I didn't have money for this. (interview with Ruvimbo, a trader, Harare, 1997)

Market traders, like women in all segments of this study, believed they had a responsibility to assist in and/or fully support themselves and their families. When asked "Why did you start this business?" several women compared market trading with other ventures in the microenterprise sector and concluded that trading offered greater prospects for financial viability and the maintenance of their families, especially because food was a necessity:

Because knitting and sewing depends on seasons, but fruit, it is always in demand. (interview with Geavy Kahondo, a trader, Harare, 1991)

Here is a good place to sell fruits and vegetables. Here there are lots of customers. You can get more money than trading clothes. When you trade clothes, it is only once a month. Selling fruits and vegetables can be done everyday. We would go to sell clothes at farms in Zimbabwe. They get paid once a month. (interview with Molly, a trader, Harare, 1994)

Because I am assured of a regular income, because the demand for vegetables and foodstuffs is on a daily basis, as opposed to other businesses where you don't get customers everyday. (interview with Choga, a trader, Harare, 1997)

These and many other similar explanations offered by vendors demonstrate the very thoughtful, rational decision making in which these women were engaged. In other words, they selected this occupation because, after much consideration, it offered the best means available to support themselves and their families. Market trading "made sense" in these difficult economic times because food was a necessity that would remain in demand among urban residents.

## Household Structure, Domestic Responsibilities, and Family Life

Unlike their sisters in sewing, hairdressing, and crocheting, market-trading women had the lowest rates of marriage in the study; nearly half (49.2 percent) were married, 23 percent were divorced, and about 5 percent were separated. Widowed and single women each constituted 11.5 percent of the sample.

Four main reasons can begin to account for the higher rates of divorce noted among market traders as compared with their sisters in sewing and hairdressing (18 percent) and those in crocheting (14 percent). First, many of the poorest women began trading establishments, particularly because they did not have partners and, as stated above, this occupation offers one of the only means of sustenance for these women and their children.

Second, the stresses and strains of this phase of globalization—which resulted in economic crisis and structural adjustment policies—have taken their harshest toll on the poorest women and children. This is so because, in several cases, their male partners were unable to fulfill their traditional breadwinning role; and with such pressures, their husbands' extended kin also abandoned their historical roles as caregivers for their sons' children. Thus, in many ways, the market-trading women in this study, and in society at large, experienced the most extensive feminization of poverty. In her feminist political economy analysis, Moghadam (2000) noted significant growth in the feminization of poverty as a result of contemporary globalization. In the case of Zimbabwean market traders, the growth of poverty is attributed to the economic crisis and the attempts to rectify this with the adoption of ESAP.

Third, as the more "middle-class" segment of this study, seamstresses and hairdressers could be expected to have higher rates of marriage. And fourth, last but not least, high rates of marriage were noted among crocheters at the Newlands Shopping Center (the largest site for crocheters in this study). This was the case because this area was adjacent to a prison and police barracks and many of the wives of the police officers took advantage of their residential location and pursued crocheting and knitting as a way to help support their families.

The businesswomen in this study who were involved in market trading were extremely committed to their families, and especially to their children. These traders had four children on average. Only five respondents did not have children at the time of the interviews (one had a child who passed away). Their number of children ranged from none to nine. As will be shown below, the dedication of these entrepreneurs to their children and their extended families was particularly remarkable given their financial status and the devastating nature of the economic crisis.

How did the market traders describe their relationship with their husbands or, in some cases, partners? Twenty-six stated that their relationships were generally satisfactory to good. Very few women, however, demonstrated any excitement in discussing their most recent marriage or relationship. In this regard, the following comments were quite rare:

> We are getting on quite well because there are no problems. Love is more important than money, even with financial problems, we get on quite well. (interview with Joyce, a trader, Manwele Market, Bulawayo, 1991)

> We have a good relationship. We don't fight and we do not quarrel. If we do, we do not for long. He shares the money with me and he shows me how much he has. When he says he has no money, I believe him. (interview with Annah, a trader, Mbare Market, Harare, 1997)[4]

Most traders described their current marriages and other relationships with male partners as difficult, mainly due to financial problems. Excessive drinking and extramarital relationships were also mentioned as reasons for unhappy relationships, and certainly in a number of cases, these factors were intertwined:

> . . . At times, there are problems here and there. Most of the problems are when my husband gets drunk. (interview with Elizabeth Monyarara, Mbare Market, Harare, 1991)

> We had a number of disagreements when I was married. My husband had a "don't care attitude"—life was tense, I just decided to get divorced. Mostly it was financial problems; my husband used to spend much of the money away. The owners of the house needed the rent. I needed money for the kids, food, and so on. I had to look after myself and the kids. (interview with Shira, Mbare Market, Harare, 1994)

---

4. This situation is indeed quite rare because in many Sub-Saharan African states (as well as in other areas of the Global South, e.g., Jamaica), both women and men attempt to keep their money separate, hidden, and generally are secretive about how much they have and how much they earn. This activity, however, is highly gendered, with men often maintaining this behavior to reinforce their power in relationships and to spend money on personal pursuits (drinking, engaging in other relationships, etc.). Women in this study and in other African nations often keep their money hidden for future investment in the education of their children, especially their daughters. See Downing (1990).

Things are difficult because of financial constraints. My husband has a temporary job, and from one day to the next, you never know when he could get laid off. (interview with Gada, Mbare Market, Harare, 1994)

Poor marriage in terms of money. Usually stayed in rural areas. [He] believed women should stay in rural areas while husband works in town. [I] liked to stay in rural areas—life in town expensive as compared with rural areas. Too expensive to raise kids in town. They were happy. (interview with Gadaga, Mbare Market, Harare, 1994)

African patriarchy—coupled with contemporary globalization, specifically in the form of ESAP and the resulting retrenchment of thousands of workers—has clearly had an impact on the level of stability and fulfillment realized in marriages.[5]

Whether a relationship with one's husband or partner was mainly positive or negative, Zimbabwean women still do the vast majority of the domestic work and are significantly involved in the rearing of children. Historically, nearly all women in urban, but especially in rural areas, could expect substantial help in these tasks from the extended family—from both relatives who lived with them and those who lived near them. Further, in the case of divorce or the death of a husband in patrilineal societies, the husband's natal family would generally raise the children. In the contemporary period, however, the economic crisis has made it increasingly difficult for extended family members on either side of a family to occupy both economic and caregiving roles, given the very major demands that globalization, particularly in the form of structural adjustment, inflicts on poor and low-income families. Thus, whereas in the past, nearly all women would receive substantial help from extended family members, today, we are likely to find that fewer women actually receive significant assistance from relatives not living with them. Further, in the case of death or divorce, children are not automatically sent to the father's family. The reduction today in support from

---

5. At a conference on gender, justice, and development at the University of Massachusetts–Amherst in 1993, Peggy Antrobus, then director of Development Alternatives with Women for a New Era (DAWN), noted that there clearly seemed to be a relationship between the adoption of structural adjustment programs and escalating violence against women in the Global South. Not only is such gender-based violence physical in scope, but it also takes the forms of economic and psychological violence. See Green (1999), Musasa Project Trust (1998), and Osirim (2001, 2003c).

Figure 4.1. Market traders at Mbare Market, Harare, June 1994

extended family members in Sub-Saharan Africa is noted by Collette Suda (2007, 66):

> The processes of modernization, globalization, delocalization, and mo-
> bility which are evident everywhere in Africa, and, indeed, across the
> world have had far-reaching consequences for the twin institutions of
> marriage and family. One of the consequences of this transition is the
> weakening of the extended family system, the decline of polygyny and
> the emergence of alternative family options which are designed to suit
> individual needs.

Although most men spend little time involved in the daily rearing of their children, many of the market traders in this study were quick to comment that their husbands or partners did play an important role in raising their children. Forty-five percent (twenty-five) of the traders who had children stated that their husbands or partners raised the children with them, while in three cases, the traders raised their children alone. The traders often used the term "raising the children" with respect to a father's financial support of his children, as opposed to his attending to their daily caregiving needs, as noted in a comment by Future Wilson: "Father helps—he pays to main-

Figure 4.2. A market trader holding her baby at Manwele Market, Bulawayo, Zimbabwe, July 1994

tain children. Children stay with me" (interview, Mbare Market, Harare, 1991). In 38 percent (twenty-one) of these cases, extended family members did assist in raising a woman entrepreneur's children, with her mother assisting more than any other relative. Though the rate of participation among extended family members might seem high, participation among such relatives would have been expected to be far higher were it not for the economic crisis.

Although many women traders in this study had children who were old enough to "look after themselves" while the women worked, several women commented that their children accompanied them to work (see figures 4.1 and 4.2):

> I bring the four year older here when the nine year older is out. The children are in school and when they are done, they join me here. (interview with Mrs. M, Mbare Market, Harare, 1994).

> I bring my youngest child here everyday. Then my other children come here after school. (interview with Runimbo, Mbare Market, Harare, 1997)

The market-trading women, as well as others in the microenterprise sector, frequently noted that work in this sphere provided them with the flexibility they need to fulfill their child care and other domestic responsibilities. Though they experienced substantial structural blockage denying them entry into formal-sector positions, they also valued the extent that market vending enabled them to combine their dual roles and responsibilities to work and family.

With respect to the businesswomen with a male partner living with them, only 14 percent of those male partners or husbands assisted with domestic tasks. Those who did provide such help were mainly involved in activities with their children, such as watching or playing with them, or occasional repair work. The husbands and male partners in this study, like men in many African and other societies, were generally not involved in cooking, dishwashing, ironing, or other daily domestic tasks, especially those centered in the kitchen. As stated above, Zimbabwean men are unlikely to assume a major role in the daily domestic tasks and are more likely to perform duties such as home repairs and yard work that do not require daily attention:

He [my husband] performs any necessary repairs to the home [it is made of wooden planks]. If a child is sick, he would give me money for the hospital. (interview with Mary, Mbare Market, Harare, 1994)

Conversely, the businesswomen in this study were likely to spend three to four hours a day on domestic tasks. These duties were begun in the morning before they arrived at the markets (they usually arrived between 6 and 7 AM). These entrepreneurs spent approximately twelve hours a day in the market and then returned home to continue cooking and cleaning for an additional two and a half to three hours or so before going to bed. Many began their day at around 4 or 5 AM. Though these women were unlikely to receive help with daily domestic tasks from their husbands or partners, their children and especially daughters were very involved with providing child care, cooking, and cleaning:

My oldest child, a daughter, spent five hours after school until I get home, doing housework. (interview with Lisa, Manwele Market, Bulawayo, 1991)

Seven hours, my eldest daughter spent on child care and housework. (interview with Tatenda, Mbare Market, Harare, 1994)

My oldest daughter spends nine hours a day washing in the morning and irons after cleaning the house. My youngest daughter spends two hours cleaning. (interview with Chipo, Mbare Market, 1997)

My older daughter would take care of the younger ones. I also used to bring some of the young children with me to the market. (interview with Mathula, Bulawayo, Manwele Market, 1997)

As can be seen from even this small sample from interviews, daughters, like their mothers before them, are saddled with many domestic responsibilities. Thus it is not difficult to see some of the major reasons why young women experience more problems in attaining their lower secondary school certificates (i.e., the successful completion of O-level exams). Though their male counterparts are also likely to have domestic responsibilities, these are more likely to resemble their fathers' duties, such as car washing and home repairs, not tasks such as cooking that need to be done on a daily basis. Thus, young men, compared with young women, have more time to devote to schoolwork. When this fact is considered in light of the persistence of African patriarchy, there is little wonder why many young women cannot pass a sufficient number of O-level exams, and thus they remain confined to work in the "second economy."

In slightly more than 26 percent of all cases (26.2 percent, fifteen women), these entrepreneurs shared expenses for their children with their husbands or male partners. Included among such expenses are school fees and school related expenses (e.g., transportation and uniforms), food, clothing, and medical expenses. In an equal number of cases, the businesswomen stated that their husbands or male partners assumed all costs related to their children. In about fourteen cases, the entrepreneurs paid for all their children's expenses alone. Six businesswomen reported that these costs were shared by them and several family members, including the fathers of their children, parents, grandmothers, and brothers. Many entrepreneurs discussed the transitions they encountered in meeting their children's expenses due to unemployment and the dissolution of their marriage or relationship:

I pay for school fees. Food is taken care of by my parents. Medicine and health care costs are paid by my elder brother. He is a teacher. My kids go to the school he teaches at. I buy their clothing and pay for whatever else they might need. When I was still married, their father paid for everything. Right now, the husband pays no maintenance and provides no money at all for the raising of his children. I have been to court twice to petition for maintenance payment. First time, he didn't pay, second time, he didn't show up to court and I didn't have the money to find him. (interview with Chiyedza, a trader. Mbare Market, Harare, 1994)

My responsibilities have not remained the same since I was married. When I was married, my husband had to support us financially, but he lost his job and could no longer do this. So, I started to work for myself and my children. (interview with Elen, a trader. Manwele Market, Bulawayo, 1994)

My mother and I pay for food. Medicine for the children is paid for by my mother. I buy clothing for the children. My husband paid for everything when I was married. Now he pays for nothing. (interview with Netsai, a trader, Mbare Market, Harare, 1997)

These market traders were further asked about responsibilities for other expenses in their households, such as paying rent, buying food and clothing, and paying for other adult expenses such as medical costs. Twenty-seven entrepreneurs reported that they shared these expenses with their husbands, whereas in only two cases did traders respond that their husbands assumed all these expenses. About 38 percent (twenty-three) noted that they alone paid for all adult-related expenses in their households. In seven cases, they shared household expenses with someone other than their husbands, such as parents, a brother, or a sister, which is understandable given that half the sample was not married at the time of the study.

Although, historically, Zimbabwean men were responsible for meeting nearly all the household expenses for their wives and children, the problems wrought by the economic crisis and structural adjustment policies have made it increasingly difficult for them to do so. In those cases in this study where the wives and husbands shared these costs, the men were usually responsible for housing and the women were more likely to pay for food and clothing. Given the reimposition of school fees, the increased costs of transportation and food due to structural adjustment policies, and their poor or low-income status, the market-trading women, like their sisters in the broader society, bore the very heavy and disproportionate weight of the economic crisis. The feelings of several market women are summed up in the experiences of Hilda:

When I first married, I used to have a housemaid, but now I cannot afford it because I have too many financial obligations. At the present moment, there is no correlation between what I get from sales and the demands at home. I'm not happy because I've been forced to make my children street vendors after they come home from school. (interview with Hilda, a trader, Mbare Market, Harare, 1997)

One example of a woman's power in a family is often demonstrated by her role in decision making for the household.[6] The market-trading entrepreneurs in this study were asked "Who makes the decisions in your family?" with regard to such issues as the use of money, bill paying, the discipline of children, and housework. All thirty married respondents stated that they shared decision making with their husbands. About one-third (twenty) remarked that they made all major decisions in their households, and approximately 17 percent (eleven) noted that decision making involved both them and extended family members, usually in cases where the latter were living with them. Although married market traders' households would appear to be democratic based on these statistics on decision making, in reality, the same division of labor that appears with respect to domestic responsibilities is apparent in decision making. Among married traders, the trend in their households is for husbands to make decisions involving money (the paying of bills, which most of them stated that their husbands physically did; and making most major purchases) and women made decisions about housework (who would do it, when it would get done, etc.):

Money spent and saved and purchasing of items, the husband does. Children and housework decisions, [I] make. (interview with Molly, a trader, Manwele Market, Bulawayo, 1991)

Husband makes decisions about money and bills. I decide on what to buy and the housework, and we both decide on children's issues. (interview with Elizabeth, a trader, Monyarara, Mbare Market, Harare, 1991)

Although the market traders in this study had many financial, child care, and other domestic duties to perform for their immediate family members residing in their households, they also had very substantial responsibilities for extended family members—both those living with them and those living elsewhere. Twenty-six percent (sixteen) of these businesswomen had

---

6. In studies of women's power within families and households in northern societies, decision-making power is most often positively associated with a woman's earnings (Pyke 1994; Andersen 1997; Lips 2005).

extended family members living with them, and 71 percent (forty-three) had responsibilities for relatives not living with them.

As has been well documented (Sudarkasa 1981a, 1981b; Kilbride and Kilbride 1990; Kilbride 1994), extended families are extremely important in Sub-Saharan Africa. Historically, they have been central in providing needed financial assistance, child care, and socioemotional support, which has sustained families, clans, and communities. Even though the vagaries of economic crisis and structural adjustment have placed added stresses and strains on extended families, forcing them to limit the amount of support they can provide, they are still a critical unit in overall family maintenance.

In her research on the Yoruba of southwestern Nigeria, Sudarkasa (1981a, 1981b) observed that a reciprocal relationship of support and obligation existed among their extended families. This example also prevails among the Shona and Ndebele of Zimbabwe, and more specifically among the market traders in this study. Thus, although 26 percent of these traders had extended family members living with them, these women did not assume all the obligations for their care but rather assumed some and received assistance in return. Typically, a relative from one's rural hometown might be sent to live with an aunt or uncle in the city to attend school, receive apprenticeship training, and/or find a job. In return, this "niece" or "nephew" might assist with housework, child care, or household expenses:

> My nephew is living with me because he wanted to. He is just being helped by the missionary and is doing Form IV studies. His mother does not have a proper space. I wanted him to stay with me. My nephew helps to sweep the floors. My nephew does not contribute money—I pay for the food and the missionaries pay for his [schooling]. (interview with Annastazia M., a trader, Manwele Market, Bulawayo, 1994)

> The two cousins (cousins of my children), my husband's nephews, do not help pay the expenses. The two cousins help to do gardening and help to look after the young ones. The twenty-three-year-old is unemployed. The elder one's father died, and the mother is married to another man. She left the child with my husband. My husband and I take care of the two nephews. (interview with Tatenda, a trader, Mbare Market, Harare, 1994)

> My cousin lives with me. I invited her to come because she can help me. She has been living with me for a long time. My female cousin helps with the housework and cooking and helps to take care of the children. Yes, I

pay for the expenses—food and clothing for my cousin. I give her money now for everything—no set amount. She does not work. (interview with Joyce, a trader, Manwele Market, Bulawayo, 1997)

The market vendors in this study were even more involved in providing support to extended family members not living with them. More than half (thirty-two) of the respondents provided financial assistance, as well as food and clothing in some cases, to their parents and/or in-laws, and another eleven entrepreneurs gave financial help to other relatives, including siblings, grandparents, aunts, uncles, nieces, and nephews. Though some of these businesswomen discussed giving money specifically to their parents, the majority mentioned their mothers because most of their fathers were deceased. In many cases, they also had far closer relationships with their mothers (especially in polygynous families), or they realized that it was far less likely that their mothers, as women, would have access to much money in their households. They also mentioned their assistance to other female relatives:

I give money to two people not living with me—my mother and my grandmother (my mother's mother). I give them Z$30 to Z$50 every month or two. I also give them food and clothing. (interview with Donorvin, a trader, Mbare Market, Harare, 1994)

Yes, [I give to] mother and two sisters. Sometimes, I give money to my mother, Every two weeks, every two months. If I find [it]. Sometimes, I give Z$100; sometimes, Z$50; sometimes, Z$20. I also buy groceries—sugar, soap, or I might bring clothes as well (sometimes, used clothes; sometimes, new clothes). Sometimes, I give my sisters money to buy things for their children. Sometimes, I give my own old clothes to my sisters. (interview with Mulaleli, a trader, Manwele Market, Bulawayo, 1997)

Therefore, given the gendered division of labor and decision making that prevailed in these market traders' households, it is easy to see how they shouldered the lion's share of domestic responsibilities. Although they were not, in the main, solely responsible for all caregiving and household/family expenses, they certainly bore more than their fair share of these tasks. In meeting their responsibilities to immediate and extended kin and running their enterprises in the midst of economic crisis and structural adjustment, they were indeed performing an incredible juggling act.

"Without a Business I Would Have No Life":
Starting and Maintaining a Trading Enterprise

Sitting in Manwele Market, Bulawayo, in 1994, the market trader Elen was asked if she had any goals as a woman. She responded, "Without a business, I would have no life." In many ways, this statement epitomizes what operating a vending establishment meant to so many women in this study. In part, many of these entrepreneurs viewed their businesses as a means to an end—a way of supporting their families and particularly providing education for their children. Conversely, for most of these women, the story did not end there. They were also very committed to the growth and development of their firms far beyond the level of simple survival. Though these market traders were less involved in major innovation than their sisters in sewing, hairdressing, and crocheting, partly due to the nature of their enterprises, they were highly dedicated to improving, expanding, and in some cases diversifying their business activities. Moreover, their work as entrepreneurs constituted a focal part of their identities. These businesses enabled them to showcase their agency and abilities in such areas as sales and to fulfill their responsibilities to their immediate and extended families.

Why and how did these women decide to begin market trading? As stated above, market vending is hardly a choice for most women in this field. Due to poverty and the structural blockage that they experienced in the educational system and the labor market, most of these women had no choice but to find an occupation that would enable them to earn a living:

> I like trading—I chose this because I did not go to school for it to satisfy me. I wanted to go for more schooling, but because of money, I had to stop school. I had to do trading because of my grade. (interview with Jessica, a trader, Manwele Market, Bulawayo, 1994)

In addition, women who find themselves heading households as single parents in Zimbabwe—most often as a result of separation, divorce, or widowhood—look to the microenterprise sector as a way of supporting themselves and their families. Further, even in the case of married women, the economic crisis and ESAP made it necessary for most of them to supplement their spouses' incomes, and starting a microenterprise was encouraged as a way to accomplish this.[7] Many women in this position view market

7. With the enactment of the ESAP in late 1990 and early 1991 and the subsequent retrenchment of about 40,000 workers over the next few years, the state encouraged the establishment of small enterprises and microenterprises to stem the tide of unemployment.

trading as more lucrative than subsistence agriculture or domestic work—the other two major alternative occupations open to women who lack the educational credentials to enter the economy's formal sector. Trading is one segment of the microenterprise sector that perhaps offers some of the fewest barriers to entry—it has low capital requirements to begin a business and is less expensive than many other firms to maintain, especially with respect to replenishing supplies and paying rental charges for a market stall. Market vending, especially the sale of food, is related to these women's domestic duties, and, for some, would be viewed as an extension of these activities. Such work further enabled some women in the study to more effectively combine their work and family responsibilities:

> This was one of the easier things to do that you didn't need a lot of money to start off with. I could watch my child and do the business. When the child gets older, I want to go back to nursing work. (interview with Beauty Ncube, Manwele Market, Bulawayo, 1991)

> To keep my children, this business I could start with little money. For other business like dressmaking, I have to have more learning and I did not have money for this. (interview with Ruvimbo, Mbare Market, Harare, 1997)

Moreover, given the realities of their lives as largely poor and low-income women with low levels of educational attainment living in the midst of economic crisis, market vending was a very rational decision, even when considering the few alternatives:

> Because knitting and sewing depends on seasons. But with fruit, it is always in demand. (interview with Geavy Kahondo, a trader, Mbare Market, Harare, 1991)

> I just wanted some money. Here is a good place to sell fruits and vegetables. Here there are a lot of customers. You can get more money than trading clothes. When you trade clothes, it is only once a month. Selling fruits and vegetables can be done everyday. We would go to sell clothes at farms in Zimbabwe. They get paid once a month. (interview with Molly, a trader, Mbare Market, Harare, 1994)

> Because I am assured of a regular income because the demand for vegetables and food stuffs is on a daily basis, as opposed to other businesses

*Table 4.1. Sources of start-up capital among traders*

| Source of capital | Number of respondents | Percent |
|---|---|---|
| Personal savings | 25 | 41 |
| Husband | 15 | 25 |
| Female relatives | 10 | 16 |
| Male relatives | 6 | 10 |
| Bank or finance agency | | |
| Multiple sources (relatives) | 4 | 6 |
| Other (church member) | 1 | 2 |
| Total | 61 | 100 |

*Source:* Author's study data.
*Note:* The blank cells indicate that banks and finance agencies were not a source of start-up capital for market traders in this study.

where you don't get customers everyday. (interview with Choga, a trader, Mbare Market, Harare, 1997)

Market-vending businesses in this study had a mean and median age of seven years, which compares quite favorably with the ages of sewing and hairdressing establishments (seven years) and crocheting enterprises (eight years). For the fifty-six traders who reported the amount of money with which they began their firms, the average amount was Z$153. Start-up capital ranged from Z$10 to Z$1,000. As was the case among their sisters in hairdressing, sewing, and crocheting, the single most important source of start-up capital for traders was personal savings. Similarly, their husbands were the second major source of start-up capital for market vendors, as was also true for seamstresses, hairdressers, and crocheters. The full list of sources is given in table 4.1.

Because the vast majority of traders (more than 75 percent) were engaged in income-earning activities before opening their businesses and were from poor to low-income families, it is easy to understand how savings were their major source of start-up capital. As stated above, given that these women lacked the essential educational credentials to enter the formal economy, the vast majority of them had previously held positions in the microenterprise sector, many working as domestics. The small amount of capital with which most of them could begin their businesses further illustrates how trading facilitates the entry of such women. And, again, their husbands were found to be an important source of start-up capital, as they were for their sisters in the other fields studied. As noted among traders in West Africa as well, husbands were very likely to provide capital for their wives to start a business in cases where these women did not have a job before marriage or if such positions were deemed "inappropriate" by their husbands.[8] Moreover, husbands frequently encouraged their wives to open a business because these activities were believed to provide ready sources of capital in the form of food, clothing, and cash to assist in supporting the family.

What did these vendors sell in the market? As stated above, women are generally involved in microenterprises that are an extension of their domestic responsibilities, and thus they are more likely to be found in the production and sale of food, cloth, clothing, crafts, and other household goods, as opposed to machinery, electronics, and high-technology goods (Downing 1990, 1995). Even African women involved in long-distance trading in the contemporary period bought and sold "gendered" goods such as cosmetics (Darkwah 2007). The market traders in this study sold fresh and/or dried foodstuffs, including tomatoes, onions, beans, nuts, eggs, carrots, cabbages, other green and dried vegetables, millet, sweet potatoes, bananas, apples, and oranges (see figures 4.3 and 4.4). Compared with their sisters in sewing, hairdressing, and crocheting, the market traders were not significantly involved in innovation. However, they were likely to innovate with respect to the types of goods they sold at particular times. In this sense, they made very rational decisions about what they sold, and they diversified production according to such criteria as season and profitability:

In 1986, I was selling only eggs. The eggs are too expensive, so I don't gain much from eggs. In 1989, I began to sell these other products— ground nuts, sugar beans, ration beans, round nuts, dried vegetables, millet, and tomatoes. (interview with Gelly Marsuku, a trader, Manwele Market, Bulawayo, 1991)

When it is cold like this, people do not normally prefer fruit, so I don't sell it now. When the weather is warm, I sell bananas, oranges, apples, and the like. I don't sell the popcorn here because each section of the market sells specific items. If I sell vegetables here, I don't sell popcorn. (interview with Elizabeth Monyarara, a trader, Mbare Market, Harare, 1991)

8. Jobs considered inappropriate by many husbands were those that made it difficult for women to fulfill their childcare and other domestic responsibilities and/or those that placed women in close working relationships with men for very long hours, particularly at night. Nursing is one such example; see Osirim (1994).

Figure 4.3. Traders and shoppers at Mbare Market, Harare, June 1994

What I sell depends on what is selling well with the people who buy. If I see that tomatoes aren't doing well, I'll buy something else to sell. (interview with Chiyedza, a trader, Mbare Market, Harare, 1994)

In 1978, I only sold fresh vegetables, not dry vegetables. I added dry veggies because customers started demanding them. Dried vegetables are used in traditional Ndebele cooking. (interview with Annastazia Mpofu, a trader, Manwele Market, Bulawayo, 1994)

In 1985, I was only selling eggs. They were too expensive; I had no profit. Changes in what I sell—from eggs to vegetables, beans and fruits. Began selling baobab fruit in 1996 because people knew this and no one was selling it. I am the only one selling it. (interview with Mathula, a trader, Manwele Market, Bulawayo, 1997)

These women understood the market. They knew who their customers were, understood their demands, and responded accordingly with the selection and timing of the products they sold. They were clear and thoughtful decision makers who took well-calculated risks in operating their market stalls.

Figure 4.4. A market trader posing in front of her stall at Mbare Market, Harare, June 1994

## The Financial Picture of Trading Enterprises

The majority of the market traders in this study did not provide precise figures when asked about the sales and profits in their enterprises during the years when they were in operation. Most of these women tried to estimate their weekly, monthly, and/or annual sales, whereas about half tried to give more specific amounts for the profits they earned at the time of the interview as well as at different intervals (of about three to five years). In discussing the sales of their firms, only about 11 percent (seven women) reported that their sales had increased over the past three to five years. They generally estimated that their daily sales were about Z$7 to Z$100. Several, however, mentioned how their sales fluctuated from the rainy to the dry seasons. Many remarked that they were experiencing declining sales due to the increased costs of goods from wholesalers, the overall increases in the prices of goods throughout society, and significant increases in competition:

> Business improves during the rainy season because people can use these goods as seeds. Therefore, I sell more during the rainy season. (interview with Beauty Ncube, Manwele Market, Bulawayo, 1991)

[I earn] about Z$7 to Z$10 a day now. Used to make more in the past than now. There is more competition now, and the prices of the commodities from the wholesaler are now very high. I used to sell about Z$20 a day when I first began in 1984. (interview with Hilda Bizure, Mbare Market, Harare, 1991)

Depends on inflation. Plus stiffer competition, because more women are selling same goods. Maybe problem with supply, so money doesn't go as far as it did before. (interview with Geavy Kahondo, Mbare Market, Harare, 1991)

The number of vendors was small compared to now. Everybody is now a vendor. Many working outside this business. It was cheaper to buy from wholesalers in the mid-1980s. Farmers have now increased their prices. (interview with Benica, Mbara Market, Harare, 1994)

Long [time] back, people were not allowed to sell on the streets outside the market; but now, they sell on the street. And unemployment is very high, so people try to support themselves by selling vegetables, and there are too many people selling. (interview with Mabasa, Manwele Market, Bulawayo, 1997)

Every trader reported earning profits over the years, especially when comparing their enterprise's performance from the first year of operation to the time of the interview. Only 54 percent (33 women) of the respondents gave figures for daily, monthly, and/or annual profits. Among these traders, profits at the time of the interview ranged from Z$0 to Z$233 a day. The average amount of daily profits was Z$33.95, while the median amount of daily profits was Z$15. Among those women interviewed in 1991, four gave figures indicating declining profits since the 1980s (the boom period in the Zimbabwean state and economy). Conversely, seven traders interviewed in 1994 and six interviewed in 1997 observed that their profits had improved since the early 1990s. Although several of the remaining businesswomen did not provide figures, they generally indicated that it was far more difficult to earn profits in the 1990s; and in several cases, they reported declining profits. Where increases were noted, profits changed by only small increments per year:[9]

9. Though it is important to remember that most figures provided by these entrepreneurs are estimates, it is also critical to note that their estimates are not adjusted figures. They do not take into account the devaluations that accompanied the structural adjustment programs of the 1990s.

[I earned] Z$15 to Z$20 per day—profits now in 1991. In 1989, [I earned] Z$52 per day. Daily profits are used to buy goods and for food, my bus fare, and bus fare for the kids to school. (interview with Gelly Marsuku, a trader, Manwele Market, Bulawayo, 1991)

About Z$1,000 profit from January to July 1994. [I] earned more last year. Have to pay to replenish stock and pay for the guys who care for the goods here. Used [them] also to pay rent, food, and clothing also. (interview with Shira, a trader, Mbare Market, Harare, 1994)

In 1987, plus or minus Z$150. In 1990, Z$200 for a season [two to three months]. In 1993, plus or minus Z$25. This is the amount per month that I was able to put in a bank account. (interview with Gada, a trader, Mbare Market, Harare, 1994)

In 1994, about Z$50 [profits] per month. In 1993, about Z$45 per month. In 1989, about Z$80 per month. In 1989, other goods were cheaper. We sold more goods, and fewer were selling in the city. Five years ago, more people were working. Now many people do not have a job. (interview with Annastazia Mpofu, Manwele Market, Bulawayo, 1994)

Perhaps the more important consideration with respect to earned profits is how they are used and who makes such decisions. In this study, 79 percent (forty-eight) of the traders reported that they made all decisions about the use of profits from their enterprises. As might be expected, given their contributions to establishing the businesses, the second-largest category of decision makers about the use of profits in these firms consisted of joint decision making by the entrepreneurs and their spouses. Ten businesspersons were in this category. In only two cases did a male relative solely decide about the use of profits—an entrepreneur's husband in one case, and a father in another. Only one other case of joint decisionmaking was noted, involving a trader and her mother.

Although a strict division between business and personal capital was not observed among the market traders in this study, they did reveal a high level of commitment to reinvest in their firms. Eighty-four percent (fifty-one) of vendors mentioned that they used profits to replenish the stocks in their stalls, as well as to meet other personal and family expenses. When considering other specific areas in which profits were used, these businesswomen most often discussed personal savings and investment in the education of their children. Seventy-two percent (forty-four) saved in bank accounts and/or rounds,[10] whereas 69 percent (forty-two) discussed paying for school fees and other related school expenses for their children, grandchildren, and other relatives. Their dedication to the success of their enterprises and to the maintenance of their immediate and extended families was evident in their comments:

> I channel the profits to the round system or reinvest this or use it at home—buy basic necessities for home. I give to my round $14 a day. These rounds are arranged based on where you are from. Both women and men can be in one round and people are members of one scattered throughout the market, selling different goods. . . . I understand that to-day's world requires people that are educated, that have gone to school and this is why I have invested in education (for my kids). (interview with Elizabeth Monyarara, a trader, Mbare Market, Harare, 1991)

> I have invested in this business because it has enabled me to send my children to school. I had to invest in their education because it is the one thing that I always considered seriously. (interview with Hilda Bizure, a trader, Mbare Market, Harare, 1991)

> I used the profits for rounds and to pay for rent, school fees, clothes, and so on. . . . My children's education is a must. No one does this for me— I have to help my sister upkeep her children. (interview with Bridget, a trader, Mbare Market, Harare, 1997)

> I used them [profits] to buy food, pay rent, and also replenish my supplies. I also save money in the banking club. . . . I help my brother sometimes pay school fees for my niece. When my brother has to buy things for my brother's children, he might ask me to help him with the fees for my niece and I help. (interview with Mulaleli, a trader, Manwele Market, Bulawayo, 1997)

Another important area of investment for these entrepreneurs was in other businesses. Fifteen traders in this study were involved in some other area of self-employment, with the vast majority engaged in sewing and/or knit-

10. "Rounds" is the term for rotating-credit schemes in Zimbabwe. These are discussed in chapter 6.

ting activities. It is easy to see why such activities would be prominent among traders, because crocheting and knitting can be done while sitting in one's stall awaiting customers. Sewing also does not involve large investments of capital and can be done with a sewing machine during the evenings in traders' homes. To supplement her earnings from trade, one vendor noted that she was engaged in subcontracting for a crocheter. As noted above, several crocheters in this study and many in Zimbabwe provide employment for relatives, neighbors, and friends through subcontracting arrangements. Though subcontracting is rare in Sub-Saharan Africa, it is somewhat commonplace in crocheting, where the production of large creations, such as tablecloths and bedspreads, can be more efficiently made with several workers each contributing pieces to the final product.

## Successes, Problems, and Aspirations for the Future

The market traders in this study did experience many difficulties operating in the midst of economic crisis and structural adjustment, but when assessing the overall performance of their enterprises from their establishment to the time of the interviews, many respondents noted that they had experienced more successes than problems in their businesses. Forty-one percent (twenty-five) stated that they had achieved success during their years of operation, whereas 37 percent (twenty-three) replied that they had encountered more difficulties than successes. Thirteen entrepreneurs commented that it was difficult to tell whether a successful or problematic experience mainly characterized their firms and that for the most part, maintaining their establishments involved some of each.

Again, the ability to provide for one's family figured prominently in a businesswoman's discussion of achieving success in her enterprise:

> I have been successful because I have managed to do a lot. I have managed to send my kids to school. I have managed to earn a better living, . . . more success. I have become very self-sufficient, self-reliant, and I can even boast that I have something to do for my own, unlike waiting for someone to give me a hand. (interview with Shira, a trader, Mbare Market, Harare, 1994)

> Overall, I have been successful because I have managed to buy a home as a result of this business. . . . I get money to buy food, also to pay rent,

and also to pay my children's school fees. (interview with Joyce, a trader, Manwele Market, Bulawayo, 1997)

Though many women discussed the overall successes they had experienced since they started their businesses, it was absolutely clear that the majority had encountered a very problematic situation in recent years under this phase of globalization and structural adjustment. These traders most often made comments such as the following:

I have got a bit of success because at least I got enough money to put some more things here. I have been able to pay up my credit when I ordered these things. . . . At times, I can't get money to order my things. At times, I come back late from the city center, the police take all my things and I have to pay a fine of Z$25, and they don't return the goods since I have started, the business is just deteriorating every month. I am getting problems; no progress, getting few customers. (interview with Tshuma, a trader, Manwele Market, Bulawayo, 1991)

More problems. People don't buy like before and so I don't make much profit. During the time we have less rains in Bulawayo, the farmers don't have much of the goods, so we have to buy the foods from the marketing board at a higher price. I used to have a car or one of the carts to get the goods—about thirty-one miles from here. I have to go to the marketing board on weekdays to get the goods. (interview with Molly, a trader, Manwele Market, Bulawayo, 1991)

I am not earning enough money to plan things in my life. My daughter had to leave school at Form I because there was not enough money. The biggest problem is when people don't buy from you because your food rots on the tables from going bad, and then you cannot sell the food that you spent money to buy and have no more money to buy fresh food. (interview with Chiyedza, a trader, Mbare Market, Harare, 1994)

The problem now is fewer customers. During the rainy season, there is no shelter for us. We could be left out in the open, and our goods would get ruined. (interview with Mary, a trader, Manwele Market, Bulawayo, 1994)

There is more failure because at first, during the beginning, people used to come buy in large quantities, but now, you sit here the whole day and no one comes. There are fewer people because there is more illegal vending. You find people selling in the roadside, and people will not go out of their way to come here and buy. (interview with Bebe, a trader, Manwele Market, Bulawayo, 1994)

Although many of these market traders have savings accounts, their poor to low-income status means that they most often do not have sufficient funds to adequately maintain themselves and their families in emergencies:

At times, we don't have money to purchase goods. Recently, my brother passed away, and I was looking after him. I had to take care of all the expenses, and I also bought food for his funeral. This really put my business at stake because I used most of the money we had aside. (interview with Primrose, a trader, Mbare Market, Harare, 1997)

Despite the dilemmas they have experienced during the nation's economic crisis, the traders in this study remained optimistic about the future—for themselves, their families, and their businesses. In fact, in addition to educating their children for a better life, the vast majority discussed their desires to expand their current businesses in the future.

I wish to further my children's education—all of them. . . . I would like to have a wholesale business. Selling these foods at wholesale, I would get more customers and a lot of money. (interview with Beauty Ncube, a trader, Manwele Market, Bulawayo, 1991)

I look forward to possibly expanding this business. Then I would have to make an establishment elsewhere and have some of my kids get involved in this business. Might have it here in Mbare—I would like to have two stands in this market. (interview with Hilda Bizure, a trader, Mbare Market, Harare, 1991)

I am investing money now so that in the future I can go to Botswana or South Africa to buy a sewing machine and pursue dressmaking. Then, I will employ a girl in this business while I am dressmaking. (interview with Elizabeth Monyarara, a trader, Mbare Market, Harare, 1991)

I want to see that my children complete school, as far as others, even the college or university. I would like to see my business expand to sell different types of nuts and beans, I do not know if I will be alive to see this. (interview with Joyce, a trader, Manwele Market, Bulawayo, 1997)

Some businesswomen expressed interest in beginning new ventures:

As a woman, I again need money. If possible, I would open a retail shop. I would sell different sorts of commodities and clothing. (interview with Joyce, a trader, Manwele Market, Bulawayo, 1991)

I'd like to have a hairdressing business. I know about hair. I know how to perm; how to do styles, makeup. Someone—my grandfather—has offered me a shop and a hairdressing business. I've already given my grandfather a deposit. My brothers have given me Z$5,000, my husband has given me Z$2,000, and I've got Z$7,000 saved of my own money. I think that in December, I'll be able to buy the two businesses. I have the total amount of money I need. My husband is helping me. He is helping me with my schoolwork. I am taking math, accounting, and English at night school. (interview with Molly, a trader, Mbare Market, Harare, 1994)

Although most traders certainly had aspirations for the future of their businesses and their positions, they generally did not express the levels of ingenuity and creativity in their ideas about the future as their sisters in sewing, hairdressing, and crocheting. These three latter types of entrepreneurs were more likely to discuss their future business aspirations in the context of beginning new and/or related activities, whereas the market vendors were more likely to discuss adding new products to the roster of goods that they sold or renting another stall. Moreover, five of the sixty-one traders interviewed mentioned that they had no future goals for their establishments, and one noted that "just surviving" was a goal for their firm. Given traders' lower levels of educational attainment, higher levels of female-headed households, and higher incidence of poverty, there is little wonder that their aspirations regarding future business activities might be less developed than their peers in other areas of the microenterprise sector.

On a more personal level, however, these traders—like their sisters in hairdressing, sewing, and crocheting—did hope to buy or build a house for themselves and their families someday. In addition to educating their children and expanding or changing their current enterprises, they were most intent on improving their own and their families' quality of life. Their optimism led them to believe that owning a house and a car would be possible one day if they maintained and possibly expanded their businesses:

If it [the business] improves, it's a result of the establishment, not my dreaming. I want to be highly educated and successful in life. Chances are sure that I will succeed. Business is going so smoothly, so I can see no problems ahead. (interview with Future Wilson, a trader, Mbare Market, Harare, 1991)

I want to diversify—into knitting and sewing with modern machines. Establish links with influential people because of business and establish something better than present situation. Assuming no problems, I will be likely to succeed. (interview with Chena, a trader, Mbare Market, Harare, 1991)

If I am successful, I would like to build a house in the rural areas. Through having a business, I want to help improve the lives of my children. I want them to have easier lives. If I have no money, then I am in trouble, but otherwise, I think that my goals are attainable. (interview with Evelyn, a trader, Manwele Market, Bulawayo, 1994)

I wish I could expand my business and be able to buy furniture for my house and buy a house of my own. I hope to be able to raise my children well and buy things for my house. I hope to put my children through school so they can find employment. I am very optimistic, but this solely depends on people buying my stuff. (interview with Horence, a trader, Mbare Market, Harare, 1997)

Unfortunately, the intensity of the economic crisis throughout the 1990s (and its continuation) made it extremely difficult for these entrepreneurs to realize their dreams.

### Government Regulations and Globalization: A Problematic Environment for Market Traders

Toward the end of the interviews for this study, the market traders were asked if there were any government policies and/or regulations that affected the operation of their businesses. These entrepreneurs were quick to report that licensing and rental fees, as well as health inspections, were government regulations that they found problematic. Several also complained about the severe negative effects that ESAP was having on their firms.

Much of the discontent that these vendors expressed about government policies were directed at the city councils of Harare and Bulawayo. These city

Figure 4.5. Makeshift market stalls adjacent to Manwele Market, Bulawayo, Zimbabwe, July 1994

councils were responsible for providing the plots of land, the sheds, and the stalls where these women sold their products. The sheds and stalls were mainly wooden structures with old wooden tables (see figures 4.3 and 4.4). The markets contained no heat, fans, or adequate toilet facilities and no refrigeration for their goods. In fact, the markets also lacked storage space, so most of the women covered their goods and left them out overnight, sometimes under the eyes of a security guard whom they paid. Some women working at Manwele Market in Bulawayo, however, traded without the protection of a shed or stalls. They sold their goods in a makeshift accommodation, largely consisting of a table and possibly a stool, outside the market (see figure 4.5). Thus, even more than their sisters trading in the sheds, they completely lacked any protection from the elements—from sun or rain—or from the fumes of cars or fires burning in the area. Working outside in this way exposed them and their customers to additional health risks (the latter from purchasing exposed food).

Although the physical conditions of the markets were difficult for these women to bear on a daily basis, they were far more likely to complain about the high costs of licenses and rental payments for stalls. The women interviewed in any of the three interviewing periods from Mbare and Manwele markets both indicated significant variation in the amounts paid monthly and annually for a license to sell in the market. In general, the range of licensing fees in Manwele Market was about Z$14 to Z$152 a year, with most women reporting a payment of Z$15 to Z$35. At Mbare Market, most estimates ranged from Z$50 to Z$216 a year. Upon payment of their licensing fee, traders received a card indicating that they were registered to sell specific goods at the market. As noted by Gada:

> The license that you get for your stand stipulates what types of foodstuffs you are allowed to sell. For example, it is a violation of the rules for me to sell any dried foodstuffs [grains, legumes, vegetables] here. (interview with Gada, a trader, Mbare Market, Harare, 1994)

Others commented on the different fees for the licenses:

> Vendors license card—price Z$50. Suspect foul play with the City Council. They seem to show partiality favors. Some get cards at Z$12, some get cards at Z$50. [You] have no choice. (interview with Sidhluzha, a trader, Mbare Market, Harare, 1994)

The vendors at Manwele stated that they paid about Z$10 a month for renting their stalls, whereas some traders at Mbare mentioned that they paid more than Z$100 a month. Because they sold food, these traders and their workplaces were examined by health inspectors before they received their licenses. Some traders talked about the benefits of this system for the public health:

> Health inspectors come through the market—tell us [we] can't store vegetables under the table. These inspectors are a good idea because they want us to keep the place clean. (interview with Tatanda, a trader, Mbare Market, Harare, 1994)

> License is Z$25 a year to sell in Manwele. We don't have enough money, but it helps to be healthy when selling food. Both the seller and the food have to be examined. Inspectors come here to check. They come in June before we go to renew out license in June. (interview with Annastazia Mpofu, a trader, Manwele Market, Bulawayo, 1994)

Others were angered by and/or resisted this policy because they observed many hawkers selling goods along city streets without licenses or inspections. This double standard seemed particularly unacceptable to some traders in Manwele Market, where traders were working under especially stressful and physically unhealthy conditions, with many trading completely outdoors. These traders had been promised a new market by the City Council in the early 1990s, but by 1997, the government had still not delivered on this promise. The traders expressed their concerns and demonstrated their resistance:

> Because I am here, I pay licenses and rentals because I am here. But the illegal vendors do not have licenses or rental fees and sell goods at a cheaper price. City Council should round up the people who are selling on the streets without licenses. (interview with Mary, a trader, Manwele Market, Bulawayo, 1994)

> Yes, we are supposed to pay for licenses to trade, but we are not paying because we don't have the money and other people are selling the same stuff at home that are not in markets. Women just decided spontaneously, no market association or rotating credit here—$27 per year for a license— because we are selling food, we have to be tested for diseases. The license indicates that the food is disease free. Someone comes from the Health Department to inspect food. Yes, if you don't pay the rent, they take the goods. We also pay $10 a month for security—private security. (interview with Joyce, a trader, Manwele Market, Bulawayo, 1997)

Although the quotation above regarding women's resistance to government regulations was reported as unplanned, it demonstrates an important example of how the perspective of feminist political economy assists in comprehending both the challenges such women experience and also their agency. These women were responding to the consequences of structural adjustment, an aspect of globalization in the 1990s, which took an especially harsh toll on poor women and children. Recognizing these negative consequences, feminist political economy urges us to also consider that in the midst of such crises, poor and low-income women have become empowered. Although they did not form an organization to voice their opposition, these vendors utilized their social capital, with their sisters in the marketplace, to resist the power of the state.

What other effects has ESAP had on these entrepreneurs? The businesswomen in this study were clearly aware of ESAP. They frequently discussed the problems of unemployment that they observed among their family members and those who typically shopped in the markets. They noted that ESAP meant higher prices for goods that they had to purchase from wholesalers, as well as increasing prices for goods and services in society at large. They also observed that in general, as a result of unemployment and the rising costs of goods and services, their customers had far less money to spend under ESAP and were coming to the markets less often:

> It has not worked [ESAP] yet. We have not noticed changes yet in the economy or socially. People have been told employment creation, inflation decrease. This has not happened yet. (interview with Shira, a trader, Mbare Market, Harare, 1994)

> Yes, the ESAP affects this business because there are fewer customers. The customers might have more expenses, so they can't buy so much in the market. (interview with Donorvin, a trader, Mbare Market, Harare, 1994)

> ESAP—it affects me because most people are not of employment and no more people are coming to buy. (interview with Mary, a trader, Manwele Market, Bulawayo, 1994)

> ESAP affects this business because people have no money to come and buy from us. They have no money because they are no longer in work. Some people are under retirement because of ESAP. (interview with Maslun, a trader, Mbare Market, Harare, 1997)

As stated above, these vendors also experienced increased competition from the many women illegally hawking and selling food along the city streets. The entrepreneurs in this study believed that they were particularly disadvantaged in their enterprises because a double standard persisted— only those who were selling in the market were subject to rental and licensing fees as well as health inspections. Hawkers escaped these additional costs and regulations, and thus they were able to sell goods at lower prices and had the flexibility to meet workers on the downtown streets. The markets studied in this work were both located in the high-density suburbs (black areas) of Harare and Bulawayo and, in general, were not located in areas where many black Zimbabweans work. Thus, those illegal sellers who traveled to the downtown areas of these cities were in some instances more likely to secure sales than their sisters in the markets. Such actions intensified the economic problems faced by the respondents.

Overall, several traders concluded that ESAP brought hardships to them and to most Zimbabweans:

> ESAP believes in destroying business. Before it came, things were easier; prices lower. It affects me very much, especially during the rainy season [when she has no shelter]. I am upset about the governmental delay [in building a shed]. (interview with Sidhluzha, a trader, Mbare Market, Harare, 1994)

> ESAP means people can be fired at any moment. I feel that the government is responsible for ESAP. Also ESAP means suffering and hunger for all. All people suffer—I am a person too so I suffer as well. (interview with Chiyedza, a trader, Mbare Market, Harare, 1994)

These entrepreneurs' daily lives were becoming more unpredictable and stressful because of the increased costs to purchase their foodstuffs, coupled with higher prices for food, clothing, shelter, and transportation due to the currency devaluation and reductions in government spending, as well as rising unemployment and more competition from illegal sellers. Given these realities of globalization, how did these women cope? How did they continue to maintain their businesses, their families, and themselves in the midst of such conditions? The paradigm of feminist political economy urges us to consider how such women can become active agents in responding to economic crises. Thus, chapter 6 will explore the coping strategies that these and other businesswomen in this study utilized to support their families and keep their activities afloat, as well as governmental and nongovernmental programs designed to assist women in small enterprises and microenterprises. But first, let us consider the activities of another segment of the microenterprise sector: entrepreneurs in sewing and hairdressing.

# Chapter 5

# Hairdressers and Seamstresses: Pathways to Success in a Challenging Environment?

Among the various types of entrepreneurs interviewed in this study,[1] hairdressers and seamstresses would appear to have the most established enterprises, those that most closely resemble businesses in the formal sector of the economy. In fact, according to several criteria, these activities would seem to lie outside the realm of the microenterprise sector. Some of the hairdressers and seamstresses interviewed in Harare and Bulawayo operated registered businesses in buildings that were often demarcated by signboards announcing the presence of the enterprises. In comparison with the market traders and crocheters examined, the hairdressers and seamstresses were most likely to have the highest levels of educational attainment in the sample, the largest amounts of start-up capital, and a greater likelihood of receiving loans for their firms and employing more workers. When one considers the size of their workforce and the registration status of most of their enterprises, however, it becomes clear why these businesses are still considered microenterprises. Those included in this study employed no more than five workers,[2] and many of these firms, especially the sewing businesses, are not registered.

Working within the feminist political economy paradigm, this chapter explores the personal backgrounds of the women who work as hairdressers

1. Due to the similarities in the size and characteristics of these firms, the characteristics of the entrepreneurs and the smaller number of hairdressers and seamstresses interviewed, they will be grouped together as one "type" in this study.

2. This subsample does include one exception to this rule. One hairdresser was interviewed in 1991 who did occasionally employ six workers, with one hairdresser working solely on commission. For this reason, this enterprise is included in this study of the microenterprise sector. This business was also unusual among the others studied in that it appeared to be far more "developed" than its sister institutions.

and seamstresses, as well as their family and household structure, the operation of their firms, and the impact of government regulations and structural adjustment on their businesses. In addition, the chapter examines how these women define themselves—what is the relationship between their work and family lives; and to what extent have they experienced success in their businesses? What problems do they face in a nation undergoing economic and political crises? What do they envision for the future of their firms?

## Why I Became a Hairdresser or a Seamstress: Profiles of Urban Women Entrepreneurs

Hairdressers and seamstresses were the smallest of the three major populations sampled for this study. A total of thirty-nine women—fifteen hairdressers and twenty-four seamstresses—were interviewed in at least one of the study's three major years—1991, 1994, or 1997. Five hairdressers and nineteen seamstresses were interviewed in Harare, while ten hairdressers and five seamstresses were interviewed in Bulawayo. Beauty salons and sewing establishments were found in the downtown areas of Harare and Bulawayo. Seamstresses tended to be clustered in one or two major buildings downtown —for example, Robin House in Harare, with each woman within a given room in the building running an independent enterprise. Beauty salons tended to occupy separate downtown buildings or at least separate sections (small flats) within a major building. Many of the beauty parlors in the center of downtown Harare, however, were white-owned establishments, whereas those in the outer rim of the downtown area were more likely to be owned by black or colored entrepreneurs. In fact, it was often quite difficult to find black-owned beauty parlors, especially in downtown Harare.

As was the case among the other subsectors studied and for the nation as a whole, the vast majority of the sample, 72 percent (twenty-eight women), was Shona. Among the thirty-nine entrepreneurs interviewed in these sectors, six were Ndebele (15 percent) and another five (13 percent) were from ethnic groups based in Zambia and South Africa. The proportion of Shona- and Ndebele-speaking women in this sample adequately reflects the composition of the overall society, which is approximately 80 percent Shona and about 16 percent Ndebele. More specifically, among the hairdressers, seven were Shona, six were Ndebele, and two were from ethnic groups based in Zambia and South Africa. The sample of seamstresses was overwhelmingly Shona, including twenty-one respondents from that group. Only two Ndebele seamstresses and one from a small minority ethnic group were included in this sample. Not only were the Shona highly represented among seamstresses and hairdressers in Harare, but they also had a significant presence in such activities in Bulawayo. The fact that some of the entrepreneurs working in these (as well as those in the other subsectors of this study, and in the nation as a whole) are not Zimbabwean by birth, coupled with the fact that many Zimbabweans are involved in cross-border trade, suggests that one needs to consider the Southern African region as a whole when thinking about enhancing socioeconomic opportunities for women and economic development.

Hairdressers ranged in age from twenty-three to sixty-five years old, with a median age of forty. Seamstresses in this study ranged in age from twenty-four to fifty-six, with a median age of thirty-seven. Unlike the market traders and crocheters, all the hairdressers and seamstresses had received some formal education. Among the hairdressers interviewed, two-thirds of the sample had received some secondary education. Three of the hairdressers had completed their secondary school Ordinary Level (O-level) examinations, which is a prerequisite for obtaining a position in the formal sector of the economy. These levels of educational attainment alone are quite remarkable, considering the situation most women face. Failing to pass five O-level examinations bars most Zimbabwean women from entry into the formal sector and is one of the major forms of structural blockage that women experience in the society.

As discussed earlier in the book, there are four main reasons why black women disproportionately fail some of these O-level examinations—hence the importance of the feminist political economy perspective and particularly intersectionality in our analysis. First, those women who were born and raised under colonialism are highly unlikely to have had the opportunity to attend secondary school in the first place, let alone take O-levels. Most black women were fortunate if they were able to obtain several years of primary education at a mission school (Seidman 1984; Summers 1991; Schmidt 1992; Osirim 1996). Formal education was a costly proposition for most families during colonialism, and if a family's resources enabled them to provide any education for their children, a preference was given to males.

Second, in the modern as well as in the colonial periods, the gender-based division of labor in the household generally saddles young girls with very significant levels of responsibility for housework and child care. Though young men also have some domestic responsibilities, these are generally less demanding and time consuming than those tasks assigned to young women.

Thus, young women have far less time to devote to their academics than young men, and in general they receive far less support for their efforts.

Third, most black families in both the preindependence and postindependence periods are poor and low income and therefore, find it very difficult to pay for a daughter's secondary education. Many young women thus end up dropping out of school because they cannot pay the school fees.[3] Further, if a student fails even one O-level examination, she must reregister in school to retake the exams, and thus parents are responsible both for tuition payments and exam fees. More recently, some women have pursued the option of trying to complete their O-levels by taking courses in evening schools, but this also carries a price tag and a time commitment that are out of reach for many poor and low-income women. Fourth, some young women become pregnant in secondary school, and under these circumstances, these students have to leave school. Therefore, completing O-level examinations successfully under such conditions is a major accomplishment.

Given that registered hairdressers generally have to obtain licenses to practice their craft, many of the hairdressers in this sample had attended postsecondary school to become skilled in this area. Eight of these entrepreneurs had specialized training in hairdressing from established schools, such as the Bulawayo Polytechnic, or through apprenticeships. In fact, seven of the hairdressers studied had previous experience as an apprentice or in a more specific role, for example, shampooer. Other hairdressers had a variety of prior work experience, including nursing, teaching preschool, sewing, typing, and working as a butcher.

Operating a beauty salon was an occupation that some women combined with other positions in the formal or microenterprise sectors. For example, one entrepreneur was a nursing supervisor, who also owned a knitting shop while managing her hair salon. Another woman owned a cosmetics factory that supplied her salon (and many others) with needed products. Two businesswomen combined hairdressing with work as dressmakers, while another ran a combined beauty salon and barbershop. One entrepreneur owned a

---

3. Under structural adjustment policies, poor and low-income families in Zimbabwe and in many other African nations have been found to disproportionately remove their daughters as opposed to their sons from schools with the reintroduction of user fees under adjustment (Kwesiga 2002; Katapa and Ngaiza 2001; Mbilinyi 1998; Assie-Lumumba 1997; Gaidzanwa 1997). In fact, businesswomen in the microenterprise sector in both Zimbabwe and Nigeria have informed me that their families are more likely to find the money to send a son to school but not to send a daughter. Thus, these women were committed to making sure their daughters received formal education.

transport business that operated between Zimbabwe and South Africa, while another owned a butchery (meat market). In general, it is quite common to find Zimbabwean women engaged in several income-generating activities simultaneously to ensure financial survival. For women with higher levels of educational attainment and skills, such as the women hairdressers referred to here, their beauty salons often serve as a form of "insurance," especially if they had lost a position in the formal sector or if the state had failed to pay civil servants.[4] Given the economic and political crisis that currently confronts Zimbabwe, such forms of insurance are very wise investments for women.

Seamstresses also had high levels of educational attainment. All the women had received some formal schooling, and 78 percent of the sample had some secondary education. Two businesswomen had successfully completed their O-level examinations. At the other end of the spectrum, seven women had either some years of primary schooling or had completed that level. Sixty-three percent of the sample (fifteen) had learned their craft in school, most notably in a postsecondary, technical training institution, such as Maury College or Specis College. Relatives are still an important source of skills transmission—four of the women commented that they learned how to sew from their mothers.

In addition to specialized courses in dressmaking, such as cutting and design, these entrepreneurs had acquired other skilled and professional credentials. Two of the women began nursing school but could not complete these programs because of pregnancy and a lack of money to pay the school fees. Another woman took a hotel-catering course after finishing her O-levels. Two businesswomen attempted to supplement their O-level results by taking courses in evening programs. Such courses have become more recently available to former secondary school students, who usually hold jobs in the microenterprise sector.

Most seamstresses held previous positions before establishing their enterprise. About 50 percent (twelve) of these entrepreneurs had prior experience as dressmakers or tailors employed in another firm. Other occupations earlier held by these entrepreneurs were domestic worker, factory employee, cashier, salesperson, and teacher. Unlike the situation among hairdressers, these women did not hold initial positions as apprentices.

---

4. The failure of the state to provide regular salaries to teachers coupled with trade liberalization in Ghana led many teachers to take up positions as traders in global consumer items to enhance their incomes. See Darkwah (2002).

As was the case among hairdressers, some seamstresses supplemented their salaries with other income-earning activities. Although none of the seamstresses studied had equivalent positions to those of the nurses among the beauty shop owners, one seamstress had a scrap metal business, which her husband later joined, and another was a part owner of a small gold mine. The latter entrepreneur belonged to the Association of Zimbabwe Small-Scale Miners and had been encountering some difficulties in paying workers and buying tools in connection with this business. Several other women were involved in knitting and crocheting in the microenterprise sector. One entrepreneur did embroidery and was engaged in long-distance trade with South Africa.

It is clear, however, even from this brief review of the educational and employment backgrounds of these entrepreneurs, that despite the structural blockage and persistent patriarchy in the society, these women were ambitious, diligent, and capable of making many important contributions to local and national development. Seventy-two percent of the sample (twenty-eight) considered themselves to be middle class or higher (two respondents described themselves as upper class) at the time of the interviews—even though, with respect to income attainment in particular, many of these women would not qualify as middle class. This is an important indicator of how far these women believe they have come, considering that their families of origin were generally lower class. One entrepreneur described her situation as

> not very rich, not very poor, so in the middle, life is good, not all that bad. Since things (are) up, . . . now life is good. Managed to send all kids to private school. (interview with Nardo, a seamstress, Harare, 1994)

Eleven of the women (four hairdressers and seven seamstresses) described themselves as lower class. The response of one hairdresser in this group to the question about self-reported social class seems to suggest her recognition of the "informal/microenterprise sector" status of her enterprise:

> Lower class—because I don't have any position. Because if I worked for government or something, I would have a job in the formal sector and I would be better. Now I might not get money; children can go hungry. (interview with Lucky Ndlovu, a hairdresser, Bulawayo, 1997)

Given their social class of origin, why did these women decide during adolescence or adulthood to enter the microenterprise sector as entrepreneurs?

How did they decide to start a business that would be their major or supplemental source of income? What factors led them to these decisions?

As discussed above, a lack of O-level qualifications essentially bars one from entry into formal-sector positions. Though some hairdressers and seamstresses did attain this level of education, the intersectionality thesis suggests that as black Zimbabwean women coming from poor and low-income backgrounds, it was quite unlikely that most of them would be successful in passing the requisite number of ordinary level examinations to receive their secondary school certificates. This in fact was the case for most respondents in this sample, and thus they had extremely limited options in the labor market. The majority of these women expressed their childhood and adolescent aspirations to become a nurse, but they did not attain adequate qualifications. Tsitsi's sentiment—"I could not be a nurse because I failed my O-levels and therefore could not qualify for nursing school"—sums up the experience of most entrepreneurs in the study (interview with Tsitsi, a seamstress, Harare, 1997).

A few women who became nurses found that the occupation seemed incompatible with raising a family, and thus they had to leave the profession. A hairdresser who worked as a nurse for twelve years stated:

I wanted to change [my job] because the nursing shifts became difficult. After I had children, I needed something which didn't require a lot of time and night duties. (interview with Elizabeth, a hairdresser, Harare, 1991)

As part of feminist political economy, the intersectionality framework further reveals how these problems were exacerbated by racism on the job for some women. A former nurse and current hairdresser experienced these problems:

I started out in a private nursing home. They didn't give married women much of a chance. First preference was given to unmarried girls in the hospital. There was a lot of racism in the private nursing home. This became a geriatric home. I wanted broader experience. We had to work three times as hard and didn't get the recognition—jobs were hard to come by and I did more. The war was going on, and I went to the semi-rural areas to work in mobile clinics. (interview with Deena, a hairdresser, Harare, 1991)

A few other businesswomen discussed their interest in becoming a teacher, a policewoman, or a lawyer, but because they failed some of their O-level exams and/or due to their parents' inability to pay school fees, these women had to give up their often more professional career aspirations. Further, several women became pregnant while in secondary or nursing school, and therefore they had to terminate their education at that time.

So how did these women finally decide to begin a business in sewing or hairdressing? Most of them needed to help support their families financially, and because the majority were unable to obtain formal-sector jobs, they turned to the microenterprise sector. They then drew on their training and experience in a field, the skills their families had taught them, and the experience and encouragement of relatives and friends in deciding to begin their own sewing business or beauty shop. The need to increase one's earnings to achieve financial independence was uppermost in the minds of most of these hairdressers:

> [I started this business] because I did not want to be working for someone else. Before I was a hairdresser, I was working for someone else. In 1993 when I was working, I had my own clients, so I thought I could make it in my own business. (interview with Mary, a hairdresser, Bulawayo, 1997)

> I wanted to have my own hair salon because where I used to work in other people's salons, I never used to get enough money. . . . When my mother saw that I had failed at school, she told me to work in other people's salons so that I could get experience and then establish my own salon. (interview with Irish Best, a hairdresser, Bulawayo, 1997)

> I discussed it with my daughter. She helped me decide. My husband said that I'd do better if I worked for myself. (interview with Lucky Ndlovu, a hairdresser, Bulawayo, 1997)

Husbands often played a key role in decisions about whether to start a business. Though black African women clearly maintain that having children is a salient part of their identities and that they have a responsibility to assist in the support of their children, black men also encourage women to begin microenterprises because it also furthers their interests in addition to the well-being of their families (Afonja 1981; Bay 1982; Osirim 1992).[5]

---

5. In an earlier study of Nigerian women and men in business, I found that husbands supported their wives' decisions to start an enterprise for several reasons including the

A husband frequently assists in providing some or all of the start-up capital for his wife's business, especially if she is unemployed at the time of their marriage or is working in a position that demands late hours or long-distance travel. A wife's business, if successful, can reduce the man's level of responsibility for the financial maintenance of his family and, at the same time, is likely to ensure that the wife will remain geographically closer to home and fulfill her domestic responsibilities. Further, because much of the microenterprise sector is segregated by gender, assisting a wife to start such a firm is likely to limit her contact with other men during business hours.

In earlier research that I conducted in urban southwestern Nigeria, such issues were of particular concern to the husbands of many businesswomen who insisted that their wives give up nursing careers to begin microenterprises (Osirim 1994a). In addition, many men who assist in providing some of the initial capital for their wives' firms also expect to occupy a role in the operation of the firm later on, often in the role of bookkeeper or accountant. This provides men with greater knowledge about the financial aspects of the business and, in some cases, clearly with greater control over these resources and their wives. Women entrepreneurs in the microenterprise sector most often try to keep the financial aspects of their businesses secret from their husbands, because the husbands are likely to reduce their contributions to the household if they believe their wives can make up the difference (Downing 1990).

Although forced by an early pregnancy to leave secondary school early, one seamstress had tried to take advantage of several opportunities that were presented to her and her family. Her story demonstrates the diligence, foresight, and perseverance of many African women and, as viewed through the lens of feminist political economy, illustrates her "agency"—how she took a problem and turned it into an opportunity:

> I didn't qualify to go and work. When I was in Form 2, I got pregnant, so I thought of doing my own work, rather than staying at home and doing nothing. Before '82, I was going to knitting and sewing clubs. We were taught how to sew and knit. If you made something, you could go and sell individually. Teachers would come to the clubs employed by the City Council. We would go to these clubs twice per week—free training.

---

fact that such types of work would provide greater flexibility for women to effectively combine their multiple roles in families. Further, these businesses also enabled women to more easily "close up shop" if their husbands' careers necessitated that they relocate. See Osirim (1992).

My husband saw another woman knitting and he asked if I'd like to have a machine. I decided to do it in town after I saw some other people doing this work in town. My auntie also encouraged me. . . . I also sell some of my products in South Africa with my friends. We go every month end—we are four women together—one goes with her husband, my sister, and me. We go to Transkei and we sell at schools and hospitals. [We] sell sweaters, clothes, doilies. (interview with Lizzy, a seamstress, Harare, 1994)

An entrepreneur who owns a hair salon and a knitting shop along with her work as a nurse-supervisor described the reason for beginning her salon in both altruistic and individualistic terms:

I established this business because my husband spent most of his time in business and I had little to do. I discovered that I could create employment, for example, for my niece. She trained as a hairdresser—didn't do well in secondary school. [I] mostly wanted to do this to create employment. My father owned a small business. I was around people in business. The high tax rate influenced me. My husband's family kept saying come and join the business. I didn't want to rely on my husband. (interview with Deena, a hairdresser, Harare, 1991)

This businesswoman is one of the very few in the entire study who by Zimbabwean standards was raised in a more middle-class household. Her parents were both teachers who were trained by missionaries and who later taught in rural mission schools. Her level of educational attainment and her combining of several different occupations are quite exceptional, even by Southern African standards. Though she clearly has egoistic interests that she is attempting to satisfy through her establishment of a hair salon, she is also contributing to the development process by expanding employment prospects in Harare. Moreover, she is meeting other personal goals and achieving economic independence in the process.

## Marriage, the Family, and the Division of Labor among Zimbabwean Entrepreneurs

Much of the research on African women, work, and development in the past decade has clearly revealed that work and family life are intimately connected in the lives of Sub-Saharan African women (Robertson 1984, 1997; Clark 1994; Osirim 1995). The split between the "public" and "private" sectors noted by structural functionalist sociologists and feminists alike based in the Global North that was mentioned above is an inappropriate dichotomy for describing the lives of African women (Parsons and Bales 1955; Sacks 1975; Hartmann 1982). Most African women view motherhood as an essential component of their identities, and they work first and foremost because they have children and believe they have a duty to help support them (Afonja 1981; Bay 1982; Osirim 1995; Darkwah 2007). This is not to say that these women do not work for personal fulfillment, to express their knowledge and creativity, or to assist in the support of their extended family members.[6] This is to suggest, however, that one cannot draw a sharp distinction between the work and family concerns of the entrepreneurs studied here. Activities regarding the family and household are often carried out in the workplace, and the many income-generating activities that these women are involved in also take place in the home. Further, there is often not a strict separation between business and household capital or between relatives and employees. Nevertheless, these hairdressers and seamstresses are indeed entrepreneurs who are committed to the development of their firms and of their nation.

In Zimbabwe, then, an entrepreneur's household composition, her roles and responsibilities within her home, and her relationship with her extended family are likely to have a notable impact on the operation of her enterprise. What were the marital statuses and household compositions of these Zimbabwean businesswomen? The majority of hairdressers and seamstresses in this study were married. Seventy-three percent (eleven) of the hairdressers and 54 percent (thirteen) of the seamstresses were married at the time of the interviews. Only one of the seamstresses described her union as a polygamous one. Other seamstresses and hairdressers, however, did discuss getting a divorce because their husbands were about to take another wife. As one previously divorced hairdresser remarked:

> I was married in 1965 and had two children. My husband took another wife, so I left. . . . [With respect to the relationship,] when two people are

6. In her study of Ghanaian traders in light manufactured items such as toys, cosmetics, and kitchen appliances, Darkwah (2007, 207) found that these businesswomen believe that work has both instrumental value and intrinsic worth—it is both "a duty and a joy."

living together, sometimes up, sometimes down. Can't say it's fine all the time. It was good; I was only disturbed by the other woman. (interview with Bere, 1991)

Only one hairdresser and three seamstresses were single in this sample. Thirteen percent (two) of the hairdressers and 21 percent (five) of the seamstresses were divorced. One hairdresser and two seamstresses were widowed. All the hairdressers in the study had children, although three of the seamstresses had no children. This is understandable given the higher marriage rate for hairdressers and the slightly younger ages of the seamstresses, although a number of single women in the study did have children. The median number of children for hairdressers was 4, with a range of 1 to 8 children. Among seamstresses, the median number of children was 2.5, with a range of 0 to 8 children. The fertility rate for hairdressers comes closer to the national average of 4.8 children per woman at the time of this study (Neft and Levine 1997). One would expect the fertility rates for hairdressers and seamstresses to be lower than the national average given the relatively high rates of educational attainment among this group and the fact that women with high levels of educational attainment generally have fewer children.

The Sub-Saharan African countries boast some of the highest fertility rates in the world. Although Zimbabwe's rate is fairly low when compared with those of other African countries, the number of children women have coupled with their extensive responsibility to extended family members poses a significant burden for many African women. In some sense, this is compounded when one considers the responsibilities that women in this study have to the maintenance of their businesses. What is the composition of these women's households? What are their responsibilities to family members?

As opposed to asking how many individuals live in your household, this study asked the question, "How many people regularly spend the night in your house?" Among hairdressers, the median number of individuals in their households was five; among seamstresses, the figure was five. The number of persons living in the homes of the former ranged from two to eight; for seamstresses, the comparable range was one to seven. Though these figures include the entrepreneur, her children, and possibly her spouse, they also often include extended family members and a domestic worker. African households are significantly more extended than those in the Global North, and thus adults in urban areas frequently provide housing for nieces, nephews, cousins, and other relatives from rural areas. There is a strong ethic of responsibility and reciprocity in these extended-family households, with payments for services sometimes paid for in cash, but often in kind (Sudarkasa 1981a, 1981b). In many homes, such relatives often receive education or employment from the entrepreneur in return for child care and housework from the live-in relative. Others might provide cash payments for their relatives who assist them with domestic duties and child care. The case of three Bulawayo entrepreneurs, two hairdressers, and a seamstress illustrate these patterns:

> I employ my cousin in the salon. She is my uncle's daughter and kind of lives in my house as well. She helps look after the house and my son. Both her parents died (she's eighteen), so she stays here while her sister stays with someone else. Sometimes I buy her clothes and toiletries. (interview with Dali, a hairdresser, Bulawayo, 1991)

> My young sister or my elder sister takes care of my children while I am at my business. Don't pay cash—I can thank them with some clothes, soap, and so on. (interview with Lucky Ndlovo, a hairdresser, Bulawayo, 1997)

> While I am working at my business, my sister takes care of my children. I pay her $60 a month. My sister does the housework and takes the whole day to do the chores. (interview with Cece, a seamstress, Bulawayo, 1991)

Most of these businesswomen have generally not shared responsibilities for housework and child care with their husbands; however, due to their more "middle-class" position (especially when compared with the market traders and crocheters in this study), most of these women have been able to hire domestic workers. Eighty percent (twelve) of the hairdressers and 67 percent (sixteen) of the seamstresses have "house girls" or domestic workers to assist them with household responsibilities. One seamstress employed her cousin as a "maid." Men are generally not found in the kitchen or engaged in other household duties, although there are a very few exceptions in this sample: "Sometimes my husband cooks and washes clothes or plates" (Ndlovo, a hairdresser, Bulawayo, 1997). Though the entrepreneurs have domestic help, they themselves are ultimately responsible for caring for their children and maintaining their homes. Husbands generally expect "everything to be in order," and if it is not, they blame their wives. In addition to overseeing the tasks of the domestic workers, women in this study were also involved in at least three-four hours of housework per day. For many businesswomen, this meant preparing breakfast for their children and dinner for the entire family as well as mending garments and, for some, possibly taking care of an elderly relative living with them.

Although the vast majority of husbands in this study (and in Sub-Saharan Africa more generally) were not involved in domestic work, some sharing of financial responsibility and decision making with husbands was noted among the seamstresses and hairdressers in this sample. Historically, most Zimbabwean husbands have regarded it as their duty to pay for such items as housing, utilities, household repairs, medical expenses, and education for their children, as well as providing an allowance for food. Feminist political economy leads us to consider how the policies of the international hegemonic powers and nation-states create significantly gendered outcomes at the local level, which disadvantage poor and low-income women. Due to the economic crisis and the Economic Structural Adjustment Program (ESAP) in Zimbabwe, women have found themselves increasingly sharing some of these expenses and paying in full for others. ESAP has meant massive layoffs of many public-sector workers and a major devaluation of the Zimbabwean dollar, in addition to the removal of price controls and major cutbacks in state support for social services (Moyo 1992; Osirim 1996, 1998, 2007). For example, though the government of Robert Mugabe essentially eliminated tuition payments for public primary school in the 1980s, resulting in a major expansion of enrollments, user fees were reinstituted with the enactment of ESAP. In this climate, Zimbabwean married women have had to increasingly provide part or all of the food and clothing for their families, as well as meet skyrocketing costs for education and health care for their children. What was the case for women in this research?

Certainly those women heading households in this study (the single, divorced, or widowed) were meeting all the expenses for their households and the education of their children. Among married women, couples were generally sharing some expenses. Those businesswomen who hired domestic workers generally paid their salaries. And the women most often paid for their own and their children's clothing. More and more, couples seemed to be sharing the costs of home repairs, with women increasing their contributions for the food bill and for medical expenses. Although some women were paying part of the rent or mortgage, men were still largely responsible for this expense. With respect to paying school fees for their children, about half the married seamstresses in the sample with children either paid part of or all these fees for their children, and in the other half of the sample, husbands paid all the school fees. The entrepreneurs generally paid for the school uniforms for their children, and occasionally they paid for some of their books. Among hairdressers, 47 percent (seven) of those married entrepreneurs with children paid all or part of their school fees, whereas in the remainder of cases, the fees were paid exclusively by their fathers.

Decision making in the households of married hairdressers and seamstresses examined was a largely shared activity among women and men, although there did appear to be a "gendered" domain of decision making. When asked the question "who decides how and by whom housework will be done," all the entrepreneurs answered that they made this decision exclusively. This further substantiates the claim that domestic work is women's work and, in this case, the responsibility for this rested with the businesswomen. Decisions about the use of money, the paying of bills, the discipline of children, and the schools they would attend were often made jointly or, in several cases, were made by the husband alone. In a few cases, the businesswomen in this study solely made these decisions, although this was a rarer occurrence. Thus, it appears that men continue to have slightly more power in the marriage. In fact, though this population's higher levels of educational attainment and more middle-class status generally would lead to higher levels of shared decision making, we are witnessing shared decision making among married women in all sectors in this study. Due to the economic crisis and ESAP, women's increased contributions to the financial well-being of the family have become pivotal, and with these greater contributions they have generally realized a stronger voice in decision making. However, this decision making is often quite gendered, as noted among the seamstresses and hairdressers here. This means that women are more powerful in making decisions about domestic matters, while men usually hold the edge in major financial decisions for the family.

When the study respondents were asked how they felt about their roles and responsibilities in their families, the market traders and crocheters largely responded that there was nothing they could do about it; this was their fate. Conversely, although a few seamstresses and hairdressers gave this response, in general, there was a much wider range of answers noted among this group. Many businesswomen interviewed in 1994 and 1997 did acknowledge that their responsibilities were arduous, particularly for those whose husbands were unemployed. Both the economic crisis and ESAP largely explain this response. For others, the tasks were found to be manageable because they received assistance from their husbands, particularly with respect to sharing the financial burden. One hairdresser remarked that Zimbabwean women do not want equality for women and men in the home. These quotations illustrate these findings:

> I have more responsibility in the family than my husband. I just think from the beginning, I spoiled my husband because he was a student. Even when he finished school, he never took life seriously because he knows I will work hard and make ends meet. I will sort everything out. Yes, I would like my husband to be more responsible. He needs to try to earn more, think of something to supplement his salary, but this is too much for me. (interview with Rudo, a hairdresser, Harare, 1994)

> If my husband works and gets a little "change," then that will help. Responsibility to be in charge of the house and all the money—too much. (interview with Nardo, a seamstress, Harare, 1994)

> It is just okay. Things are tough in Zimbabwe. We have got no money. Just because I am a mother—this is our customary law in Zimbabwe. A woman works twenty-four hours a day. I think it is our culture here. A woman works most of her life. We have equal rights in work because of the government. We don't want it at home. You have to follow your culture. Our culture is not for equal rights for women and men at home. (interview with Susan, a hairdresser, Bulawayo, 1997)

> I am not really happy, because you really cannot ensure that groceries will last for a month and the house is small. I would like to see some roles changed. I want also for my husband to listen to my point of view also in the family. (interview with Marjorie, a seamstress, Harare, 1997)

> Sometimes I feel overburdened. Yes, I wish my father-in-law would take over the responsibility of looking after his two sons—my husband's brothers—whom we are looking after. (interview with Kuda, a seamstress, Harare, 1997)

The family responsibilities of these entrepreneurs do not end with their nuclear family members who live with them. As stated above, for some businesswomen, the nexus of responsibility and reciprocity extends to relatives that they employ in their enterprises and/or within their homes as domestic workers. These "employed" relatives might receive cash or in-kind payments for their services. They are frequently poorer relations from rural areas who hope to increase their educational attainment and/or their prospects in the labor market by migrating to the cities and assisting their more established relatives. With regard to the former, the entrepreneurs are likely to pay the school fees, as well as the indirect costs of going to school, such as uniforms, books, and transportation expenses for younger siblings and/or nieces and nephews. A seamstress from Harare explained her support for a niece living with her:

> I pay school fees for my niece. She is in secondary school. She finished O-levels and didn't come out with good passes. She needed the help I'm giving her. Her mother is in a rural area. Her parents don't own a home. She needed a place to stay, and I could help her. Maybe one day she will make out. Everyone needs to be given an opportunity. (interview with Winnie, a seamstress, Harare, 1991)

These women also have significant responsibilities to other extended family members, particularly their parents and their in-laws. Only 13 percent (two hairdressers and three seamstresses) did not provide financial support for extended family members. The remainder of this sample most often provided support for several family members, with parents and in-laws named first on their lists. According to the entrepreneurs, payments to their parents and in-laws were not necessarily made on a regular basis but generally averaged about Z$50 to Z$100 every time a payment was made. Some entrepreneurs gave these payments to their parents and in-laws every month or quarter, whereas others provided such funds whenever they had a few extra dollars. Payments to relatives were also made in the form of gifts of food and/or clothing. Other relatives that received financial support from these businesswomen were siblings, uncles, nieces, and nephews.

Thus, although many of the seamstresses and hairdressers studied here do receive assistance with housework and child care from nonrelated domestic workers and from relatives, and those who are married share some expenses and decision making with their spouses, these businesswomen still bear the major responsibility for the domestic front. Though many entrepreneurs would like to see a decrease in their duties in these areas, fulfilling their responsibilities to their families also constitutes an important aspect of their identities. Several of these women have faced greater financial strains with the intensification of the economic crisis and ESAP. This chapter now examines how their roles in their households and families intersect with their duties as businesswomen.

## Hairdressers' and Seamstresses' Operation of Their Enterprises

The hairdressers and seamstresses in this study were very committed to the establishment, maintenance, and growth of their enterprises. Beauty salons and dressmaking firms were not merely survival activities for these women, who primarily defined themselves as middle class. These were serious business endeavors in which they invested and reinvested substantial amounts of capital, sustained a labor force, and demonstrated innovation in production.

The average age of beauty salons and sewing establishments in this study was seven years. Beauty salons in this study ranged in age from six months to thirteen years. In comparison with market traders and crocheters, these entrepreneurs began their firms with substantially higher initial investments. The start-up capital for hairdressers ranged from Z\$500 to Z\$36,000, with a median initial investment of Z\$3,000. Most of these entrepreneurs obtained this capital from their own savings, though husbands and other relatives were also important sources. These women were frequently able to save this money from earlier or simultaneous positions they held in the formal and/or microenterprise sector. In general, capital provided by husbands and female relatives was given in the form of a loan, with the clear expectation of repayment. Table 5.1 indicates the sources of start-up capital for this sample. Given the nature of the hairdressing business, most firms would have to start with some capital in order to buy equipment and some basic products that are essential to performing the services, such as a hairdryer, hair creams, and shampoos.

The vast majority of entrepreneurs owned machines in their businesses. Ninety-three percent (fourteen) of the salons owned such equipment as

*Table 5.1. Sources of start-up capital among hairdressers*

| Source of capital | Number of respondents | Percent |
| --- | --- | --- |
| Personal savings | 6 | 40 |
| Husband | 3 | 20 |
| Female relatives | 2 | 13 |
| Other male relatives | | |
| Bank or finance agency | | |
| Multiple sources[a] | 4 | 27 |
| Total | 15 | 100 |

*Note:* The blank cells indicate that other male relatives, banks, and finance agencies were not a source of start-up capital for hairdressers in this study.
[a]This category includes combined contributions from a husband and one's personal savings, loans and gifts from siblings and friends, and a loan from a bank.
*Source:* Author's study data.

*Table 5.2. Sources of start-up capital among seamstresses*

| Source of capital | Number of respondents | Percent |
|---|---|---|
| Personal savings | 14 | 58 |
| Husband | 4 | 17 |
| Female relatives | 2 | 8 |
| Other male relatives | 1 | 4 |
| Bank or finance agency | | |
| Multiple sources | 3 | 13 |
| Total | 24 | 100 |

*Note:* The blank cells indicate that banks and finance agencies were not a source of start-up capital for seamstresses in this study.
*Source:* Author's study data.

hairdryers, blow dryers, steamers, electric clippers, curling irons, hot combs, electric scissors, and hot brushes. Given the range of hairstyles that these businesses provided, it would be nearly impossible to maintain these enterprises without machines. The one exception to this is found in a salon that only does braiding, a type of hairstyle that does not require machinery.

At the time of the interviews, the vast majority of hairdressers rented the spaces in which their salons were located. Eighty-seven percent (thirteen) of the rooms/buildings were rented, compared with 13 percent (two) hairdressers who purchased or were buying their buildings. With regard to the latter, one entrepreneur's building was in her son's name and was bought for Z$2,500, and the other paid Z$1,300 a month toward the ownership of her building. Those who rented their spaces paid from Z$335 to Z$2,285 a month. Some of these women rented one or two rooms in a multiple-occupancy building, whereas other salons were the size of a small building or flat (apartment).

Dressmaking businesses ranged in age from three months to seventeen years. Initial capital investments in their firms ranged from zero to Z$3,000, with a median start-up capital of Z$500. The initial capital investments in the dressmaking firms were lower than in the beauty salons. This is because the seamstress shops require less machinery and other products than beauty salons, and they thus have fewer barriers to entry. One can begin a dressmaking business with only one sewing machine, which some women might have owned before they began their firms. The entrepreneurs in the study obtained their start-up capital from the sources given in table 5.2. Unlike the hairdressers, one seamstress entrepreneur's brother was the sole source of money for beginning her business. Included among the multiple sources of capital are a husband, a mother, a sibling, and the entrepreneur's personal

Figure 5.1. A seamstress at her sewing machine, Robin House, Harare, June 1994

savings. No one in this sample received any loans from a bank or financial agency.

All the dressmakers had some machines in their enterprises at the time of the interviews, most notably sewing machines (see figure 5.1). Some firms had more specialized machinery, such as zigzag sewing machines, sewing and overlocking machines, and knitting and embroidery machines.

Among the seamstresses studied, no one owned the space in which they operated their business. Everyone rented spaces, which ranged monthly from Z$200 to Z$6,200. Most spaces were rented for a few hundred dollars per month. Many seamstresses shared their worksites, which were frequently limited to one room, with other entrepreneurs in the dressmaking business. Thus, their workspaces were generally much smaller than the beauty salons. The one exception at the high end of the spectrum, with rental payments of Z$6,200 a month, was an establishment that included a dressmaking college where women received instruction in the craft.

Unlike the typical images of entrepreneurs in the microenterprise sector as persons who lack business knowledge and are engaged in survival activities, these businesswomen demonstrated that they clearly had business acumen. Since the establishment of their enterprises, these women had

Figure 5.2. Hairdressers braiding hair at a beauty salon in Broadwell Lodge, Harare, June 1994

innovated in their firms in the methods utilized and the goods and services produced. They were creative entrepreneurs who were aware of the supply-and-demand parameters of the local populations they were serving. Conversely, they kept abreast of the latest styles in hairdressing and in dressmaking, often drawing on examples of new styles from South Africa and Britain.

Only 27 percent (four) of the hairdressers had not made changes in the styles and the methods used in their salons since their inception. The remaining eleven businesswomen had made several changes in the products used, the styles they created, and the goods that they sold in their salons. Though the majority of salons now provided a wide range of hairstyles for their clients, including braiding and permanent relaxers, some salons only began with either braiding or perming hair and later increased the number of procedures they performed. As braiding became more popular, for example, more salons added various styles of braiding to their repertoire (see figure 5.2). Other salons added hair dyeing or tinting and facials to the services that they provided. As stated above, these entrepreneurs became aware of and incorporated styles from abroad. Comments such as the following were quite common among hairdressers as they described innovation in their enterprises:

> [I do] braiding, perms, relaxers, and weaving. Now, I do weaving, tints, and highlights. I introduced new products. Use Revlon and Dark and Lovely products now. Used to use only local products. (interview with Rite, a hairdresser, Bulawayo, 1991)

> I would like to get more new products but can't get in Zimbabwe. Have made fashion changes. Get some ideas from magazines and girls when they go to South Africa. They get ideas and model on workers to show customers. (interview with Constance, hairdresser, Bulawayo, 1991)

> When I went to the U.K., I came back with ideas and different chemicals. I concocted some hair treatments, scalp treatments and braiding styles. When I went to the U.S., I learned more braiding styles and treatments. (interview with Deena, a hairdresser, Harare, 1991)

In addition to the new ideas for styles that these businesswomen themselves obtained directly through observations in their travels, they also benefited from their social capital. The women relatives, friends, and employees in their networks also brought back new ideas for hair products, hair, and dress styles from their travels to South Africa and elsewhere. Such travel for women based in Bulawayo was actually quite commonplace, given its proximity to South Africa and the persistence of ethnic ties among the Ndebele on both sides of the border.

Some businesswomen also sold hair products and hair accessories in their salons, whereas others regarded their salons as an opportunity to expand the range of products they provided for women and to increase their profits. Thus, some women sold handbags and secondhand clothing in their beauty parlors. In general, these entrepreneurs were very attuned to the need for innovation and some diversification of their activities to maintain their firms in a competitive field and to advance their businesses beyond the level of "simple survival." As the perspective of feminist political economy reveals, these women were active agents of change not only in their enterprises but also in their families and their communities as a result of their business acumen, their social ties, and the employment opportunities they created.

All the hairdressers in this study provided paid employment, while one also provided training for apprentices in this trade. Ninety-three percent (fourteen) of the businesswomen studied had between one and five employees, clearly qualifying them for inclusion in the microenterprise sector. The median number of employees in these salons was four. One additional hairdresser stated that she had six workers—five salaried employees and a sixth who was a hairstylist working solely on commission. Because the latter was not a regular salaried employee, she was included in this study. Another example of the business acumen of these entrepreneurs was the division of labor in their firms. In addition to the entrepreneurs, several of the employees in these salons were certified hairdressers, indicating that they had received formal training in cosmetology. Other employees occupied the positions of trained hairdresser, shampooer, braider, cleaner, receptionist, and bookkeeper. Twenty percent (three) of the hairdressers reported that they employed one of their relatives—a cousin, a niece, and a nephew.

Do such enterprises provide stable employment? In Northern as well as in Southern countries, small enterprises and microenterprises have historically had a high rate of failure, especially in the first year of operation. Many of these firms cannot be expected to provide long-term employment. Conversely, though each of those businesses that survives only provides a small number of jobs, collectively they are responsible for employing the largest number of workers in such countries as the United States. In Zimbabwe, work in microenterprises is the second major source of income for women after agriculture. Under ESAP, the Zimbabwean state also suggested that recently retrenched workers from the civil service look to the small enterprise and microenterprise sector for employment opportunities, particularly as entrepreneurs. How much change has been noted in the labor force among those hairdressers studied?

Sixty percent (nine) of the hairdressers had changed the number of workers in their firms at some time. In 47 percent (seven) of these cases, entrepreneurs increased the number of workers. Some entrepreneurs noted that their busiest months were around the holiday season in November and December and that they often had to increase the number of workers they had at that time. Only two entrepreneurs reduced the number of workers since they opened their businesses. Such decisions by these entrepreneurs were clearly linked to the economic crisis and ESAP, which made going to a salon an out-of-reach luxury for many former and potential customers:

> Business has decreased, so I hire less. Business is less because of ESAP. People can't afford to get hair done. . . . I have achieved success in my business, but ESAP has made things difficult. People have little or no

money for extras. Up until 1989, things were good. (interview with Williet, a hairdresser and seamstress, Harare, 1994)

Unlike the hairdressers, the seamstresses were less innovative in their methods of production, their choice of materials, and the goods that they made. Only 29 percent (seven) had innovated since they began their businesses. Most of the changes in their enterprises involved making new lines of clothes, for example, adding men's clothing to their repertoire of goods produced:

> I have improved with time because I can sew jackets and trousers. When I began, I just used to sew skirts and other small things, but now I have diversified in line with my experience and growing demand. (interview with Tsitsi, a seamstress, Harare, 1997)

In a few cases, the addition of machinery meant that a seamstress could change the finishing of a garment:

> Used to do zigzag stitch for finishing, have an overlocking machine now, began using this in June 1991. (interview with Winnie, a hairdresser, Harare, 1991)

In discussing innovation, these entrepreneurs also expressed their reliance on imports, which posed some problems for businesspersons under austerity and structural adjustment programs. Under these policies, bans are placed on some imported products and import licenses are often difficult to obtain, especially for women. One entrepreneur discussed her preference for imported raw materials:

> First started with dresses, umbrellas, and pompons. Then, I started doing different and more things. I use imported materials now. Before used bad materials. The imported materials are a lot more expensive but better fabrics. (interview with Beluah Thsuma, a seamstress, Harare 1991)

Perhaps most interesting among the comments made by seamstresses were the coping mechanisms developed by them to deal with the increased competition and declining sales and profits resulting from ESAP. Several crocheters adapted to the increasing poverty and declining market for their goods in Zimbabwe by becoming a cross-border trader selling handmade crocheted and knitted goods in South Africa. For years, a significant market for such goods existed among both black and white South Africans, who were most accustomed to machine-made sweaters, bedspreads, and other items. As discussed above, white South African women were often seen purchasing such handmade goods at the major market for crocheted and knitted goods in Harare at the Newlands Shopping Center along Enterprise Road. Black Zimbabwean businesswomen identified this demand among South Africans and seized the opportunity to improve the profitability of their enterprises through cross-border trade. The perspective of feminist political economy again draws our attention to such acts of agency and empowerment among women, particularly those who experience the interactions of race, class, and gender in their daily lives—which, in both the historical and contemporary periods, has positioned them at the bottom of the socioeconomic hierarchy.

Cross-border trade was also a coping strategy utilized by some seamstresses experiencing economic problems under ESAP. Such women were likely to divert some of their attention toward the production of crocheted items for sale throughout the region:

> Began making the doilies last year. My friends were making and taking doilies down to South Africa. They told me to make some and join them selling the doilies to individuals who work in hospitals and schools. (interview with Lizzy, a seamstress, Harare, 1994)

Seamstresses in this study did provide paid employment, although fewer of them hired workers than their counterparts in hairdressing. Nearly 46 percent of seamstresses (eleven) had employees in their businesses, with a median of two workers per firm (the range was one to five). There is some division of labor in these establishments, with a few of them hiring a tailor, an embroiderer, a knitter, or a sales clerk to assist with specific tasks. Most employees, however, are usually individually engaged in the complete sewing of garments. These employed seamstresses are often very talented, as noted by one entrepreneur:

> She is very experienced. Can make a dress from a picture. No pattern necessary. Used to knit when working at Sanders also, but only makes dresses. (interview with Catherine, a seamstress, Bulawayo, 1991)

Five of these enterprises employed relatives. The businesswomen usually relied on social networks to locate and hire workers. And in a very few cases, they placed advertisements in the daily newspapers. They also sometimes hired people who came looking for work, especially if they are short-staffed during a peak period, such as the beginning of the school year (especially if they have a contract to provide school uniforms) or during the Christmas holidays. After a few years at these enterprises, some employees did leave to begin their own businesses, including a woman who began her own dress shop. Worsening economic conditions also led some entrepreneurs to reduce the size of their staff: "In 1995–96, I had two employees. I decided to let them both go because I had less orders at that time" (interview with Libra, a seamstress, Harare, 1997).

## Hairdressers' and Seamstresses' Responsibilities as Entrepreneurs

The businesswomen in this study generally had multiple responsibilities for operating their enterprises, despite the fact that almost all of the women studied had employees and some division of labor existed in their firms. Small enterprises and microenterprises are frequently characterized as establishments where the specialization of tasks is absent and thus the entrepreneur is burdened by too many disparate responsibilities. Under such conditions, businesses are likely to fail. In these Zimbabwean firms, however, the businesswomen had knowledge of all aspects of the enterprise and were able to juggle several responsibilities. Fourteen of the fifteen beauty salon owners interviewed stated that they combined hairdressing with accounting and management functions in their enterprises. The majority of the hairdressers (about 53 percent) remained fully involved in doing hair on a daily basis, in addition to many other duties, whereas some of them occasionally completed a hairstyle begun by their workers, such as braiding. Several hairdressers noted that though they did assume a variety of responsibilities in their enterprises, they really enjoyed the creativity and social relationships developed in their work:

> I manage to see the overall. Sometimes people come with complaints. I have to instruct apprentices; I also ask questions of them on the spot to see if they know their jobs. . . . I enjoy work; I like it, it keeps you up

to date. You meet lots of women and they have problems and they tell you their problems. You can give them advice. They know you; you can't afford to make mistakes. . . . I like to do relaxers the most. It is quicker. Just have to relax, rinse, and set. When you finish, you see the art in it. (interview with Rite, a hairdresser, Bulawayo, 1991)

I manage books and do hair. My duties have changed since I first began business. At first, more work because training all the employees, but now have qualified workers. The job suits me—I enjoy very much to be with other people. I can talk. I like my job more as time goes on. When I started hairdressing was not my aim, but I ended up enjoying it. (interview with Constance, a hairdresser, Bulawayo, 1991)

I like my job. It is nice to meet so many different people and see how they appreciate what you've done. I like the creativeness. If someone comes with kinky hair and you straighten it, you see a lot of change in them and it makes it interesting. (interview with Elizabeth, a hairdresser, Harare, 1991)

I enjoy my job. It keeps me occupied and fit. I entertain and educate because of my contact with others. I used to want to quit when I worked for others. I see more of the benefits of self-employment now. (interview with Williet, a hairdresser and seamstress, Harare, 1994)

Only one hairdresser reported that she no longer did hair and was primarily involved with the accounting and management functions in her enterprise. She had delegated many of the duties in her business to her staff of three, which includes two professionally trained hairdressers, one of whom is her niece. In her role as entrepreneur, however, she recognized how the hairstyles created in her salon could alter the self-esteem of her customers and certainly affect sales in her business:

I don't do too much. I set the standards. I keep accounts; I give them ideas because I learned quite a bit. I really do public relations. I do less now than in the beginning. I now have confidence in the staff I have. I like to see people looking beautiful and different than when they came in. I like it when they feel good about themselves when they have been to the hairdresser. . . . Now I take it easy a bit. I realize it can be very stressful. I try to delegate most chores; I try to tolerate it when things are not perfect as long as workers are fair to the clients. (interview with Deena, a hairdresser, Harare, 1991)

Seamstresses also assumed a range of responsibilities in their firms—including sewing, design, pattern making, bookkeeping, and management. These entrepreneurs generally enjoyed their position and the creativity that it afforded, although several noted that life had become more difficult as more firms entered the microenterprise sector and competition increased during the economic crisis and ESAP:

I do part of designing, part of pattern making, a bit of grading. There are not enough machines for me to sew also. I deal with the customers. I can make a pattern cutting. If the person is very big, the pattern might be too small and grading means "making the pattern bigger." I like it because I am very much into fashion, and I like to make fashionable clothes. . . . I understand a lot; I want to please my customer. I want to do what the customer wants, not what I want. Design it, sketch it out—I like this the most because it makes me think. (interview with Winnie, a seamstress, Harare, 1991)

I work for anyone. I am not very busy. Too many people doing the same job. . . . Problem is that there are too many people doing the same job so I don't get many customers. (interview with Apollonia, a seamstress, Harare, 1991)

I find it interesting because I love dressmaking. . . . I love my sewing. I love making wedding dresses, decorating and making them fancy, not like men's clothes. (interview with Salu, a seamstress, Bulawayo, 1994)

Engaging in cross-border trade with South Africa also led some seamstresses to develop positive sentiments about their work. Many of those who sold crocheted and knitted goods in Zimbabwe discovered that they could improve the profitability of their enterprises by selling their goods in South Africa, as well as in other Southern African nations on occasion. Such cross-border trade has become an important coping strategy for women who were encountering a declining market for their goods at home but were committed to the maintenance and growth of their enterprises for themselves and their families. To supplement their incomes, some seamstresses made crocheted and knitted items at home for sale in local markets or in South Africa. Knitted sweaters and crocheted tablecloths made by hand for example, were in high demand in South Africa, where consumers were accustomed to mass-produced, machine-made goods. Moreover, the Zimbabwean-made goods were more reasonably priced than the clothing manufactured in South Africa, and the prices of the former were also negotiable in transactions between Zimbabwean entrepreneurs and South African customers. In addition to the sale of handmade knitted and crocheted goods, seamstresses also found a market for their Zimbabwean-made clothing in Johannesburg and in the townships. Not only was the Zimbabwean clothing more reasonably priced, but South Africans could also place orders for clothing and household goods that would meet their specifications. On subsequent visits to South Africa, the Zimbabwean businesswomen would often hand deliver these goods, especially to those residing in the townships.

A seamstress with four employees explained her multiple duties and the need for cross-border trade in her enterprise:

> I do sewing, check cash, help correct workers. . . . My duties have changed because I have employees to help out. Right now I enjoy my job because of where I get money [from]. Get more money from going to South Africa. Not a big market in Zimbabwe. If I relied only on Zimbabweans to buy goods, would have closed up shop. (interview with Pricillar, a seamstress, Harare, 1994)

## Economic Indicators of Firm Performance

As in many other works on small enterprises and microenterprises, entrepreneurs in this study were unable to provide accurate, reliable data on the financial status of their firms. Like their sisters in the other areas studied, many of the seamstresses and hairdressers interviewed did not keep up-to-date records of their firm's financial profile. And in those cases where such records existed, the entrepreneurs were unlikely to share these data with the interviewer. Thus, this investigation obtained data on sales, assets, and profits from entrepreneurs' verbal estimates, which relied extensively on their powers of memory. Businesswomen were asked to estimate annual sales and profits, as well as the value of assets in their firms and to note changes in these figures from the establishment of their enterprises to the time of the interview. Therefore, in many cases, the answers to such questions did not reveal the pattern of recent declines in sales and profits in most enterprises under ESAP, because sales, profits, and assets during the start-up phase (the first year of operation) were compared with estimates at the time of the interview.

The majority of seamstresses interviewed for this study revealed that the economic performance of their firms improved from the time of their businesses' start-up to the time of the interviews. Of the twenty-four seamstresses studied, three-quarters provided information on sales within their enterprises. Of the eighteen firms for which sales figures were given, fifteen reported increases in sales from start-up to the interview. Sales estimates ranged from a low of Z$1,200 a year during the first year of operation to a high of Z$70,000 at the interview date. For most sewing establishments, sales averaged around Z$2,000 to Z$4,000 a month at the time of the interviews. One seamstress explains the change in her sales over time:

> Annual sales—I started in 1982 at Z$400 per month. Now in 1991, [I earn] Z$3,000 to Z$4,000 per month. I don't have proper books. I roughly write down what is coming in. . . . I am earning more now. Trying to get ourselves to the best standard we can get. We try to satisfy the customer, do the work quickly, do the proper thing the customer wants, and we can cope with our work. We are running away from this cheap labor thing. With that you have so much work to catch up with and won't be doing good-quality work. (interview with Winnie, a seamstress, Harare, 1991)

Nineteen of the seamstresses answered questions on the value of their businesses' assets, with sixteen reporting increased assets since they began their firms. Start-up capital for these firms ranged from Z$20 to Z$3,000, which were on average seven years old at the time of the interviews. Current assets ranged from Z$500 to Z$150,000, with the estimated assets for most businesses around Z$7,000 to Z$10,000. Though the seamstress entrepreneurs were encouraged to think about assets in terms of all the capital they owned for the business, including all profits saved for the firm, most discussed assets in terms of the machines they owned. In the case of sewing establishments, such capital usually consisted of sewing machines, and in some cases embroidery and overlocking machines, with an occasional knitting machine. These entrepreneurs spoke with pride about their machines and stated that they had them regularly serviced, generally at least once or twice per year.

The vast majority of the seamstresses did provide some information on the profits earned by their firms, although of the three categories of financial indicators, profits were the least specific. In fact, many provided no actual figures for profits but did indicate that profits were earned and generally described how they were used. Of the twenty-three seamstresses who did give some information on profits, nineteen reported that profits had increased since the start-up phase. There is little wonder why entrepreneurs in the microenterprise sector are reluctant to reveal information about the profitability of their firms, because many are attempting to avoid state policies—particularly taxation—by remaining very small and "informal" (Portes, Castells, and Benton 1989). Conversely, unlike many of the earlier studies that maintained that women's microenterprises were largely survival activities, the vast majority of seamstresses (nineteen) reported that they first reinvested profits in their enterprises, before investing in other areas. Their profits were used mainly to purchase raw materials and machinery, as well as saved for later reinvestment in their firms.

In addition to reinvestment, in what other ways did these seamstress entrepreneurs use profits from their firms? They had many responsibilities for assisting to support immediate and extended family members as well as maintaining their households. The majority (twenty-three) stated that they invested in the maintenance of their households, including the purchase of durable goods for their homes, the provision of child care, and, in a few cases, domestic help. Three of the seamstresses were using some of their profits to build a home or an addition to an existing home either in the city or in their family's ancestral homeland in the rural areas. Many commented that some of their profits were used to pay rent on their existing home and/or to buy groceries. Among the various subsectors of entrepreneurs interviewed in this study, increasing numbers of women in all categories reported that they were making greater contributions toward the purchase of food for their immediate families during the economic crisis and structural adjustment. Many husbands had not increased their food allowances to their wives in this period of increasing costs, particularly those resulting from the removal of price controls from staple products. During this period of economic decline, many men also lost their positions in the formal sector, especially in the civil service, and therefore they were unable to provide food allowances or meet their responsibilities for other household expenses. In these cases, the women had to increasingly make up the difference in providing daily meals as well as household necessities.

The next major areas of investment of profits for seamstresses were in education, in meeting obligations to extended family members, and in contributions to their personal savings accounts. There is no doubt that entrepreneurs were strongly committed to providing education first for their children. Women frequently discussed their payment of school fees and their purchase of uniforms and books for their children's classes. Such costs increasingly fell within the purview of women during this period of economic crisis and structural adjustment, particularly the costs associated with their daughters' attending school. As more men lost positions in the formal sector, and as school fees were reinstituted, many families removed their young girls from school to reduce the financial burden. For many Zimbabwean men in particular, investments in the education of their sons and young male relatives was a rational choice, because these young men remained a part of their families and were obligated to take care of them in their old age. Daughters, however, eventually joined their husbands' families, and thus historically made more limited contributions to the support of their natal families. Therefore, in difficult economic times, low-income fathers preferred to invest in their sons', rather than their daughters', educations.

The women entrepreneurs in this study, however, were determined that their daughters would be educated as much as possible, and they were adamant in saving as much as they could for this purpose. These businesswomen also invested in further education and short-term training courses for themselves, as well as in the education of their younger siblings, nieces, and nephews. In a few cases in this study and throughout the society more broadly, some entrepreneurs provided apprenticeship training in their own enterprises for younger, often poorer, relatives from rural areas.

In addition to providing educational opportunities for relatives, these seamstresses were also committed to the financial support of their extended family members. Women frequently discussed that they send money to their parents and their in-laws on a monthly or quarterly basis. Although in marriage, women did leave their natal families and joined the families of their spouses, these entrepreneurs maintained close connections to their families of origin through frequent visits, in which they brought money, clothing, and food to their parents. Further, the seamstresses were equally determined to establish and maintain personal savings accounts. No matter how little they had, they managed to save some money each month, which they placed in a bank or postal savings account. Often they saved for their children's educations, for a new home or household goods, and/or for their old age.

Finally, five businesswomen in sewing stated that they bought a car with some of their profits, while four women each invested in jewelry and other businesses. In one case, a seamstress mentioned that she invested some of her profits from sewing in her hairdressing establishment; but in the other cases, the entrepreneurs generally invested in their husband's or other relative's businesses. Though cars and jewelry were generally considered luxuries, among this more "middle-class" segment of the study, investing in gold jewelry was considered a significant form of savings for the future by some women. Gold was a commodity that, when compared with other items, such as the Zimbabwean currency, was generally viewed as a good investment—an object that would likely increase in value.

The vast majority of the seamstresses, 83 percent of the sample (nineteen), were the sole decision makers about the use of profits from their businesses. In only four cases were decisions about the use of profits either made jointly with their husbands, or occasionally made by their husbands. Decisions about the use of profits and control of the proceeds from an enterprise are very important concerns in African women's entrepreneurship. In general, women and men generally have separate financial lives in African societies. Women frequently do not know what their husbands earn, and in some cases, they are not even aware of the different types of work in which their husbands are involved. Women entrepreneurs often attempt to keep secret information about the financial position of their firms (Downing 1990). There are several reasons for this, including that businesswomen often prefer to maintain control over financial matters in their enterprises rather than cede such control completely to their spouses, and that men will generally decrease their financial contributions to the family, especially in the areas of providing money for food and school fees, if they believe their wives can assume these expenses (Osirim 1992, 1994b). Zimbabwean women are also frequently concerned that husbands who decrease their material contributions to their families might be spending money on "outside wives" and possibly other children from such relationships (Suda 2007). For all these reasons and more, women entrepreneurs attempt to keep information about the financial position of their firms secret, particularly from their husbands.

The fifteen hairdressers in this study contributed some information on the financial profiles of and trends within their firms, although in a few cases, no actual figures were given. In twelve beauty salons, sales had generally increased, whereas three entrepreneurs complained of declining sales, most especially in the last few years. Monthly sales for the salons ranged from about Z$1,500 to Z$10,000, with most averaging around Z$3,500. Fourteen salons provided information on assets, with thirteen reporting increases in their total value since the start-up phase. Two of the fourteen salons that provided figures noted that in the last few years, the value of their assets had declined due to the economic crisis and the accompanying structural adjustment program. The hairdresser entrepreneurs estimated the current values of their firms as ranging from Z$7,000 to Z$60,000. Most of the businesswomen attributed the increase in the worth of their enterprises to the increased numbers of machines they had purchased since they established their firms, including hairdryers, steamers, and electric hair clippers.

All but one of the hairdressers reported that the profits from their enterprises had increased since the first year after they opened their salons. The one woman who stated that her firm currently "earn[ed] no profits" attributed this to the change in the size of her business. A year before her interview, her salon had moved to a much smaller shop, and she noted: "The place now is small, too small to fit all the customers." The size of the shop appears to have had a negative effect on the number of customers that now come, because she later stated: "I have to write for customers in the paper sometimes" (interview with Susan, a hairdresser, Harare, 1991). Very few entrepreneurs gave actual figures for the profitability of their salons, but those that did generally discussed profits that ranged from Z$30 to Z$2,800 a month.

Like their sisters in sewing, the vast majority of hairdressers reinvested profits in their businesses. Eighty percent (twelve) of the salon owners stated that their profits were first and foremost used in this way. They were also engaged in many other investments related to their responsibilities as mothers, wives, and members of extended families. Again, entrepreneurs were very involved in maintaining their present households and in trying to build homes in their rural areas of origin. During this period of economic crisis, they also found themselves investing in major appliances for their current homes, because husbands were increasingly unable to provide such goods as new refrigerators and stoves. For more than 80 percent (thirteen) of these salon owners, education for their children, their relatives, and themselves was a very high priority. As one hairdresser noted:

> I have tried to educate myself in an effort to supplement the O-levels. I am educating myself to improve this business. (interview with Irish Best, a hairdresser, Bulawayo, 1997)

Supporting members of their extended families, particularly their parents and in-laws, was a major concern for these women. In many respects, tradition and decency dictated that they did not have a choice. As one hairdresser recounted:

Why do we invest in our relatives? Because we have to do it, it is a must. There is nobody else who can look after my mother and my mother-in-law. They are old; there is not really a choice. (interview with Susan, a hairdresser, Bulawayo, 1997)

The businesswomen in this study also discussed the need to open and maintain personal savings accounts as a means of security for the future. In many ways, they reflected on their experiences in assisting in supporting their aging parents and in-laws and realized how essential it was for them to save for their old age, in addition to any support they might receive from their children. In fact, higher levels of educational and occupational achievement for their children, coupled with greater geographical mobility, meant that one could not count on her children for support in the same way as her parents had expected of her. As was the case among seamstresses, a few hairdressers did invest in other businesses—those that they owned and, in one case, a knitting and sewing shop owned by her sister. The latter entrepreneur, however, was emphatic that she only made a one-time investment in this enterprise and now that it was in operation, she expected her sister to maintain that business. Nearly half the sample had invested in a car and some had invested in jewelry, again as a form of insurance to support them in their senior years.

In response to the question "Who makes decisions about how profits are used in your business?" the majority of hairdressers (60 percent) stated that they were the sole decision makers regarding the use of profits in their firms. In three cases, women noted that the use of profits was a joint decision between them and their husbands. In only one case did a husband alone make the decision about how profits would be used. As stated above, women and men in African societies generally do not pool their financial resources. This is especially the case for women in the microenterprise sector, who feel that they need to control the profits from their enterprises as much as possible to maintain their businesses and invest in the future of their children. A similar finding was observed by Downing (1990) in her work for the Growth and Equity through Microenterprise Investment Project (GEMINI). She argued that women entrepreneurs in Southern Africa, as well as in the Caribbean nations such as Jamaica, try to conceal information about the profitability of their firms from their spouses. This not only enables women to reinvest such profits but also to invest in the development of human capital in their families and communities.

## The Problematic Face of Adjustment and Globalization

The Economic Structural Adjustment Program in Zimbabwe had a devastating impact on women and children, especially those at the bottom of the socioeconomic range. The Mugabe government in Zimbabwe, at the behest of the International Monetary Fund and the World Bank, instituted ESAP in an effort to strengthen the national economy and to enable the nation to receive further loans. The IMF and the World Bank have at least strongly encouraged, if not mandated, such programs to improve national economic performance as well as meeting the aims of globalization.

In this study, the overwhelming majority of hairdressers and seamstresses claimed that ESAP had had a negative impact on their businesses. As a result of ESAP, many entrepreneurs witnessed a declining customer base and shrinking profits. Some of the specific conditions of ESAP that have been most problematic for women entrepreneurs are the devaluation of the currency and rampant inflation in the cost of raw materials for production as well as consumer goods, government bans on certain imported products, increasing cost of import and business licenses, increasing competition and a declining customer base, and increasing unemployment. Therefore, through the establishment of ESAP, globalization has negatively affected the operation of microenterprises in Zimbabwe.

Several hairdressers in this study complained about the difficulties they experienced in obtaining needed hair products for their firms. Hairdressers in Harare and Bulawayo provided a number of specialized treatments for black Zimbabwean women, including various forms of hair straightening, permanent relaxers, hair weaving, and braiding. Each process requires the use of specific products, many of which are not produced locally. Thus, hairdressers were dependent on imports to perform many of these operations in their firms.

Under austerity and structural adjustment programs, governments frequently ban many imported items or make it more difficult to obtain the import licenses to get such goods. In some respects, this is clearly understandable, given a declining economy and the high premium placed on foreign exchange. The feminist political economy paradigm provides us with the tools to analyze how women entrepreneurs in Zimbabwe, as well as those in many other nations in Sub-Saharan Africa, have experienced far greater structural blockage in obtaining the needed resources to successfully operate their enterprises compared with their male counterparts (Osirim 1992). The lack of access to import licenses is one of these areas, which intensified under structural adjustment. Ella, a hairdresser, expressed the discrimination she experienced in trying to obtain the necessary inputs for her salon:

> If I were a man, I wouldn't have as hard of a time getting chemicals that I have now. Right now, I travel once or twice a month [to get the goods]. My husband doesn't always like my traveling away from home, but it is for the sake of the business that I go. (interview with Ella, a hairdresser, Bulawayo, 1991)

Other businesswomen also noted the problems with getting the needed supplies for their establishments:

> Problems with the Zimbabwean economy. We can't get supplies—imported hair extensions and hair ointments. We can only get local items. (interview with Susan, a hairdresser, Harare, 1991)

Elizabeth, in her interview in 1991, further echoed this problem: "I can't get a license to order imported hair creams. These are considered luxury items." Deena expressed her desire to innovate with hairstyles in her salon, but she discussed her frustration with the bans on some imported goods. She further suggested a means of addressing the problem:

> Because of all the bans on imports, then what is happening is that there are magazines available for new products which you want to introduce and become the most popular. It is a problem because you can't get these products and it is very frustrating. I have considered going into manufacturing of hair products, but premises would be a problem and I would have to be a hairdresser full time. (interview with Deena, a hairdresser, Harare, 1991)

In addition to the difficulties in obtaining import licenses and the necessary inputs for production, the hairdressers and seamstresses were especially hindered by increased costs for raw materials, business licenses, and rental fees. The economic crisis—coupled with massive currency devaluations in the 1990s and the removal of price controls from some essential goods as part of the structural adjustment program—did affect the operations of beauty salons and sewing enterprises. As Elizabeth remarked:

A business license is now $115 per year. I think this is too much. Until last year, I used to pay $10 per year. If I wanted to sell chemicals, it would be an extra $300. (interview with Elizabeth, a hairdresser, Harare, 1991)

In an attempt to reduce the costs of materials and to enhance the overall profitability of their firms, some entrepreneurs have taken greater advantage of their proximity to other more affluent, Southern African countries, including Botswana and South Africa, to purchase goods for their enterprises and obtain other products to sell in Zimbabwe. As Mary noted, "I have to go to Botswana to buy dryers and chemicals. Our rent is also too high." The experiences of these businesswomen suggest the growing importance of cross-border trade between Zimbabwe and its Southern African neighbors for many self-employed women. Increased cross-border trade is a further indication of the impact of globalization in the region. Such trade, however, is not without its costs:

I get more money from going to South Africa. Not a big market in Zimbabwe. If I relied only on Zimbabweans to buy goods, would have closed up shop. . . . When I get my money for me to get goods with rand, import duty is very high. There is a 30 to 45 percent tax on goods. . . . That's why [I] end up getting more to sell on black market or hiding things so customs can't find it. Have to lie about prices to get past customs. We earn money by selling but still have to pay twice for things. (interview with Priscillar, a seamstress, Harare, 1994)

ESAP is further responsible for a declining market for the "luxury" goods provided by seamstresses and hairdressers. With the removal of price controls from staple foods, rampant inflation on all consumer goods, and massive unemployment, the customer base for entrepreneurs in this study has been drastically shrinking in recent years. The businesswomen in this study were very conscious of this growing problem:

Under ESAP, retrenchment resulted in loss of customers. With hairdressing as a luxury business, no one can make themselves attractive while the stomach growls with hunger. ESAP has destroyed so many families; some of my relatives are out of work, and people have lost property due to inability to pay the increase in rates. They tell us that it will end next year, but who knows. I see the government as being responsible for ESAP.

They have cheated us. Ministers live rent free with healthy allowances and they back dated a 64 percent pay hike by seven months. They live well, and the rest of us suffer. (interview with Miriam, a seamstress and hairdresser, Bulawayo, 1994).

Profits are decreasing because of lack of business. I have to pay more rent and pay employees who are actually not working. (interview with Williet, a hairdresser and seamstress, Harare, 1994)

ESAP affects business—we lose customers because they have no money to come in, because ESAP closes factories. These other people are possibly stranded; this affects business here. If you have a job in the formal sector, you have to look nice—have your hair done. But, if you are selling tomatoes, you don't have to get your hair done. If people are out of work in Bulawayo, they can't afford to do their hair. A person who does their hair is a person who is working. (interview with Susan, a hairdresser, Bulawayo, 1997)

Most people in Harare are no longer working; therefore, our old customers no longer demand our service, and this is a great hindrance in our business. In Zimbabwe, the removal of food subsidies has affected us indirectly because food is very expensive now and clothing is just a luxury for most people. (interview with Tsitsi, a seamstress, Harare, 1997)

The significant increase in unemployment throughout the 1990s was directly linked to the economic crisis and the government's structural adjustment program. The state encouraged retrenched workers to begin small enterprises and microenterprises to support themselves and their families and to contribute to national development. Small enterprises are responsible for generating employment in the North and the South. In the case of the seamstresses and hairdressers in this study, however, more women were beginning microenterprises in their fields and thus increasing the competition for customers. This was particularly problematic in a period of decreasing demand for these services due to the economic crisis and structural adjustment policies:

I am not very busy. There are too many people doing the same job. Sometimes I do not get customers. (interview with Apollonia, a seamstress, Harare, 1991)

There is a lot of competition, especially from establishments which can afford to charge lower prices for garments. This means that those who place orders for resale from the Republic of South Africa will flock there to buy at lower prices. I have no embroidery machine and therefore must go and get this done at an extra charge. This machine is about $25,000. (interview with Tenda, a seamstress, Harare, 1994)

ESAP is affecting us because prices of things are too high—things like food, transport, and clothing. There are obstacles to growth such as financial problems. There are many vendors, so people are getting secondhand things because they are cheaper than the things I make. (interview with K. Todds, a seamstress, Harare, 1997)

## Views of Success and Aspirations for the Future

Despite the many problems that the seamstress and hairdresser entrepreneurs in this study experienced during the economic crisis and ESAP, the majority also revealed that since they had begun their firms, they had overall experienced more successes than failures in the operating their businesses. More than 58 percent (fourteen) of the seamstresses in this study and 60 percent (nine) of the hairdressers reported that their enterprises had more successes than failures since the start-up period. Their definitions of success pertained to the economic performance of their firms, their material contributions to their families, and their professional development. The businesswomen first discussed their successes in terms of accomplishments for their firms in the economic realm, namely, the addition of capital and in some cases, increases in their customer base. Although several entrepreneurs reported losing customers under ESAP, Marjorie's experience differed:

My business is successful just a little bit because I have more customers than when I started. (interview with Marjorie, a seamstress, Harare, 1997)

These women entrepreneurs equally defined their success with respect to their contributions to their families and households. They were proud of the purchases of household goods that they bought for their families and the items they were able to afford for themselves. These were significant accomplishments for women in this society, who were historically dependent on their husbands for the purchase of major household items and who seldom had the time or resources to further their education. Their expenditures for themselves often included further education and training in their field, which contributed to their firms' profitability and enhanced their self-esteem. Some described their views of success:

> Yes, more success because we ended up having the factory from the salon. It is an achievement. End up getting an extra car or something. (interview with Rite, a hairdresser, Bulawayo, 1991)

> I achieved a lot of success. I learned in London about hairdressing. I have confidence in what I am doing, learned new styles, techniques, deal with customers. More success. Doing very well, but too much responsibility. (interview with Rudo, a hairdresser, Bulawayo, 1994)

> [The year] 1996 was . . . successful . . . because I was able to buy a fridge and sofas from the profits I had made. I have had more successes because most of the time I have work to do. It's only a few times when you don't have customers. (interview with Tendai Maswerera, a seamstress, Harare, 1997)

> Success? Yes, I managed to mold my talent as a good dressmaker. I also get enough money to afford me the basic necessities. More success than failures. (interview with Shauiso, a seamstress, Harare, 1997)

Although their firms' economic performance was important, the women entrepreneurs in this study did not define success solely in financial terms. In fact, their responses indicate the critical intersection of their professional and personal lives. Although many reported that they received satisfaction from their ability to maintain their firms, engage in creative enterprises, and expand their skills, they also acknowledged their substantial responsibilities to their households and their families. As demonstrated by many feminist social scientists, African women worked primarily because they have children and believe they have a responsibility to assist in their support (Afonja 1981; Bay 1982; Osirim 1998; Darkwah 2007). Their positions and responsibilities as mothers and as members of extended families are major components of their identities. Achieving financial success in their firms enables them to make material contributions to the well-being of their families and, in turn, to their communities. As entrepreneurs, these women not only contribute to the expansion of human capital in their societies but also to local and national development. Thus, the profitability of their firms is not the sole criterion of success; nor is it the end in itself for which they are striving. Profitability in this sense is a means to an end.

Although Zimbabwe's economic downturn in the 1990s placed severe strains on the operation of microenterprises, the women entrepreneurs in this study continued to have many aspirations for the future. The majority wanted to advance their businesses *and* their households, as well as their professional achievements. Many expressed particular desires for their households and families, which often involved building or buying a new home and investing in new household goods. In addition, they were committed to the expansion of their businesses and to the further development of human capital—for themselves and their children:

> [I want to] go abroad . . . to Britain and combine further hairdressing knowledge and spread to girls and customers. Want kids to have something and have good education. (interview with Constance, a hairdresser, Bulawayo, 1991)

> New business, then end with a big complex with a big, beautiful boutique [with] cosmetics and hairdressing. And further, whatever I am doing. Further education, not necessarily academically, but pursuing whatever I am doing. (interview with Margaret, a hairdresser, Bulawayo 1991)

> I want to renovate Smart Girls Salon next year (new mirrors, towels, chairs). I want to grow to a mini-factory and manufacture children's wear. I want to see myself and my family happy. (interview with Miriam, a hairdresser and seamstress, Bulawayo, 1994)

Some of the women discussed desires for further independence, which, when compared with their attitudes about some aspects of their family responsibilities, appeared feminist in orientation:

> I have goals to expand but not into hairdressing as such, possibly something more scientific. Either manufacturing hair products and beauty products or set up a consultancy business and public relations. Set up a gym or beauty care business, health and mind improvement. As a woman, for myself, continuing education. Can't get this out of my system. In October 1992, I might go to college again. Haven't decided what I might study. Like to be totally independent and self-supporting to be

able to have options. Certain that I can pay for myself if I go to college for a year. (interview with Deena, a hairdresser, Harare, 1991)

[I have] many goals: refurbishing, new furniture. I would like to give the salon another look, carpeting the foyer, changing the counter, new chairs to give more comfort to the ladies. As a woman, I want to be more independent. To make my own decisions about what to buy for myself. (interview with Rite, a hairdresser, Bulawayo, 1991)

One seamstress discussed aspirations that were largely beyond her own personal and professional desires but involved philanthropy:

I want to be very successful, to have a lot of cash to donate to companies and institutes. So many organizations need a lot of help. You can donate a few dollars there if you are successful. For example, [in] the program, "A Dream Come True," the people need help. I want to be very successful. I want to be known. You have money; you have achieved your goals. Helping people if I get the money. (interview with Winnie, a seamstress, Harare, 1991)

From the perspective of feminist political economy, we can see the many challenges faced by these seamstresses and hairdressers in their work and family lives during the 1990s—problems that were exacerbated by the economic crisis and the resulting ESAP instituted at the beginning of the decade. Given the devaluation of the currency, the increase in formal-sector unemployment, the removal of government subsidies from vital social services, and the increase in competition in the microenterprise sector, these women entrepreneurs found themselves making increasing contributions to their households and extended families. At the same time, many of them experienced a shrinking consumer base, increasing costs for raw materials for their firms, and greater difficulties in obtaining import licenses—factors that negatively affected their firms' operations.

Despite these difficulties—which can be partly explained by the low social status of these hairdressers and seamstresses, resulting from their gender, race, and class and the impact of globalization in the 1990s—they remained committed to their enterprises, and many looked forward to the possibilities of expansion in the future. Most of them innovated in their enterprises and saw themselves as involved in a creative process, which requires particular knowledge and skills that they continued to develop. They viewed education as a lifelong process, and though many of them had experienced blockages in attaining educational goals in the past, they continued to pursue opportunities to advance their knowledge and skills in their craft. Moreover, they invested their profits in both their businesses and their families, particularly to further the education of their children and other relatives, thereby contributing to the growth of material and human capital in their communities. They further contributed to human capital development by providing employment in their firms. In all these endeavors and more, these businesswomen were active agents in their lives who faced many challenges, but, through their diligence and ingenuity, weathered the storm and empowered themselves. They indeed moved beyond the level of simple survival, and in this process, they defined themselves as dynamic entrepreneurs.

# Chapter 6

# To Support or Not to Support Women's Microenterprises: The State, NGOs, Informal Associations, and Coping Strategies

During the postindependence period in Zimbabwe, several state and non-governmental organizations (NGOs), as well as informal associations, were created to assist women's microenterprises. As one of its aims in fostering equality between women and men after the nation's Liberation War, the Zimbabwean government established several programs beginning in the early 1980s to support women's income-generating activities. About a decade later, in response to the economic crisis and the severe toll that the Economic Structural Adjustment Program (ESAP) had taken on the poor, the state instituted additional programs to assist families, especially women and children, in coping with the maladies of adjustment. In the wake of massive public-sector layoffs, the Zimbabwean state encouraged women and men to begin small enterprises and microenterprises as a way to support themselves, their families, and their communities during the economic crisis and structural adjustment. At the same time, Zimbabwe, like many other African nations in the 1980s and 1990s, saw a major increase in the number of both international and locally created NGOs, which emerged to assist women in dealing with the vagaries of crisis and adjustment. In addition, poor and low-income entrepreneurs developed their own informal associations and coping strategies to assist them in responding to the crisis.

This chapter explores the contributions that each of these spheres—the state, NGOs, and informal associations, and coping strategies—played in the lives of the women entrepreneurs studied in Harare and Bulawayo. Which institutions were most useful in their efforts to maintain their businesses and contribute to their families? This chapter concludes that although several governmental and nongovernmental services and institutions existed to assist Zimbabwean women in business, the vast majority of these services did not assist the women in this study. Though these women were aware of some of these institutions, most were not familiar with the specific government programs that existed to assist them; instead, most respondents were aided in their enterprises by networks and associations of their own creation. Social class played an important role here—established NGOs have been found to play a key role in supporting middle- and upper-class women in business, as opposed to their poor and low-income sisters.[1] The women in the former income categories are likely to have relatively high levels of educational attainment and financial and social capital to assist them in not only establishing but in expanding enterprises in Zimbabwe as well as in other areas of Sub-Saharan Africa.

## State Programs to Enhance Women's Microenterprises

One of the earliest efforts of the postindependence Zimbabwean state was to establish the Ministry of Community and Cooperative Development and Women's Affairs in 1981. This ministry was designed to work on the elimination of all forms of discrimination against women in society and to promote women's meaningful participation in the national and local economies. In this regard, the ministry recognized women's pivotal roles in the informal economy and worked to integrate women's activities in this sphere, as well as in others, into the state's macroeconomic policies. Moreover, the ministry was charged by the government to mainstream women's issues into every other ministry. An example of the ministry's success in this regard can be noted in the efforts of the ministries of education to promote nontraditional education and training for young women (Osirim 1994b).[2] In many ways, this message certainly trickled down to the local level, where I observed young women who were recent school-leavers in Harare and Bulawayo receiving instruction in welding and carpentry often alongside their male counterparts. Unfortunately, such training largely existed for recent

1. In previous works on this subject, I, as well as other social scientists, have discovered that middle- and upper-class women have been the major beneficiaries of the works of many NGOs on the continent. See Gordon (1996) and Osirim (1998, 2001).

2. At the time of this research in the early 1990s, the Zimbabwean government had two ministries of education—one for primary and secondary education and one for higher education.

school-leavers and was not available for older women who had already established businesses, such as the entrepreneurs in this study.

Other ministries were even more directly involved in providing support to women's small and microenterprises. The Ministry of National Resources and Tourism was charged with providing assistance to women in marketing their crafts. The Ministry of Trade and Commerce provided vital support services to women in establishing and maintaining their businesses. Included among these services were facilitating access to loans and credit facilities, opening up new opportunities for women in trade, and keeping an updated registry of women's businesses in the small business and microenterprise sectors (Osirim 1994b; Ministry of Community and Cooperative Development and Women's Affairs 1991).

Providing loans to women for business development was a central feature of the state's activities. The state created several programs to provide funding for women's income-generating ventures. First, through Zimbank, in which the state was a major shareholder, women in business could receive loans up to Z$6,000 with no collateral required.[3] However, realizing that the provision of capital was rarely enough to promote successful business development, the state worked with the Small Enterprises Development Fund (SEDCO) to provide training for women in business. Loans were also provided for small enterprises and microenterprises through the reorganized Ministry of Community and Cooperative Development.[4] In keeping with the state's earlier socialist orientation, the government was committed to encouraging the formation and maintenance of cooperatives. Loans of under Z$25,000 were available from the state for established cooperatives whose members could convince the state that they were capable of succeeding. The ministry also provided six short training courses in such areas as accounting and entrepreneurship and attempted to foster cohesion among members of cooperatives (see figures 6.1 through 6.3). In an interview with one of the ministry's major officials, Dr. Mabokwa, he reported that the majority of loan recipients repaid their loans, although about one-third of those who received loans in the immediate postindependence period did not repay. Larger loans, known as establishment grants, were also available from SEDCO, but these were generally for small and medium-sized businesses and required feasibility studies.

3. At the beginning of this research in 1991, US$1 = Z$2.30. By 1999, US$1 = Z$37.00.

4. By 1994, Women's Affairs was removed from this ministry and established as a separate department within ZANU-PF, the major political party in power.

Figure 6.1. Women working at a bead making cooperative, making jewelry, key chains, and the like in traditional Ndebele designs, Greater Bulawayo Area, July 1994

As discussed above, with the passage of the Economic Structural Adjustment Program in late 1990 or early 1991, poor and low-income families in Zimbabwe faced significantly increased hardships. In an attempt to cushion the blow of the economic crisis and ESAP, the Zimbabwean state established a Social Development Fund in 1991. This fund was designed to support social welfare programs as well as employment- and income-generating projects. It had two major components: the Social Welfare Program, which aimed to compensate the poor for increased user fees for health and education and for higher food prices, especially for the staple, maize; and the Employment and Training Program, which was established to provide assistance for workers retrenched as a result of ESAP. Over an eight-year period, the Social Development Fund supported 2,705 microenterprise projects, which created about 10,600 jobs. It was estimated that these loans met the needs of 28 percent of the targeted population. Further, in the first phase of the program (after five years after the enactment of ESAP) the Education and Training Program had retrained only about 28 percent (using official statistics) of those who were retrenched, nearly 13,000 workers.

Figure 6.2. A government training program in pottery making, Harare, June 1994

This figure is quite low when one considers that the official statistics of those who lost jobs under ESAP were believed to be grossly underestimated (Kanyenze 2003).

At the local level, the city councils of Harare and Bulawayo provided plots of land, and in some cases sheds and stalls, for crocheters and market traders. When asked if there were any institutions, programs, and organizations that could assist women in businesses such as hers, a market trader in Bulawayo stated:

> Yes, government [helps us]. In 1987, I was one of the representatives to President Mugabe organized by Social Welfare and Women's Affairs. I went to ask that this place be established as a regular market. Then we got these protective coverings. We used to have to sell outside. (interview with Tshuma, Manwele Market, Bulawayo, 1991)

As was noted above, however, the provision of stalls and sheds was insufficient for the demand on such facilities by the traders. For example, many women trading at the Manwele Market site in this study, especially in the

Figure 6.3. A weaving cooperative in Harare, June 1994

mid-1990s, did not work under the protection of a shed or a stall. They completely lacked protection from the elements. At the time of this research, the crocheters did not work in sheds but sold their goods on City Council–provided land and, in some cases, conducted their business from makeshift stalls. At such sites as the Newlands Shopping Center in Highlands, Harare, and at City Hall in Bulawayo, the crocheters either worked on the bare ground or sat on trash cans or steel drums to avoid sitting on the dirt with no protection from the elements. These City Council–provided sites also lacked toilet facilities, refrigeration, and storage facilities.

On a more positive note, taking the lead from the federal government, the City Council of Bulawayo did provide sites and support for some women's cooperatives. One such example was a bead-making cooperative in a high-density suburb of the city, where women made belts, key chains, change purses, and other items in traditional Ndebele designs (see figure 6.1). With the help of the City Council, these items were sold in local department stores, and, at the time of my visit, the cooperative was seeking to establish trade linkages to sell these goods abroad. The financial returns from their sales were shared among the members of the cooperative, with a portion saved as working capital for their activities.

In addition to promoting the work of women in bead-making cooperatives, a crocheter from the Newlands Shopping Center observed that on occasion, the government did assist with the sale of crocheted goods as well:

> Sometimes the government advertises in small shops in hotels, the knit-
> ting and crochet work, and this helps. People come there to buy. (inter-
> view with F. Tekenende, crocheter, Newlands Shopping Center, Harare,
> 1994)

When asked about their knowledge of programs to assist them in business, the hairdressers, seamstresses, crocheters, and traders almost never
mentioned any federal government program by name. The only major
program noted by a few hairdressers and seamstresses was Zimbank, which
they realized was a possible source of business loans. A few crocheters and
traders mentioned that they had heard of the Social Welfare, but that they
did not receive any assistance from this source. In fact, they believed that
those who did receive help were likely to be civil servants who had access
to the information about these services. One exception to this was a trader
in Manwele Market, who noted these problems but also acknowledged that
she had received some assistance:

> [I] know that the government is there to help people, but they choose the
> people they know. Clothes are donated to the poor, but they don't receive
> anything. People in the offices help their relatives. [I] was under the so-
> cial welfare. I was given clothes, blankets, corn meal for the children.
> (interview with Sijhiwe, Manwele Market, Bulawayo, 1997)

Other traders from Mbare and Manwele noted that there were government cooperatives that could help. Members of these groups shared money
among themselves and also provided each other with loans:

> Mugabe's government is trying to help women in business to form co-
> operatives. I have never come across this myself, but some women have
> been assisted as a group of grocers. (interview with Annastazia Mpofu,
> Manwele Market, Bulawayo, 1994)

In general, several of these businesswomen believed that though government
programs did exist that could help them and their enterprises, they did not
know the names of such programs or what they had to offer.

For at least three main reasons, there is little wonder that the entrepreneurs in this study lacked sufficient knowledge about the federal government programs that could assist them. First, the federal government did little or no advertising about these programs; nor did it engage in outreach efforts to target groups such as market traders or crocheters. In fact, these populations often seemed to be those written off by both public and private loan programs as not possessing the business expertise or creditworthiness to be successful. Further, as scholars such as Raftopoulos and Compagnon (2003, 20) have explained, although the state created programs like SEDCO, the government did not vigorously promote them, fearing that "an autonomous black private sector would provide an alternative power base" to the black nationalist base that controlled the state.

Second, the government's training programs to assist poor and low-income populations, especially those providing nontraditional skills training to women, were aimed at recent leavers from secondary school—those who had not received their Ordinary Level certificates. These programs were not designed for women age thirty-five to forty years who perhaps needed to retool their skills to attain better jobs and higher wages. Thus, the women in this study by definition were excluded from such state-sponsored training programs.

Third, the women entrepreneurs in this study, who for the most part had low levels of educational attainment, also lacked the formal-sector connections and the higher-level social capital that might have enhanced their knowledge base about such programs. With the possible exception of hairdressers and seamstresses, the businesswomen in this study did not operate in circles that provided them with access to federal-level institutions, and thus they lacked important sources of information about business programs in this sphere that could possibly assist them. Therefore, it is not surprising to discover that in 1993 only 0.4 percent of all small enterprises and microenterprises in Zimbabwe received support from nine of the largest government programs (Daniels 1998).

At the local level, however, some traders and crocheters were quick to mention the city councils of Harare and Bulawayo as government bodies that provided services to assist them with their businesses. As noted by traders in Mbare Market:

City Council helps in general maintenance and provisions of stalls. It also helps with hygiene conditions. (interview with Future Wilson, Mbare Market, Harare, 1991)

City Council provides shelter and garbage collectors, those responsible to maintain the area. (interview with Geavy Kahondo, Mbare Market, Harare, 1991)

Conversely, as stated in the previous chapters, many of the crocheters and vendors were very irritated with the city councils, which in some cases provided them with no protection from the elements, and in other cases provided only inadequate shelter. This was in addition to the lack of toilet facilities and refrigeration for their products, as well as frequent exposure for women, at sites like Manwele Market, to fumes from adjacent burning fires. Therefore, many of the traders and crocheters believed that the sources of their current problems were twofold, both the responsibility of the local and the national governments:

> The municipal authorities are the ones who regulate our activities, making us pay rent out here in the open. ESAP has caused the price of wool/cloth to rise. Even when we increase the prices of our goods, it doesn't help because all other things are more expensive and our money buys less. (interview with Ndaizioeyi, Kamfinsa Shopping Center, Harare, 1994)

> Because of ESAP and the rising cost of living, the money I earn does not go far. We have no shade/shed, and in the rainy season, there is nowhere we can go. (interview with Tsitsi, Kamfinsa Shopping Center, Harare, 1994)

> ESAP, I believe, is destroying business. Before it came, things easier; prices lower. City Council promised us shelter four year ago and still has not delivered. It affects me very much, especially during the rainy season. I am upset about the governmental delay. (interview with Sidhulzha, Mbare Market, Harare, 1994)

Although the hairdressers and seamstresses in this study were buying or renting space in buildings in which to conduct their business, they also felt that there were major problems with the government at both the local and national levels. With respect to the latter, as noted in an earlier chapter, these entrepreneurs clearly understood that ESAP and the related maladies of additional government regulations were the sources of many of their problems. However, a businesswoman with combined activities in sewing and hairdressing also noted how the federal government, based in Harare, was neglecting the development of Bulawayo:

> I feel Bulawayo is being neglected by government. There is no invest-
> ment coming into this city, unlike Harare. I feel that it is the fault of the
> government—they should start building and opening up investment op-
> portunities. (interview with Miriam, hairdresser/seamstress, Bulawayo,
> 1994)

Therefore, given these realities, the majority of businesswomen in all the occupational categories of this study concluded that, for the most part, government programs and policies were not supporting them in their enterprises. Most of the efforts at the federal level were invisible to these women. When the term "government" was mentioned, both ESAP and the city councils came to mind immediately and evoked negative feelings in the minds of many.

## NGOs and Commercial Banks of the Global and National Kind

Zimbabwe, like many other nations in Sub-Saharan Africa, witnessed a major increase in its number of NGOs, especially after the onset of the economic crisis and the enactment of ESAP in response to this crisis in the late 1980s and 1990s. State-sponsored programs, such as the Social Dimensions Fund and Social Welfare Program, were substantially underfunded, given the significant needs in the greater society. Thus, the Zimbabwean government, like other African states, counted on NGOs to address many of the social and economic challenges, such as unemployment, underemployment, and the inability of poor and low-income populations to afford social services.

The proliferation of NGOs in this phase of globalization was especially targeted at women's issues, because women and children were most negatively affected by the economic crisis and structural adjustment policies. Working from a feminist political economy perspective, Moghadam (2005) has convincingly argued that this period has sparked both globalization from above, in the actions of multinational corporations and international financial institutions, and from below, in the efforts of NGOs and transnational feminist networks, to name just a few examples. In the case of Zimbabwe during the period of this study, NGOs were some of the major agents attempting to combat globalization from above with efforts to encourage the empowerment of women. These women-focused NGOs addressed the grow-

Figure 6.4. The Zimbabwe Women's Bureau (a nongovernmental organization) in Harare, June 1994

ing inequality wrought by the globalizers from above, such as corporate capital and the international financial institutions.

There are several different types of NGOs operating in Africa and other regions of the Global South. Some are established as national-level organizations, while others work at the grassroots level (see figure 6.4). Those NGOs generally working to promote women's empowerment can be classified as service organizations, professional associations, development research centers, human rights and women's rights groups, women in development organizations, and associations affiliated with political parties (Moghadam 1997; Osirim 2001).[5] What is this "empowerment" that these groups have been striving to promote?

During the past two decades, the "empowerment"—which I believe is a critically important term in considering what many women and NGOs have been attempting to accomplish in the Global South—of women has become

5. I have written elsewhere about two examples of NGOs that could serve as models in the Southern African region, indeed in Sub-Saharan Africa, for addressing women's and gender issues in the 1990s, viz., the Zimbabwe Women's Resource Center and Network and the Musasa Project Trust; see Osirim (2001).

a buzzword in much of the development literature and has generally been defined in terms of women's access to and control of capital (Longwe 1989; Blumberg 1995). Moser (1991, 168), however, has added a nonmaterial dimension to her definition of "empowerment":

> [Empowerment means] giving women the right to determine choices in life and to influence the direction of change through the ability to gain control over crucial material and non-material resources.

Adding "nonmaterial resources" to the definition of empowerment means that a woman's sense of identity and self-perception will be important determining factors in whether she considers herself empowered. One important source for empowering women in Sub-Saharan Africa, indeed in the Global South more generally, has been the establishment of social networks, grassroots organizations, and other associations that address their needs. Such linkages with other women through NGOs and other local efforts can assist in personal growth and with gaining strength through numbers, and can lead to the realization of women's material and/or nonmaterial goals. In this regard, such efforts could hopefully combat the vagaries of globalization and strengthen women's abilities and self-esteem in the process.

This study sought to uncover, in part, whether NGOs had provided assistance to women in the microenterprise sector, generally in the form of business loans, technical training, and support, as well as management training and entrepreneurial development. Researchers, such as Berger (1995), have demonstrated that many NGOs in the Global South have had an excellent track record in providing credit for women's microenterprises. In this study, however, only 10 percent of the businesswomen (fifteen respondents) received business loans from NGOs or banks—four market traders, four hairdressers, one seamstress, and seven crocheters. With the exception of some training provided as a condition for receiving a loan from the Zimbabwe Women's Finance Trust (ZWFT) and the Zambuko Trust, the women in this study had not received technical or management training from any sources. Not all the fifteen entrepreneurs who received loans revealed the source of their funding. Those who did provide information on the source of their loans had received assistance from commercial and government banks, such as Standard Chartered Bank and Zimbank, and from NGOs, such as the ZWFT, the Zambuko Trust, and the Zimbabwe Women's League.

For the most part, the loans provided by NGOs usually ranged from a few hundred to a few thousand Zimbabwe dollars, for example, a loan of

Z$3,000 for a market trader from the Zimbabwe Women's League with a repayment period of about one year. Interest rates were generally quite high—around 30 percent or more a year. A few businesswomen, particularly those working as hairdressers or seamstresses, sometimes received loans in the form of overdraft coverage from their banks. The one businesswoman who received a large loan from a commercial bank—a hairdresser who received Z$50,000 from Standard Chartered Bank—had a fairly high level of educational attainment compared with her peers in this study. She had received her Ordinary Level certificate and was a trained nurse. In fact, her previous occupations included work as a nursing supervisor, a community nurse, and a family planning trainer. In addition to her nursing diploma, she also had certification in occupational health and safety, family planning, and training in accounting. What is more, she owned a knitting shop, which provided her with a significant source of collateral in applying for a business loan from a commercial bank. Given this source of collateral, combined with her more middle-class status as a trained nurse, there is perhaps little wonder that she had been successful in getting such a substantial business loan.

As discussed above in reference to the entrepreneurs in this study receiving government assistance for their businesses, there are five similar reasons for the lack of loans and business support services that entrepreneurs received from NGOs and other private institutions. First, women working in the microenterprise sector often lack knowledge about the existence of many business support programs. Although many NGOs existed in Zimbabwe to assist women with their enterprises, they generally engaged in little or no advertising about their programs.

Second, some women in this study, most especially seamstresses and crocheters, were aware of a few NGOs that provided assistance to women in small enterprises and microenterprises: the Zambuko Trust, the ZWFT, Zimbabwe Women in Business, and the Indigenous Businesswomen's Organization. These women, however, rarely had much specific information about the programs offered by these NGOs, and given their myriad responsibilities for their enterprises, their households, and their extended families, they maintained that they had little or no available time to find out about these organizations and their services.

Third, loan transaction costs for low-income businesswomen are often prohibitively high. Berger (1995) notes that these costs include transportation expenses, special fees, and bribes. In addition, women who have to travel long distances to apply for such loans also incur the cost of the forgone wages they would have earned in the time it takes to make the trip

(Berger 1995; Snyder 2000). Furthermore, such activities also create difficulties for these entrepreneurs who are taken away from their domestic responsibilities in applying for these loans. This results in further stress for these women, who generally spend many more hours than men per day in such household tasks as child care, cooking, and cleaning (King and Evenson 1985; Leslie 1987; Berger 1995).

Fourth, the high interest rates—not just among informal moneylenders and formal institutions but also among NGOs—act as barriers against women applying for loans. Many NGOs have interest rates of 40 percent or more, which can be very off-putting to low-income entrepreneurs, especially when considered in light of the other transaction costs they encounter (Snyder 2000). Raftopoulos and Compagnon (2003) further confirmed that under ESAP, small business entrepreneurs faced both exorbitantly high interest rates from banks and generally conservative policies.

Fifth, a long history of discrimination in borrowing from banks has existed for entrepreneurs in the small enterprise and microenterprise sectors in Sub-Saharan Africa and the Global South more generally (Schatz 1977; Osirim 1992, 1997; Berger 1995). The perspective of feminist political economy illuminates the gendered component to this discrimination, which makes it particularly difficult for women entrepreneurs in micro-level activities to obtain business loans. Lacks of collateral, education, and training; lower class status; and a lack of social capital all work against women in attempting to secure business loans from commercial banks. If a woman lacks adequate collateral and other requirements, some banks will insist that she get her husband to cosign a loan agreement. This is also problematic for many women entrepreneurs, who not only believe they need to keep their capital distinct and secret from their husbands (for fear that such knowledge would lead their husband to reduce his contribution to household expenses) but also because husbands who cosign a loan are likely to thus gain greater control of their wives' enterprises. This control by husbands is often manifested in them taking over bookkeeping and accounting functions in the business and/or decision making about the use of profits. Moreover, some husbands will refuse to cosign loan agreements for their wives for fear of losing their own assets if their wife's business falls into default (Snyder 2000).

For all these reasons, many businesswomen were denied loans as well as failed to apply for them, given their knowledge of how the system works. Such experiences with formal institutions also lead some women not to apply to NGOs for microcredit, fearing that some of the same policies will apply. Thus, several NGOs were created in countries such as Zimbabwe to address the credit needs of women in this sector. Some of these organizations, such as the ZWFT, a division of Women's World Banking, have made an important contribution in addressing the needs of those locked out of commercial banks. And as argued by Yunus (1999, 199) in discussing the work of the Grameen Bank in Bangladesh, "People are able to reach their full potential much more easily after accessing credit." Such credit, which can significantly assist in the maintenance and growth of microenterprises, also aids in the empowerment of women, particularly those from poor and low-income backgrounds, as is the case for most women in this study. Conversely, Zimbabwe, like other nations in the Global South, also has its share of associations that do not address the credit needs of its poorest citizens.

One such example of such a limited association is Zimbabwe Women in Business (ZWIB), which was established in 1988 as one of the first organizations to provide support to women's enterprises. ZWIB also worked with the state to enable businesswomen to gain access to vital imports for their firms, an area where women experienced severe structural blockage. ZWIB sponsored national conferences and seminars and provided training in financial planning, accounting, and management. However, those businesswomen who have received loan assistance from ZWIB have mainly been those in the middle and upper classes who already had established enterprises and were members of ZWIB. On the basis of an interview with the leader of ZWIB in 1999, it appeared that its members were the major businesspersons aware of their loan fund, because no major advertising of this, or any requests for loan applications, had been made by women outside ZWIB (Osirim 2001).

On a more positive note, some NGOs in Zimbabwe have provided assistance to women in this study, as well as to other businesswomen in the small enterprise and microenterprise sectors more generally, namely, the ZWFT and Zambuko Trust, two national-level NGOs. In two interviews with the executive directors of the ZWFT in 1994 and 1999, I discovered that the organization was clearly committed to providing loans and other forms of business assistance to poor and low-income women in the country. The ZWFT was begun in 1989 as a division of Women's World Banking, with the goal of

> empowering women, to give them a sense of self-control and a sense of their environment. We wanted to help them determine their own destinies and that of their children and that in turn, this would help stabilize society. (interview with S. Meda, acting executive director, July 1999)

The ZWFT provides training in management, business, and vocational skills and seeks to promote savings among entrepreneurs. Training is also offered in exporting and importing.

In 1992, the ZWFT began its microlending facility with grants from the Swedish International Development Assistance and Norwegian People's Aid.[6] Although the lending program started by providing loans to individuals, which averaged around US$375 in 1994, the ZWFT shifted to a group-lending methodology around 1996. This methodology enabled the ZWFT to operate as a community bank, where women in a solidarity group could put pressure on each other to repay. "In the worst case, the joint savings of the group can be attached by the ZWFT to repay the individual's loan" (Bango et al. 1999, 23).

In other studies, solidarity groups were found to be an excellent method of providing credit to women in the microenterprise sector because they reduce the cost of lending to NGOs and encourage significant participation among several women (Berger 1995). Solidarity groups consisted of at least seven members where each member is a coguarantor for the others. These women were each entrepreneurs who have been in business at least twelve months. Solidarity groups in the ZWFT also participated in a savings program as well as a six-week orientation in which the ZWFT system of microfinance is explained (Bango et al. 1999). Initial loan appraisals were done at the group level, where, in groups of seven women, the first four would receive loans of about US$107 each and the remaining three would qualify for loans when the first four had made their first payment. After the initial loan, further loans from the ZWFT could go up to about Z$20,000. Once a group qualifies for a loan, it is also eligible for business and training assistance. The ZWFT has provided loans to a wide range of microenterprises, including those in knitting, crocheting, and poultry farming, as well as women in nontraditional areas, such as brick making. The acting executive director in 1999 stated that

> they wanted to explore the possibility of women taking a role in the production of herbal medicine and herbal tea, rather than all of them buying and selling. (interview with S. Meda, July 1999)

Like many microlending programs for women in the Global South, the ZWFT has an excellent repayment record of about 96 percent for its business loans, with no loans written off. Loans are granted for a six- to twelve-month

---

6. This information is from the ZWFT proposal, 1999.

period, with an interest rate of about 5 percent per month on the outstanding balance. In 1996, the Austrian government joined other national governments and international NGOs in providing assistance to the ZWFT by channeling funds through CARE Zimbabwe, which was extremely involved in overall capacity building for the ZWFT and assisted in the development of computerized record keeping, management information systems, and staff training programs. By 1998, the ZWFT had made nearly 5,600 loans since its establishment, totaling nearly Z$18 million, with more than Z$4 million still expected in repayment (Bango et al. 1999). By that period, 5,000 women had participated in the ZWFT's savings program, which had total deposits of more than Z$2.2 million (Bango et al. 1999). At the time of the interview for this study in 1999, the ZWFT had dispersed about 200 loans to women entrepreneurs each quarter.

In addition to the institutions mentioned above, the ZWFT also received funding from Women's World Banking, the African Development Foundation, and the Canadian International Development Agency, as well as many other organizations. To inform the general public about its activities, the ZWFT distributed pamphlets about the organization and advertised at trade fairs. In addition, the ZWFT encouraged linkages and outreach among its members. The savings, lending, and training opportunities provided by the ZWFT helped not only to develop poor and low-income women's microenterprises but also to stimulate the growth of social capital and advanced the empowerment of these women. Unfortunately, many women in this study as well as in Zimbabwe more broadly also found applying for loans from the ZWFT prohibitive. Though this NGO was certainly one of the very best in removing many barriers in the lending process for low-income women entrepreneurs and providing a more comprehensive program of savings, lending, and training, it also charged interest at a rate of 60 percent per year, a significant deterrent for many poor women.

Another national-level NGO focused on the poor was the Zambuko Trust, which was founded in 1992. This organization provided loans, training, technical assistance, and project monitoring for women's and men's microenterprises. The trust aimed to facilitate the growth and advancement of microenterprises by providing these services and helping entrepreneurs transition their establishments into formal-sector firms. In addition, the trust focused on generating employment- and income-producing opportunities for the poor, first in the cities, with the intention of expanding its services to the rural areas. Although this NGO provided services to women and men, it was particularly committed to providing microcredit to women, who continued to experience discrimination from commercial banks. The Zambuko

Trust provides loans to individuals, solidarity groups, and to women's trust banks operated through Opportunity International, a global NGO, which provides funding to the poor in several Global South nations (Bango et al. 1999). Trust banks are similar to but generally larger than solidarity groups and include at least fifteen women coming together over an eight-week period to discuss all aspects of operating a business. A more comprehensive approach to training is provided by such groups, which surpasses bookkeeping and management of the firm per se and includes the social aspects of entrepreneurs' lives outside the business. It is also another way for women to expand their social capital—they come to know and to some extent to rely on their trust bank members in operating and sustaining their businesses. Loans given within the rubric of trust banks, however, are generally smaller than those provided to solidarity groups, although in both types of loans, the other members of the group or bank are coguarantors of each other's loans. The Zambuko Trust loans money to be used for raw materials and working capital for a business as opposed to funding the creation of buildings or the purchase of major equipment.[7]

In providing training, advice, and loan assistance, the regional manager of the Zambuko Trust noted that it served about 14,000 clients in a year. Lending was its major activity, with first loans averaging around Z$500 to Z$5,000 and an upper limit for all loans of about Z$100,000. Entrepreneurs had six to eighteen months to repay at an interest rate of 42 percent. Loans were given to both individuals and groups. As with many similar community-banking establishments, trust and the personal character of the applicant were important criteria in assessing loan requests. Recipients received business training for free (interview with the regional manager, Zambuko Trust, July 1999). Due to the very high interest rate charged and a lack of formal follow-up on training, there is little wonder that 15 to 20 percent of all loans fell in arrears. Further, given that the trust disbursed loans to both women and men, it is more likely that men were more responsible for failing to repay their loans, because women in the Global South have demonstrated a very high repayment rate over the past two decades (Reichmann 1984; Tendler 1989; Berger 1995; Neft and Levine 1997; Yunus 1999).

Loans and training assistance have been given to entrepreneurs in carpentry, food production and distribution, agriculture, trade, services, and other manufacturing establishments. Several international government agencies

---

7. According to Bango et al. (1999), clients also used money for family and household expenses such as the payment of school fees, utility bills, and funeral costs, among other expenses.

and private foundations have provided donor support to the Zambuko Trust, including the Australian Agency for International Development, the Canadian International Development Agency, CARE Zimbabwe, the German Technical Corporation for Developing Countries, Opportunity International, the Mennonite Economic Development Agency, the Ford Foundation, and the U.S. Agency for International Development. One of the future goals of the Zambuko Trust was to become a bank and to provide savings training for entrepreneurs, a service that it maintained was sorely needed.

## Coping with Economic Crisis and Structural Adjustment: Informal Associations and Other Strategies

Given the difficulties that most businesswomen encountered in accessing credit from banks and from NGOs, and considering the grave financial needs that many entrepreneurs had during the economic crisis, several women entrepreneurs in this study joined savings clubs or rotating credit schemes at their workplaces. In Zimbabwe, these informal associations are called "rounds" and are found at many sites, but especially in locations such as markets where large numbers of individuals trade in foodstuffs, clothing, and other goods. Rounds were also a prominent savings activity among crocheters in this study. Nineteen percent (eleven) of the crocheters and 15 percent (nine) of the market traders stated that they participated in rounds. The fact that these businesswomen turned to the rotating credit scheme as a means of maintaining their businesses during the economic crisis demonstrated that they are indeed creative and strategic in the decisions that they made about their enterprises and in response to structural adjustment policies.

Rotating credit schemes have been especially important in assisting women in maintaining businesses in Zimbabwe as well as in West Africa, the Caribbean, and East Asia (Gabianu 1990; Berger 1995; Snyder 2000; Osirim 2001). There were more than 10,000 rounds in Zimbabwe with more than 50,000 members, and more than 97 percent of them are women (Safilios-Rothschild 1990). Such rotating credit schemes (also referred to as *esusus* in West Africa) have been defined as

an indigenous system through which people join hands to save money and help each other to meet credit needs. *Esusus* involve a group of people coming together and saving a mutually agreed upon amount of money on a predetermined day at regular intervals. The money realized after collection is given on a rotating basis to a member of the group and the process is repeated until everyone in the group has had a turn. (Gabianu 1990, 123)

Among Zimbabwean entrepreneurs, these associations were most often found in the markets with a woman or man at the site serving as banker and collecting deposits from members on a daily or weekly basis. Business-women frequently mentioned how the lump-sum payments from these accounts most often assisted them in meeting their business and family expenses. For example, crocheters noted that they were able to purchase raw materials, replenish their supplies of other items, such as carvings, and pay subcontractors with the payments they received from rotating credit schemes. These rounds also enabled them to meet their responsibilities to their children by providing them with needed cash in the form of large lump-sum payments in December or January, in time to pay school fees at the beginning of the academic year. Therefore, rotating credit schemes were notable as coping mechanisms that not only sustained businesses but also contributed to national development through the expansion of human capital.

Another useful mechanism for coping with the strains of economic crisis and structural adjustment for some crocheters and seamstresses in this study was participation in cross-border trade. During my fieldwork visit to Zimbabwe in 1997, I traveled by bus to Johannesburg to interview Zimbabwean cross-border traders there.[8] Businesswomen in Zimbabwe regarded cross-border trade as a significant means of improving the profitability of their businesses, although they also realized the heavy costs associated with such activities. Despite the sacrifices that cross-border trade entailed, engaging in this activity illustrated another example of the creativity and ingenuity of Zimbabwean women entrepreneurs in the face of economic crisis. Increasing numbers of crocheters and seamstresses from urban Zimbabwe transport their goods—such as sweaters, doilies, tablecloths, and dresses—mainly from Harare to Johannesburg. These entrepreneurs sell their wares to the residents of the former black townships, such as Soweto, in addition to customers who pass though Park Station, the city's major railway terminal. Some crocheters also sell their goods in the stalls of flea markets in largely white areas of Johannesburg, such as the Bruma Lake Flea Market.

Cross-border traders in crocheted, knitted, and sewn goods encountered

---

8. A Bryn Mawr College undergraduate student accompanied me on this visit and assisted in the interviewing of cross-border traders and participant-observation at their sites.

very different sales situations, depending on whether they sold their goods at established flea markets, at Park Station, or in the townships. Entrepreneurs selling in the townships generally carried their goods from door to door to a black South African clientele. Customers in the townships were generally poorer than those at the other types of business sites at which the Zimbabweans traded. Township residents thus were more likely to bargain with the entrepreneurs to arrive at an agreed-upon price, pay on credit over time (often over weeks or months), or provide used clothing in exchange for the new knitted and crocheted goods. Upon returning to Zimbabwe, the businesswomen would often sell such used clothing at the secondhand clothing market in Mbare, the largest high-density black area in Harare.[9] Crocheters who sold their goods at flea markets in Johannesburg generally encountered a largely white South African clientele who might bargain in their negotiations with Zimbabweans or might accept a price closer to the entrepreneur's asking price. These flea markets often contained stalls and were located in white suburban areas of the city. Mainly black South Africans purchased goods at Park Station, where Zimbabwean and South African traders established a makeshift market behind the station, which generally met the needs of low-income black South African customers.

Handmade crocheted and knitted goods were not generally made or widely available in South Africa, with the major exception of those goods made by Zimbabweans. These items were more affordable than the machine-made goods found in the major department stores for much of South Africa's poor black population, because these residents bargained with their Zimbabwean sisters and paid them in cash or with used clothing. Upon completing their sales in Johannesburg, the crocheters and seamstresses most often purchased computer software, other high-technology goods, and housewares such as machine-made bedspreads in South Africa for resale in Zimbabwe. Some women were even involved in broader networks of trade that included buying blue jeans made in Zimbabwe or South Africa for sale in Zambia.

The Zimbabwean businesswomen who sold their goods in South Africa and/or throughout the region also incurred many problems. Like black male

9. In studying the role of microenterprise and small enterprise clusters in Kenya, scholars such as McCormick and Kinuanjui (2007) have noted the substantial growth in secondhand clothing markets. These markets, however, have exploded throughout Sub-Saharan Africa due to the economic crisis. Needless to say, such markets do affect the demand for new machine and handmade clothing, the latter as produced by entrepreneurs in my study, while meeting the needs of the poor.

migrant laborers during the colonial period, they were frequently separated from their children for long periods of time. Though their extended family members and those with whom they had established social capital were still major sources of support in caring for their children, the economic crisis weighed heavily on these families and made such arrangements more stressful and less stable.[10] In addition, black Zimbabwean women were frequently harassed by South African immigration officials upon entering and leaving the country, as well as by the police near Park Station. All too often, the crocheters were fined for trading without appropriate visas and permits, and their goods were confiscated by the police and often not returned upon the payment of fines. These Zimbabwean entrepreneurs also had to endure weeks or months in overcrowded living quarters, often sleeping on floor mats, with Zimbabwean or South African friends and relatives. Further, for those who worked at Park Station in Johannesburg, their workplaces posed even more environmental problems than their worksites in Harare or Bulawayo. At Park Station, these entrepreneurs were trading on absolutely bare ground, or at best sitting on one of their pieces of cloth, with no market stalls and no protective covering, not even on land provided by the city government.[11] Moreover, they were breathing in the sickening fumes from the large vats of burning refuse in the area, which they often tried to sit near to keep themselves warm in the winter season. Despite the cold, these Zimbabwean businesswomen were likely to travel to South Africa at this time of the year, because this is when their handmade knitted sweaters would be in high demand.

Despite these problems, however, these Zimbabwean women entrepreneurs engaged in cross-border trade argued that it was worth it because they earned more money than if they sold their goods solely in Harare or Bulawayo. As the economic crisis intensified, more and more women utilized such creative and strategic coping strategies as selling their goods in Johannesburg to maintain their enterprises and their families—again demonstrating that they were, indeed, enterprising women.

10. One important means through which crocheters established strong social networks was through hiring relatives, neighbors, and friends as subcontractors in their firms. Such social capital illustrates the strong relationships of reciprocity and responsibility among Zimbabwean women that Sudarkasa found earlier among Nigerian women. See Sudarkasa (1981a, 1981b).

11. In Harare and Bulawayo, crocheters sat on the ground provided by the city councils of those cities, for which they paid rental fees and fees to "security guards" to protect their goods at night.

# Chapter 7

# Conclusion: Moving beyond Simple Survival in the Microenterprise Sector

The previous chapters have shown how Zimbabwean businesswomen in hairdressing, sewing, crocheting, and market trading demonstrated that despite the major problems posed by the economic crisis and the subsequent Economic Structural Adjustment Program (ESAP) during the 1990s, they were able to maintain their enterprises and households and contribute to community and national development. How did they succeed in these tasks? These entrepreneurs revealed in their own voices that they possessed the business acumen, creativity, and ingenuity to cope with the numerous challenges that they encountered in their business and personal lives. As black women who experienced both the travails of intersectionality of gender, race, and class, and the effects of 1990s globalization, many of them still managed to be innovators in their firms, contribute to material culture, and generate employment. Although these women were located in different segments of the microenterprise sector, they encountered many commonalities in their experience as women, entrepreneurs, mothers, and wives. Given their different positions in the microenterprise sector and their somewhat different occupational statuses, they also experienced some distinct challenges in running their enterprises. This chapter explores some of the major similarities and differences in their experiences by subsector and offers policy recommendations to improve their position in the nation and in the global economy, when the current turmoil subsides, and in the meantime may also apply to women entrepreneurs in other countries of the Global South. Finally, the chapter discusses some of the changes and challenges in the state and the economy in recent years that make advancement for Zimbabwean businesswomen and the broader society highly unlikely in the foreseeable future.

## Our Commonalities Outweigh Our Differences:
### The Experiences of Hairdressers, Seamstresses, Crocheters, and Traders in Their Families and Enterprises

The intersection of race, gender, and class in the lives of Zimbabwean women entrepreneurs working as hairdressers, seamstresses, crocheters, and traders from their youth meant that they experienced a great deal of structural blockage in their society, especially in the educational system and the labor market. British colonialism and British and African patriarchy severely restricted the opportunity structure for these women and limited their educational attainment. The race-based system of stratification that existed under the British forced most of them to remain in the Tribal Trust Lands eking out a living in subsistence farming. Only a relative few had the opportunity to attend mission schools, where most received a few years of highly gendered education. For some of the women in this study, this meant no formal schooling or at best a few years of primary school, whereas several hairdressers, seamstresses, and crocheters were able to complete a few years of secondary school, and, in some cases, complete the first level of secondary school, given the financial support of their parents and/or extended family members. Despite the achievement of the latter group, the lack of sufficient educational attainment among the vast majority of women in this study meant that they had no choice but to enter the microenterprise sector of the economy. For these young women, either their parents were too poor to keep them in school and/or the women failed to pass at least five Ordinary Level (O-level) examinations. British and African patriarchy and British colonialism combined were very responsible for the educational experiences (or lack thereof) that the women received and the highly gendered curriculum, behaviors, and attitudes that severely restricted their performance in school. Their failure to successfully complete the first level of secondary school and receive their O-level certificates barred them from entering the economy's formal sector. Furthermore, the perspective of feminist political economy reminds us that the time and manner in which Zimbabwe (Rhodesia) entered the world economy in the first place, coupled with the race-based system of stratification under British colonialism, explain the severe restrictions placed on the social and economic mobility of these black Zimbabwean women.

In addition to receiving at least some formal education, the women in this study benefited from the informal training that they received in hairdressing, knitting, crocheting, and/or sewing from local clubs, community centers, and churches. These organizations also taught them some important business skills, such as bookkeeping. Moreover, networks of female relatives also taught these young women such crafts as knitting, crocheting, and sewing and such skills as typing either within their households or via apprenticeships. Such networks of immediate and extended family members as well as friends were vital to these women as entrepreneurs—assisting hairdressers in locating employees, crocheters in hiring subcontractors, and many of these women overall in providing child care while they were involved in cross-border trade or other business activities at home.

The women entrepreneurs in this study also gained capital and valuable experience in the world of work and in operating a business from the several occupations that they had previously held or held simultaneously with the business that they owned at the time of this research. These businesswomen were previously employed in occupations ranging from domestic worker to schoolteacher, including such activities as salesperson, factory worker, and nurse.[1] Hairdressers and seamstresses, some of whom enjoyed higher socioeconomic status in this project, were more likely to occupy multiple positions, as opposed to those involved in market trading and crocheting. Thus, a few hairdressers and seamstresses also held positions as nurses and owners of other businesses, such as a barbershop, a knitting shop, or a meat market. There was also the exceptional case of one seamstress who owned a small gold mine.

## *The Domestic Sphere*

On the home front, the women entrepreneurs in this study bore the vast majority of responsibilities for housework and child care. (Only in a few cases would Zimbabwean men, like their counterparts throughout most of Africa, be found in the kitchen.) Even when some of these hairdressers, seamstresses, and crocheters could afford to hire domestic help, the full responsibility of arranging and paying for such services generally rested with these respondents. For the majority of the women in this study, however, housework and child care rested on their shoulders, and although they did not have expectations that this situation would be otherwise, it did pose significant burdens for them when considered in light of the nation's economic crisis

---

1. Needless to say, those who occupied positions in such fields as teaching and nursing were small in number in this sample. With respect to nursing, I generally refer to those few women who did successfully complete the first level of secondary school. Teaching at the primary school level for some did not require the successful completion of lower or upper secondary school.

and structural adjustment (Mbilinyi 1992; Adomako et al. 2004). Though, in the past, most of the women could have expected significant assistance with housework and child care from their extended family members, financial strains from the economic situation during the 1990s made it increasingly difficult for the latter to provide such help in the majority of households for extensive periods of time. Thus, for many of these women—especially those poorer women involved in market trading and crocheting—their business and domestic responsibilities required them to begin their days at about 4 or 5 AM. Poverty, unemployment, and underemployment for spouses and other relatives and the removal of subsidies from transportation meant that many of the women had to leave their homes very early to ensure a long day of work in the market.

Most of the women interviewed for this research reported that they faced increased financial responsibilities in their households under globalization and structural adjustment in the 1990s. Although, historically, Shona and Ndebele men were responsible for paying the household expenses, this had become exceedingly difficult given the economic crisis and the resulting unemployment and underemployment plaguing many poor and low-income men. At the same time, the many stresses and strains posed by the economic crisis led to greater family instability, marked by separation, divorce, and/or physical, economic, or psychological violence in many households (Green 1999; Osirim 2003c).[2] In this study, the highest rates of separation and divorce were noted among market traders, the poorest segment of the study. Therefore, even in cases where some assistance was provided by their extended families, many separated or divorced market traders found themselves heading households and experienced far greater pressure to support their families.

The married entrepreneurs in this study remarked that they were increasingly sharing household expenses with their husbands. Unlike the expectations held for Zimbabwean men historically, most men were not solely paying for food and shelter and, in fact, women were particularly feeling the pressure to meet the increased costs of user fees for their children's educations and the related costs of books, uniforms, and transportation to school.

---

2. As previously noted at the conference, "Gender, Justice, and Development," held at the University of Massachusetts–Amherst in January 1993, Peggy Antrobus, then director of Development Alternatives with Women for a New Era (DAWN), stated that there clearly seemed to be a relationship between the adoption of structural adjustment programs in the Global South and the increasing incidence of violence against poor women in these societies, who were disproportionately carrying the burdens of adjustment.

Though husbands more typically provided food allowances to their wives, in many cases, these payments had decreased and given the escalating costs of food due to the economic crisis and ESAP, these women were left to endure this burden.

Among the married women in the study, decision making in their households also appeared to be shared significantly with their spouses. The women's increased contributions to the financial upkeep of their households and families accounted for much of their increased decision making power in these relationships (Blood and Wolfe 1960; Andersen 1997; Lips 2005). Conversely, a gendered division of labor that favored men persisted with regard to those issues for which one's decision really seemed to matter: the economic issues. For example, the women were found to largely make decisions about housework and child care issues, and although women contributed to decision making about financial issues, men appeared more powerful in such matters.

Understanding the division of labor within the households of these women revealed only part of their personal stories. These women had substantial responsibilities for extended family members, both those living with them and those not living with them. The majority of the businesswomen in all the entrepreneurial categories were providing financial and in-kind support to extended family members, with market vendors constituting the smallest percentage of women providing such support. This again indicated the poorer status of traders in this study. Many entrepreneurs had some extended family members living with them, whereas the majority provided cash payments, food, and/or clothing to relatives not living with them, most especially to parents and in-laws. Several hairdressers, seamstresses, and crocheters also hired relatives to work in their enterprises, and for some this served as a type of apprenticeship training for siblings, nieces, and nephews.[3]

## The World of Work

The businesswomen in this study demonstrated that they were indeed dynamic entrepreneurs in their creativity, in their business acumen, in their knowledge of local and sometimes other Southern African markets, and in their contributions to material culture. To what extent had these women

---

3. In West Africa, particularly in nations like Nigeria, there is a long history of such apprenticeship training by relatives in small enterprises and microenterprises. This has been an important training ground for future entrepreneurs. See Osirim (1992, 1994a).

exhibited these characteristics in the daily operation of their firms? From the start-up phase to the time of the interviews, the women were involved in a variety of business practices that illustrated their commitment to the growth and development of their enterprises.

This chapter now comparatively examines how these respondents were dedicated to the advancement of their firms in the provision of start-up capital, in generating employment and/or opportunities for subcontracting, in the specialization of functions, and in their examples of innovation and their control and reinvestment of profits. Although not all the hairdressers, seamstresses, crocheters, and market traders in this study exemplified these traits in the operation of their businesses, many did. This is quite a remarkable feat when one considers the severity of the economic crisis that affected poor and low-income entrepreneurs in this study and in society at large during the 1990s. Moreover, many of these businesswomen had aspirations for the future that clearly revealed their commitment to the growth of their enterprises, far beyond the level of simple survival.

## Establishment Capital

First and foremost, the businesswomen in this study were entrepreneurs precisely because they started their enterprises and were responsible for their operation. They are not categorized as entrepreneurs because of particular business traits that they manifested, but rather because they established, owned, and controlled their firms.[4] With respect to starting their businesses, the largest single source of establishment capital was the entrepreneur's personal savings (see table 7.1). In most cases, this referred to money they had saved from previous occupations and, to a lesser extent, to cash that they had saved from household money. For most women in this study, starting a business with one's personal savings was a rather bold move in either the first postindependence decade or in the period of economic crisis and structural adjustment, considering their status as poor and low-income women. For most of these women, their personal savings was the only significant material capital they owned. Thus, the success of their investments was very

4. Many of the earliest theorists who examined the critical role occupied by entrepreneurs in promoting development in Global South societies characterized entrepreneurs as those businesspersons who possessed particular traits, attitudes, and aspirations. E.g., Schumpeter's entrepreneurs expressed "a joy in creating," "the dream and the will to found a private kingdom," and the "will to conquer." See Schumpeter (1959) and Kilby (1971).

Table 7.1. Sources of start-up capital among Zimbabwean women entrepreneurs (percentage and number of respondents)

| Source of capital | Hairdressers | | Seamstresses | | Crocheters | | Traders | |
|---|---|---|---|---|---|---|---|---|
| | Percent | Number | Percent | Number | Percent | Number | Percent | Number |
| Personal savings | 40 | 6 | 58 | 14 | 39 | 22 | 41 | 25 |
| Husband | 20 | 3 | 17 | 4 | 26 | 15 | 25 | 15 |
| Female relatives | 13 | 2 | 8 | 2 | 21 | 12 | 16 | 10 |
| Other male relatives | | | 4 | 1 | 11 | 6 | 10 | 6 |
| Bank or finance agency | | | | | | | | |
| Multiple sources | 27 | 4 | 13 | 3 | 3 | 2 | 6 | 4 |
| Other (church member) | | | | | | | 2 | 1 |
| Total | 100 | 15 | 100 | 24 | 100 | 57 | 100 | 61 |

*Note:* The blank cells indicate that none of the hairdressers, seamstresses, crocheters, or traders obtained start-up capital from a bank or finance agency. Male relatives, other than husbands, did not provide start-up capital for hairdressers. Finally, church members were not a source of start-up capital for entrepreneurs, with the exception of one trader.
*Source:* Author's study data.

important to them not only for the future development of the business but also in their efforts to support themselves and to provide their children with the opportunity for a better life.

Husbands were also a very important source of initial capital investment in these women's businesses, as might be expected given the historic role of men's support for such enterprises, particularly as noted among such West African populations as the Yoruba. Husbands recognized that if their wives started and successfully maintained a business, this would assist in financially supporting the family and household and, perhaps, lessen the breadwinning burden somewhat for them. Also, such microenterprises are often closely linked to women's domestic responsibilities or are flexible in ways that enable women to bring their young children to work with them. With the exception of those women who engaged in cross-border trade, women's microenterprises tended to be located close to home and did not involve long-distance travel. Husbands (as well as the businesswomen themselves) generally viewed these issues as beneficial for the family and thus were quite supportive of such business ventures.

Other relatives, especially mothers and sisters, were another major source of start-up capital for these firms. Not only were female relatives supportive in starting such businesses, but they also provided important social capital for women in this study, which assisted in advancing their enterprises. Such relatives (and friends) frequently worked as subcontractors for crocheters and assisted in the care of the entrepreneurs' children, especially those engaged in cross-border trade. To a lesser extent, male relatives also assisted in providing initial capital for these firms. Needless to say, given the multiple sources of structural blockage that poor and low-income women experienced in Zimbabwe, there is little wonder that banks and other formal institutions were not an important source of start-up capital for these women.

## Employment Generation and the Division of Labor in Firms

More than one-third of all the entrepreneurs in this study provided employment (see table 7.2). Only the market traders did not hire workers. The hairdressers were most likely to hire regular full-time employees and had the largest number of workers; they employed a median of four workers.[5]

---

5. An additional hairdresser in this study did employ six workers, with one of these employees working solely on commission. She is not included in this study.

*Table 7.2. Employment generation among Zimbabwean businesswomen*

| Type of business | Number providing employment | Percent |
|---|---|---|
| Hairdressers | 15 | 100 |
| Seamstresses | 11 | 46 |
| Crocheters[a] | 30 | 53 |
| Traders | | |
| Total | 56 | |

*Note:* The blank cells indicate that market traders in this study did not provide employment.
[a]Because crocheters hired women largely on a subcontracting basis, they did not provide regular, full-time employment for their workers.
*Source:* Author's study data.

Forty-six percent of the seamstresses also provided employment, with a median of two workers per firm. The crocheters were quite unique in this work, and in Sub-Saharan Africa as a whole, in providing subcontracting opportunities. As was earlier noted by Portes, Castells, and Benton (1989) and other scholars, subcontracting has not been a major activity in Sub-Saharan Africa. The crocheters in this study, who employed a median of two workers per establishment, often relied on their social networks of relatives, friends, and neighbors to assist as subcontractors. These subcontractors were involved in piecework for the entrepreneurs, often crocheting hundreds of 3-by-3-inch squares to be later stitched together in making tablecloths and bedspreads. The businesswomen were most likely to hire subcontractors during the very busy winter months and Christmas holiday season (Zimbabwe's summer), when the demand for knitted and crocheted goods was highest.

Although wages for workers in these occupational categories were low, by providing employment on a regular or subcontracting basis, the entrepreneurs in this study contributed to the development of human capital, which in turn benefited their communities and their society. Whether working in a beauty salon, a crochet market, or a sewing establishment, these business owners helped employees in further developing their skills as well as in providing them with incomes to assist in supporting their families. Some seamstresses, for example, after gaining experience in respondents' firms, left to begin their own businesses with the knowledge and skills they gained working in the sewing establishments in this study. In addition, hiring workers, especially during the holiday seasons for hairdressers, seamstresses, and crocheters, increased the efficiency and the overall sales performance of their enterprises. Generating employment in these ways further developed and strengthened the social capital of these entrepreneurs because they often hired from and directly identified other potential employees through their social networks. On some occasions, these networks included relatives who were hired to work in sewing firms.

In addition to assistance with hiring, social networks were also important vehicles for marketing one's product. Very few seamstresses in this study, for example, received contracts to make school uniforms, but for those who did, knowledge about and referrals to schools and large businesses making such requests generally came from social networks. Such connections also assisted other businesses in increasing their sales, because many customers knew about these enterprises via word of mouth, particularly those South Africans who traveled to Zimbabwe to purchase sweaters. Local customers and tourists were often attracted to specific market stalls and/or crochet markets by their enticing, colorful displays of goods. Also, for example, market traders over time developed relationships with repeat customers who were assured of the good quality of their products. In providing employment and in developing social capital, these entrepreneurs exhibited their knowledge of the market and their strong business acumen at a time when their nation's economic crisis was escalating.

Microenterprises are often regarded as businesses that function as one-person operations, in which the owner-entrepreneur is the sole employee. In addition to hiring workers to improve their establishments, several entrepreneurs in this study also demonstrated their shrewd insights as businesswomen by hiring workers for specialized duties in their firms. The division of labor was most notable in beauty shops, where business owners hired licensed hairdressers, bookkeepers, and receptionists. Salons also hired shampooers, hair braiders, and cleaners. Although sewing firms illustrated less specialization of tasks than their counterparts in hairdressing, some seamstresses had employed tailors, embroiderers, knitters, and sales clerks to fulfill specific responsibilities.

Although a division of labor existed in these firms, the entrepreneurs also assumed many major responsibilities themselves. Most hairdressers and seamstresses continued to perform the basic functions in their businesses—namely, doing hair and sewing—which they also combined with the accounting and management functions in their enterprises. In addition, the majority of seamstresses also designed clothing and made patterns for the garments they created. In fulfilling a myriad of responsibilities to their businesses (as well as their families), these business owners further demonstrated their fortitude in the midst of many challenges.

*Table 7.3. Innovation in Zimbabwean women's microenterprises*

| Type of business | Number who innovated | Percent |
|---|---|---|
| Hairdressers | 11 | 73 |
| Seamstresses | 7 | 28 |
| Crocheters | 39 | 68 |
| Market traders | 45 | 74 |
| Total | 102 | 100 |

*Source:* Author's study data.

## Business Innovation

The majority of businesswomen in this study were dynamic innovators who experimented with different products and styles in trying to meet the desires of their customers (see table 7.3). They clearly understood their customers' needs and wants, and they attempted to meet the customers' demands to the fullest extent possible. The seamstresses were the least likely to innovate in this study, but those who did were most likely to introduce new lines of clothing or introduce new methods of production. For example, one seamstress crossed gender boundaries and added men's clothing to the roster of items that she made, and another respondent purchased a zigzag sewing machine that enabled her to add a new finishing to her clothes.[6] Some seamstresses especially looked forward to importing cloth and other small items that they used in accessorizing their garments.

The market traders were not as creative in innovation as their counterparts in the other occupational categories of this study. The traders largely innovated by changing the goods they sold, often responding to the change of season and the profitability of particular products. Thus, market vendors often reported that they sold fruit in the summer, not in the winter, because their customers preferred to eat fruit in the warmer months and were more likely to purchase it then.

The hairdressers frequently created new styles, used new products, and sold different goods in their salons. Several hairdressers relied on imported hair products, and some tried new styles based on what they saw in magazines from abroad. Their social networks also served them well here, because those customers who traveled to South Africa and Europe frequently brought back ideas and magazines that included new hairstyles. Because some

6. For clothing that is not mass-produced in factories, tailors are most likely to make men's garments in many Sub-Saharan African nations, including Zimbabwe.

hairdressers were more "middle class" in their incomes, educational attainment, and overall status, a few had traveled and brought back new ideas from Britain. These as well as other strategies assisted hairdressers in achieving the greatest economic success in their enterprises.

However, the crocheters were the most innovative, in the broadest sense, in this study. First, by the mid-1990s, they began to add vibrantly colored yarns, as well as white yarn, to their garments, which were far more expensive than the beige yarn noted in my earliest visits to Zimbabwe. This made their doilies far more attractive to the eyes of customers in the shopping centers and major streets where they were located. Second, they changed the styles of their hand-knitted sweaters, which were especially appealing to tourists and buyers from South Africa. Third, they recognized the increase in tourism to the region, with the coming of majority rule to South Africa in 1994, and they began to make brightly colored batiks to cater to the tourist market. The crocheters often included national symbols on these batiks, such as the Zimbabwe bird, which in some ways, had even greater appeal for tourists interested in "street" art. The production of batiks, as well as crocheted goods, came to be widely identified in the region as the work of Zimbabwean women and illustrated their contributions to tourist art and material culture. Finally, these crocheters crossed gender boundaries in the selling of Shona soapstone carvings. They recognized that these goods were in especially high demand among tourists from the United States and Europe, and therefore they added these artworks to their repertoire of goods. Shona carvings often depicted nurturing family relationships and thus illustrated the centrality of family life in the broader society, a major element in the national culture. In selling such items as well as the batiks, these businesswomen made Zimbabwean culture more visible around the globe. Selling Shona carvings, however, marked a significant "boundary crossing" for these women, because these goods were historically and more typically sold by the artists, who were generally young Zimbabwean men.[7] The negative effects of globalization, experienced largely by living under ESAP, led to the crossing of gender boundaries in several segments of the microenterprise sector in Zimbabwe, as well as in other parts of Sub-Saharan Africa.[8] The

7. One could certainly find "high-quality" soapstone carvings available for sale in the galleries in downtown Harare sold by storeowners, who were disproportionately white Zimbabwean men.

8. During fieldwork visits to Zimbabwe from the mid-1990s onward, I noticed increased numbers of men selling "women's" products, usually food, in the markets in Harare and Bulawayo. Men displaced from the formal economy and recent school-

innovative strategies of the entrepreneurs in this study were important coping mechanisms, which enabled these businesswomen to sustain their firms beyond the level of simple survival.

Decision Making and the Use of Profits

With respect to the economic performance of their firms, most entrepreneurs in this study did not keep accurate records of financial transactions. Though the majority of firms in all categories had earned profits since their establishment, profits as well as sales had not been increasing every year, largely due to ESAP. Several women reported declines in sales and profits from the middle to late 1990s. Many businesswomen commented on the challenges of selling their goods or services, especially those viewed as providing "luxury" items, such as new clothes and household goods and regular visits to the beauty salon, during a period of economic belt-tightening.

Despite these problems, however, the majority of entrepreneurs in this study were strongly committed to the maintenance and growth of their firms, as noted in their decision making about the use of profits. The vast majority of the women in all occupational categories stated that they were the sole decision makers regarding the use of profits from their enterprises (see table 7.4), thus illustrating their significant empowerment as businesswomen. Some mentioned that their husbands assisted in deciding how to use profits, but these women were clearly in the minority among their peers. For what types of investments were their profits used? They stated that they first and foremost reinvested profits in their enterprises (see table 7.4). These businesswomen remained very dedicated to this task, even though profits had not been steadily increasing in their establishments due to the economic crisis and because a strict division between business and personal capital had not existed for them. The majority of businesswomen in each category noted that they reinvested profits in their firms, using these to replenish supplies, purchase raw materials and machinery, and/or hire more workers or subcontractors. A few of the businesswomen used the profits from their enterprises to invest in other activities—for example, those hairdressers,

---

leavers often found market trading to be one of the few viable options for them under adjustment. Clark (1994), *Onions Are My Husband,* found similar conditions in Ghanaian markets under adjustment. Under such circumstances, however, women run the risk of losing control of the one urban domain in which they were dominant: urban food markets; see Clark (1994).

*Table 7.4. Reinvestment and decision making about profits for Zimbabwean businesswomen*

| Type of business | Reinvestment in firm | | Sole decision maker | |
|---|---|---|---|---|
| | Percent | Number | Percent | Number |
| Hairdressers | 80 | 12 | 60 | 9 |
| Seamstresses | 79 | 19 | 83 | 20 |
| Crocheters | 51 | 29 | 72 | 41 |
| Traders | 84 | 51 | 79 | 48 |
| Total number of entrepreneurs | | 111 | | 118 |

*Source:* Author's study data.

seamstresses, and market vendors who invested in additional knitting and sewing enterprises and/or in cross-border trade with South Africa.

Given the intersections between their work lives and personal lives, the women in this study also stated that they used profits to meet their obligations to immediate and extended family members. Therefore, education for their children and/or other extended family members—to pay school fees and purchase uniforms and books—was the second major area in which most of these women invested profits. In all the occupational categories of this study with the exception of crocheters, most entrepreneurs invested first in their businesses and then in education, contributing to the development of human capital. Though their desires for educational attainment were highest for their children and then other relatives, these entrepreneurs were also very determined to advance their own knowledge and skills. Thus, it was not unusual to find some seamstresses, hairdressers, and crocheters enrolled in continuing education programs to complete their lower-level secondary school certificates or to gain further skills in sewing, knitting, hairdressing, or other fields. In addition, as noted above, the respondents were also strongly committed to assisting in financially supporting their extended family members, especially parents and in-laws; thus, the majority of them used profits from their firms to provide support to their parents and others on a monthly or quarterly basis. Sometimes, this meant cash payments; at other times, purchasing food and clothing.

Because, in most cases, the entrepreneurs in this study had not collected a regular salary, and because strict divisions were lacking between business and personal capital, it was not unusual for these women to indicate that they used profits to pay their rent and to buy food, clothing, and household goods. These businesswomen were also wedded to maintaining personal savings accounts, in which they deposited the profits from their enterprises. Even the women who appeared to be the poorest traders managed to establish and save in personal bank accounts and/or in rotating credit schemes. Finally, about 20 percent of the seamstresses and 50 percent of the hairdressers did purchase a car with profits from their businesses, an action that was beyond the financial reach of crocheters and market traders. The range of categories in which these businesswomen invested profits with their first-level commitment to their firms demonstrated the fluidity of their identities and their myriad responsibilities as entrepreneurs, mothers, and wives—as well as their remarkable strides in balancing these roles and maintaining their firms. These examples further illustrated their creativity, tenacity, and dynamism as entrepreneurs.

In assessing the development of their businesses over the years, most of these entrepreneurs expressed their belief that they had experienced more successes than failures. With the exception of market trading, in all the other occupational categories, the majority of the businesswomen stated that they had achieved success in their enterprises over the years. About 40 percent of the market traders noted that they experienced more successes than problems. When entrepreneurs in all the categories discussed their successes, however, they again demonstrated the multifaceted, intersectional nature of their business and personal lives. Success in one's business was closely tied to the ability to provide for one's family, particularly providing education for one's children. Thus, hairdressers and seamstresses, for example, described success in terms of the financial performance of their firms, while at the same time including their contributions to human capital development for themselves and their families among their achievements. They also discussed their success in terms of the additional machines they were able to purchase for their firms and the goods they bought for their homes. In many ways, their ability to make purchases of major household appliances and furniture marked a great achievement for them, and again the crossing of gender boundaries, because such purchases were largely the domain of men.

In discussing their aspirations for the future, these entrepreneurs again revealed that they did not view their enterprises as "simply survival" activities. Rather, they were committed to the growth and development of their businesses over the long term, and some hoped to diversify production. Several crocheters and traders wanted to open shops for their businesses and expand the range of goods that they sold. Others hoped to add new activities to their current ones, such as crocheters hoping to expand into sewing and hairdressers planning to open boutiques to sell cosmetics as well as continue their ongoing activities. Many hairdressers and seamstresses discussed their desires to improve the infrastructure of their current operations—to add new machines and products. Several hairdressers hoped to study abroad in Britain to advance their knowledge and skills in cosmetology. A few entrepreneurs mentioned their intentions to pursue large-scale manufacturing—one hairdresser wanted to make hair products and reduce her dependence on imported goods, and a crocheter wanted to start a sweater factory. Although the market traders did not express the same level of creativity in their future aspirations as was noted among their sisters in sewing, hairdressing, and crocheting, they were very determined to see their children complete school and to expand their enterprises.

## The Impact of the Economic Structural Adjustment Program on Women's Microenterprises

Although the women in this study had certainly encountered difficulties in operating their firms from the start-up period, most of the problems they faced in the 1990s were due to ESAP. The entrepreneurs in nearly every occupational category, but especially the traders and crocheters, complained about the increasing competition they faced due to significant increases in the number of businesses in their field. The market vendors were especially hard hit by the increase in women hawking foodstuffs along the major city streets, whereas those in this study sat in (or outside) markets in the high-density suburbs. In fact, though the two major city governments in this study had made promises to both market traders and crocheters that they would build new markets for them, this construction was not forthcoming due to the government's decreased spending under ESAP. The massive devaluation of the Zimbabwean currency resulted in major increases in the costs of raw materials for production and of goods for sale in every category of businesswomen studied. Government bans on some imported products especially hurt hairdressers, seamstresses, and crocheters. These entrepreneurs, especially the hairdressers, experienced gender-based discrimination in obtaining import licenses for hair products. The crocheters were faced with higher customs duties in their activities as cross-border traders. Increased unemployment and underemployment under ESAP resulted in fewer customers for these businesswomen, especially when the goods or services they produced were considered luxury items, such as hairdressing and clothing.

Under ESAP, the problems faced by these entrepreneurs in their businesses were also frequently reflected in their personal lives. Unemployment and underemployment in their immediate and extended families placed greater responsibilities on these businesswomen to assist in financially supporting their families in many areas—from purchasing food to paying school fees. The removal of state subsidies from social services such as education, health care, and education also resulted in higher user fees for these entrepreneurs and their families. All in all, ESAP took a high personal toll on these businesswomen and contributed to an overall decline in their quality of life. Despite all these challenges, however, these businesswomen remained steadfast in their entrepreneurial pursuits, sustained their enterprises, and held onto their high aspirations for the future.

## Support and Coping Strategies for Women's Microenterprises

Although government programs did exist to assist women in small enterprises and microenterprises, as well as poor and low-income women more generally, both before and after ESAP began, very few women in this study knew about or were aided by such programs. Among the few government- or state-related institutions that had assisted a very small number of businesswomen were Zimbank, in which the state was a major partner, and the Social Welfare Fund. A similar story can be told about nongovernmental organizations (NGOs), many of which exploded onto the scene in Zimbabwe, as well as in many other African nations, during the 1990s period of economic crisis and structural adjustment (Moghadam 2005; Osirim 2001). The women entrepreneurs in this study were aware of some of these NGOs—such as the Zimbabwe Women's Finance Trust, the Zimbabwe Women's League, the Indigenous Businesswomen's Organization, and Zambuko Trust—but few were successful in gaining assistance from any of them. Only 10 percent (fifteen) of the women received a loan for their businesses from either a bank or an NGO. The women praised the activities of the Zimbabwe Women's Finance Trust and Zambuko Trust in these efforts.

In general, however, entrepreneurs in the microenterprise sector, such as those interviewed for this study, did not appear to be a major target of the state's or NGOs' efforts to assist poor and low-income women. In fact, I would argue that recent school-leavers (those who had not successfully completed secondary school), as well as those who did finish school but were unable to find work, were often sought after in the government's efforts. Conversely, more middle-class and upper-middle-class women with established enterprises and significant social capital often benefited from both NGO and state efforts to assist women in business.

Despite the problems they faced and the general lack of formal support for their activities, the women entrepreneurs in this study exhibited the creativity and ingenuity to persist in business and to move beyond the level of simple survival. In addition to innovation in their enterprises, the development of human and social capital, the reinvestment of profits in their firms, and contributions to material culture, several women were involved in other strategies to maintain their businesses. These efforts were generally more informal, such as establishing rotating credit schemes in food and crochet markets to which they made daily and/or weekly contributions and from which they later received lump-sum payments in return. Such payments helped them replenish supplies for their markets, pay subcontractors, and meet family and household expenses, particularly school fees.

The businesswomen in this study also developed social networks that assisted them not only in maintaining their enterprises but also in successfully fulfilling their domestic responsibilities. This process had four particularly notable aspects. First, social capital assisted hairdressers, seamstresses, and crocheters in identifying potential employees to hire for their firms. In the case of hairdressers and seamstresses, such workers often provided specialized skills in such areas as embroidery and hair braiding that enhanced the development of these microenterprises. Conversely, the addition of subcontractors in crocheting, as well as the employees who assisted in the division of labor in beauty salons and in sewing establishments, enhanced the efficiency of these enterprises, which led to increased production and generally advanced business performance.

Second, for hairdressers, their social networks with customers benefited their firms in the area of innovation. Customers who traveled abroad frequently returned with new ideas for hairstyles and products, and brought back magazines featuring new hairstyles, which contributed to the repertoire of services and styles provided by the hairdressers. Such innovation was important in attracting new customers to the beauty shops and in solidifying their customer base.[9]

9. If this had not been a period of economic crisis and adjustment, such innovation would have likely resulted in significant expansions in the number of customers, because the women who patronized such establishments in downtown Harare and Bulawayo were very intent on keeping up with the latest styles. The desire of women in the Global South, specifically in Sub-Saharan Africa and in the Caribbean, to keep up with current styles and engage in transnational trade in such areas as fashion can be seen in Freeman (1997) and Darkwah (2007).

Third, social capital also assisted entrepreneurs in identifying potential customers. In a few cases, some seamstresses received contracts to make school uniforms as a result of such connections. Social networks also spread the word about the quality of goods produced by these entrepreneurs in Zimbabwe as well as in South Africa. Fourth, the development of social capital among crocheters and seamstresses was also important in providing needed assistance with child care, especially for those engaged in cross-border trade in Southern Africa.

Such cross-border trade was another ingenious effort of entrepreneurs in this study largely undertaken by some crocheters and seamstresses. Previous research on cross-border traders in South Africa discovered that more than 66 percent of such traders were women. "South African immigration officials in Zimbabwe and Mozambique indicated that 80 to 95 percent of those who applied for visitors' visas for trading or shopping were female" (Peberdy and Rogerson 2000, 31; also see Nethengwe 1999). Drawing on their social networks in Harare and Bulawayo, which frequently involved relatives, neighbors, employees, and subcontractors, these entrepreneurs identified women living in Johannesburg who could often provide letters of invitation and short-term accommodations for them. The letters were used to obtain visitors' visas for these businesswomen in South Africa. The Zimbabwean entrepreneurs shared flats on a short-term basis with other Zimbabweans and South Africans, often enduring very crowded and uncomfortable living conditions. Experienced Zimbabwean cross-border traders and South African residents informed the entrepreneurs in this study about where to purchase goods to sell in Zimbabwe (and/or Zambia, if this was part of their trade route) at the best prices.

Cross-border traders—who sold their wares at the Johannesburg train station, at urban flea markets, and in the townships—were major risk takers in their actions, which sometimes drew the attention and wrath of the South African police. They took many risks crossing international borders, frequently without the appropriate travel documents; risked their health in working in difficult outdoor conditions at the railway station; and faced frequent harassment from city police for selling goods without proper work permits. Cross-border trade also meant that these women were away from their families for several weeks or months at a time, while drawing on their social capital, leaving their children in the care of relatives and neighbors who were also facing multiple responsibilities. Such situations brought greater stresses and strains to the entrepreneurs in this study, which they were willing to endure for the well-being of their businesses and their families.

Moreover, most of the businesswomen in this study were optimistic about the future of their enterprises. They planned to continue their operations and looked forward to expansion, growth, and, for some of them, diversification of production and sales. Some hairdressers sought to accomplish their desires through further education abroad in their field. In addition to their commitment to the future of their enterprises, these entrepreneurs, who were also mothers, were strongly dedicated to their children's educational attainment. This dedication was a very strong incentive for these businesswomen to maintain and further develop their enterprises and, as a result, contribute to both community and national development.

## Whither the Future? Policy Recommendations to Improve the Lives of Zimbabwean Women Entrepreneurs

What of the future? Reflecting on the findings from this study summarized above, it is possible to offer several policy recommendations to improve the lives of Zimbabwean women entrepreneurs in the microenterprise sector. To improve the lives of these businesswomen and, in turn, their contributions to development, several plans and policies are needed at the local, national, and global levels. However, given the current political and economic breakdown in Zimbabwe, these recommendations likely will only be able to be implemented there in the future. Nevertheless, this section explains how improvements can be made when they are practicable; the subsequent section considers the current situation in Zimbabwe. In the current period, these policy recommendations provide a model that could be useful in improving the lives of businesswomen in the microenterprise sector in other Sub-Saharan African societies. This is especially the case because more than forty African nations experienced adjustment policies in the 1980s and 1990s, and because the microenterprise sector is the second major area of income-earning activities for women on the continent.

In Zimbabwe, at the micro level, market traders, especially those working at Manwele Market in Bulawayo, and crocheters in all locations were in desperate need of adequate markets in which to sell their goods. This situation was especially problematic because of the lack of adequate shelter from the elements. Many women at Manwele Market and the crocheters in general had no places to sit, and those at Manwele faced even greater perils because their goods were likely to perish due to the lack of protection from the sun and rain. Market traders at Mbare and Manwele markets, as well as traders in general, lacked refrigeration and adequate spaces in which to store their goods. Adequate restroom facilities were also needed in all the market sites in this study. The creation of new comprehensive urban markets that include child care facilities would constitute a major step forward in providing adequate worksites for traders and crocheters. Given the economic problems in Zimbabwe, the building of these markets could be accomplished through self-help projects, in which NGOs could perhaps assist businesswomen to secure the needed supplies and the entrepreneurs and their families could provide the labor. Such markets could reduce the health risks for women and children, improve the working conditions and performance of their businesses, and enhance the overall care of their children.

Local and national governments and NGOs need to make their programs for small business and microbusiness development visible and accessible to the broadest public, especially those women at the bottom of the socioeconomic hierarchy who are most in need of assistance. At the very least, advertising needs to be undertaken in all branches of the media—print, radio, television, and even the Internet. Conversely, poor and low-income women do not have access to some of these media outlets, and thus more personal, direct efforts, such as community outreach workers, are needed to provide information about business services. These outreach workers could provide information to both individuals and groups and also engage communities in meetings to inform them about the available microlending, technical assistance, and entrepreneurship training programs. Moreover, these outreach workers should ascertain the needs of this population by asking the entrepreneurs directly. Furthermore, the state and NGOs also need to target their efforts more fully toward poor and low-income businesswomen who already run enterprises, as well as recent school-leavers and those who are trying to establish a business. The former should not be written off as too old to benefit from training and credit programs, but rather they should be regarded as valuable resources who actively sustain communities and contribute to the nation's development.

Zimbabwe also needs to identify new markets for its products and outlets for the goods produced by women in the microenterprise sector. Some doilies, sweaters, and key chains made by women in this sector could be found in the major department stores in downtown Harare and Bulawayo. The state, however, should assist women in exploring the possibilities of markets for these handmade goods in stores in other African nations, such as South Africa and Kenya, and beyond the African continent, particularly in Global North businesses. Special care has to be given to avoid the exploitation of small producers and microproducers that often occurs when goods made by poor and low-income populations with little knowledge of international markets are sold abroad. Galleries in major U.S. cities already sell Shona carvings, and a range of artworks and other crafts from the African continent can be found in a number of African shops in the United States and Europe. A good example of an organization that could partner with Zimbabwean women entrepreneurs is Ten Thousand Villages, the nonprofit chain of stores in North America that works with artisans in more than thirty Global South nations and practices fair trade. Selling the items produced by Zimbabwean seamstresses and crocheters abroad would not only enhance the profitability of their enterprises but would also increase the visibility of the nation on a more global scale.

As demonstrated in this study, educational attainment is a high priority among entrepreneurs—for their children, other relatives, and themselves. The vast majority of women in Zimbabwe and those in this study in particular faced significant structural blockage and gender-based discrimination in the educational system, which restricted women to the microenterprise sector in the first place. Education needs to be more accessible to and affordable for all Zimbabweans, with particular attention given to the plight of poor and low-income individuals. To improve the situation for women requires national-level attention in the form of a complete reform of the system. The colonial (British) system of education needs to be eliminated and replaced with a comprehensive system of education that emphasizes learning over the life course and includes a range of curricula—from academic to technical courses. At the very least, a universal free primary education system needs to be established, and there needs to be a goal to provide universal secondary and preschool education as well. Gendered educational messages and programs—which track girls and women into courses in domestic education and the humanities, leading them away from the natural and social sciences and technology—need to be abandoned. The state, in partnership with the private sector, should create affordable programs to enable those who did not complete secondary school to later have the opportunity to acquire equivalency certificates or diplomas.

Further, the state, the private business sector, and the NGO community should continue to create and support education and training programs for women entrepreneurs that will enable their businesses to grow beyond the level of survival activities. In other words, women and men of all ages should have access to continuing education over their life course, based on the understanding that education beyond secondary school is unlikely to be free but could be more available and affordable than at the time of this study. At its very foundation, this new system of education would strive to remove all discriminatory barriers from the learning process, including patriarchy, classism, and ageism, and lead to a society that promotes social justice.

To accomplish any of these goals and improve the development prospects for Zimbabwe, significant attention needs to be given to the macro level of the economy. With respect to economic development, the state needs to fully examine its position regarding neoliberalism and the broader agenda of contemporary globalization. What are the advantages and the shortcomings of this system? What are the trade-offs? During the 1990s, the efforts of the international financial institutions and the Northern hegemonic nations severely intensified the economic crisis for poor and low-income women and children, as evidenced by the experiences of the businesswomen in this study. Though the tide has certainly changed somewhat for some African nations and their relationships with the international financial institutions—such that they have now moved away from structural adjustment loans and policies—Southern nations still need greater freedom and authority in the global marketplace to set their own agendas and determine their own development goals (Faiola 2008).

Moreover, once the downward spiral of the state and the economy is reversed, such an agenda and goals need to be discussed in the broader national arena of Zimbabwe to seek a consensus on the major issues and to pave the way forward for the nation. In a world that is becoming increasingly interdependent, Zimbabwe needs to strengthen regional cooperation in the Southern African Development Community and participate fully in the African Union, as well as in other Africa-focused organizations. Though increasing domestic production and achieving less dependence on the North are viable goals, it is also important to recognize that in this age of globalization, a nation needs to participate in the international community to pursue trade and security.

## The Zimbabwean State, Development, and the Microenterprise Sector since 1999

Since the completion of my fieldwork in Zimbabwe in August 1999, the likelihood of the Zimbabwean state and society enacting any of the recommendations listed above in the short term has become extremely remote. In fact, since late 1999 and early 2000, the economic crisis has been joined by a political crisis, which, along with the HIV/AIDS pandemic, has more seriously jeopardized Zimbabwe's development prospects. Today, the Zimbabwean state under Robert Mugabe and his elite corps of top political officials has wreaked havoc on a nation that in the 1980s and early 1990s was still regarded as the "breadbasket" of Southern Africa, with a highly developed economy second only to South Africa's on the continent.

Although the international community, particularly the international financial institutions and the Northern hegemonic powers, also bears some responsibility for the crises that now beset Zimbabwe, especially the economic crisis of the 1990s, the Mugabe government has turned the country into a pariah state on the world stage. In fact, some journalists, such as R. W. Johnson of the London *Sunday Times,* have gone so far as to accuse the Mugabe regime of genocide in the past few years (Johnson 2007). What happened to this nation, which held out so many prospects for sustainable development in the first postindependence decade? And what has this meant for Zimbabwe's poor and low-income women entrepreneurs?

In recalling my fieldwork in Harare in 1999, I remember being pleasantly impressed by what appeared to be a highly democratic process at work in drafting a new Constitution. I attended a Catholic Mass at Saint Martin's in Harare at which the congregation was asked to provide recommendations for issues they would like to see addressed in a new Constitution. At the same time, in conversations with some leading academics and activists in Harare, I was told that the nation was possibly on the brink of civil war. Although ESAP and the overall economic crisis had inflicted a very heavy toll on the poor, especially women and children and those in my study, I would not have characterized the situation as one that was ripe for civil war. However, the events that followed in the new millennium have turned out to be far worse in many respects.

The current economic and political devastation afflicting Zimbabwe stems from the administration's failed constitutional referendum and Mugabe's Zimbabwe African National Union–Patriotic Front's (ZANU-PF's) significant loss of seats in the parliamentary elections of 2000. After the state appointed a Constitutional Commission to draft a new "more indigenous" Constitution (because the Lancaster House Agreement could be and needed to be revised), the new version presented failed to win the majority support of the electorate. In February 2000, the referendum failed, with 55 percent of the voters rejecting it. Later that year, the Movement for Democratic Change (MDC), the major opposition party to ZANU-PF, posed the first major electoral challenge to the state since independence. In the parliamentary elections of June 2000, ZANU-PF won sixty-two seats to the MDC's fifty-seven (Booysen 2003). Shortly after this defeat, the "war veterans" began the process of seizing commercial farmland owned by whites.[10] The Zimbabwe state had ceased to be governed by the "willing seller" / "willing buyer" policy of the Lancaster House Agreement, whereby the British government had funded part of the land reform during the first postindependence decade. Even by the end of the 1990s, 11 million hectares of the best farmland were still owned by 4,500 white commercial farmers. As was noted above, however, the British did not consider land reform in the early Mugabe years a success, because much of the land that had been reallocated was given to those in the government's inner circle.

Although there is no doubt that land reform was sorely needed in Zimbabwe if the nation was to reduce its massive social inequality and really embark on a path to sustainable development, the way the process of "reform" ensued brought further misery and hardship to an already-beleaguered society. As land was seized from white commercial farmers, much violence ensued. Both black farmworkers and white farm owners suffered under the forced land seizures from beatings, torture, and sometimes death (Sithole et al. 2003; Osirim 2003c). By the end of 2002, some 11.5 million hectares had been transferred to black Zimbabweans; however, government ministers and elites were still the primary beneficiaries.[11] Although some black subsistence farmers did acquire land as a result, overall, the land was not placed in the hands of those who were experienced with large-scale farming, nor were those who received land able to benefit from any government programs to assist them in producing what was needed to feed the nation, let alone export.

What the subsequent land seizures and the establishment of a regime of violence in a state that was "above the law" did achieve were "victories" in subsequent elections that further solidified Mugabe's control. The reallocation of land to black Zimbabweans (both poor farmers and political officials) shored up Mugabe's rural base, the major source of his political support in the country, at the same time that it "bought" support among the political elites. His regime claimed victory in the seriously flawed presidential elections of 2002 and, needless to say, in all the elections that followed.

10. Included among those seizing white-owned farms and inflicting violence on large-scale farmers and workers were Zimbabwean youth, who certainly did not participate in the Liberation War, and thus were not war veterans.

11. See http://www.american.edu/TED/ice/zimbabwe.htm.

At the same time, the state continued to arrest the leaders of its archrival, the MDC, and to inflict violence on both these leaders and the MDC's rank and file.[12]

Over the next several years, as the economy continued its free fall and the agricultural sector was unable to produce sufficient food to feed the country, political affiliation became all the more important because food rations were often limited to those who were card-carrying members of ZANU-PF. Throughout this period, however, many Zimbabweans in the formal opposition and others continued to resist the power of the state. As their meager salaries were further and further eroded by hyperinflation, workers organized many strikes, including strikes in January 2007 of major medical personnel, civil servants, and university lecturers.[13] By early 2007, the Consumer Council of Zimbabwe reported that the steepest price increases were in education (261.9 percent), bread (179.7 percent), cooking oil (78.3 percent), and white sugar (166.7 percent)—items that are important for the entire population but whose pricing takes its harshest toll on the poor, as well as the women in this study.

Women in the microenterprise sector in Harare and Bulawayo as well as poor residents in the other cities of Zimbabwe were also affected by the increasingly violent Zimbabwean state in this period. In May 2005, the government conducted Operation Murambatsvina, which in the Shona language means Drive Out Filth. This was a campaign to remove the supposed "shantytowns" regarded by the state as "eyesores" that bordered the major cities—what the Mugabe administration termed its effort at urban renewal. In addition, the state billed this action as an attempt to reconnect poor urban residents with their rural roots. In reality, however, this project was the Mugabe regime's response to those who had not supported ZANU-PF in the parliamentary elections of March 2005—this was the state's retaliation for poor people's support of the opposition. Moreover, not only had many poor urban residents voted against the Mugabe government, but they were also becoming restless and highly likely to strike out against the state. Instead, the government cast the first blow, which wreaked further devastation and malnutrition on an already-beleaguered population. The government demolished homes in these high-density suburbs and also forced residents at gunpoint to destroy their own houses. Though some of the demolished

12. See Amnesty International Canada (http://www.amnesty.ca/themes/zimbabwe_overview.php).

13. See the *New York Times,* January 30, 2007.

homes were small wooden dwellings, others were actually well-constructed brick homes with electricity and running water.

Many respondents in this study lived in the high-density suburbs that suffered under Operation Murambatsvina, an action that resembled the destruction and displacement of black South African townships under apartheid. Though such destruction is not new to Sub-Saharan African societies, Zimbabwe was the worst offender with regard to forced evictions in the new millennium. From 2000 to 2005, an estimated 2.4 million Zimbabweans were displaced (Meldrum 2006). In his reporting for the London *Sunday Times,* Johnson interviewed Philomena Makoni, a survivor of Operation Murambatsvina, who lived in the Hatcliffe settlement in Harare, where some died as a result of the hardship and malnutrition:

> They came at night, shouting and yelling, made us get out of the house and just leveled it to the ground. Then, we were carted off into the countryside and dropped there. The president has said that people like us had lost our roots and that we must rediscover them. My baby that I was nursing died—I had no food and could give her no milk. We buried her in the bush. My other two children are terribly thin and sick. We walked all the way back to Hatcliffe, it was many miles but things are much harder even then before. My husband lost his job through being sent away and we have no income. We are only alive because the churches give us some food, but I am very frightened for my children. They are no longer in school and they are now begging at the roadside. I cannot see what will become of us. (Johnson 2007)

According to Amnesty International Canada, in the year since the demolition of many high-density suburbs, the displaced residents had not received any assistance from the state. Moreover, the state repeatedly hindered UN efforts to provide emergency assistance.[14]

Unfortunately, Operation Murambatsvina did not end with the destruction of many high-density suburbs but proceeded to directly attack street vendors and market traders, a segment of the microenterprise sector included in this study. In May 2005, the Zimbabwean police destroyed makeshift stalls and beat and arrested more than 9,000 traders and street vendors in Harare. This action was a direct attempt on the part of the Mugabe state

14. See Amnesty International Canada (http://www.amnesty.ca/themes/zimbabwe_overview.php).

to destroy much of the microenterprise sector, a part of the economy that the state had encouraged the unemployed and underemployed to enter in the early years of economic crisis and structural adjustment. The government now accused the vendors of "selling scarce goods at three times the rate of controlled prices" (Meldrum 2005). Of course, by this period, inflation was already running in the triple digits and the state's economic measures were clearly not working. Many Zimbabweans, however, recognized this crackdown as another of the state's attempts to punish those who had supported the opposition, this time in the March 2005 elections. Meldrum—in quoting Morgan Tsvangirai, the leader of the MDC, and others—noted that such actions were waging war against the opposition, as well as protecting other interests:

> Harare residents also allege that Mr. Mugabe is protecting Chinese businesses selling cheap, shoddy goods that have sprung up throughout the capital over the past two years. "The country has been mortgaged to the Chinese," Morgan Tsvangirai, leader of the opposition MDC, said in a statement. "How can we violently remove Zimbabweans from our flea markets to make way for the Chinese? The majority of Zimbabweans depend on informal trade to feed, clothe and educate their families." (Meldrum 2005)

At the same time, however, entrepreneurs in Zimbabwe's microenterprise sector were determined to maintain their businesses and support their families to whatever extent possible. In the midst of the reign of terror and violence, the massive food shortages, the out-of-control inflation (which is now more than 100 million percent, the highest in the world), an unemployment rate of 80 percent, and the HIV/AIDS pandemic, most urban women in this sector (and poor and low-income women more generally) believed they had two choices: either to begin or continue to trade or operate their enterprises in such cities as Harare and Bulawayo, because the urban population at the very least still had to eat; and/or to continue or begin cross-border trade with such nations as South Africa or Zambia or seek permanent refuge there. Although some more middle- and upper-class Zimbabweans migrated to Britain, Australia, the United States, and South Africa, their poorer sisters most often had fewer choices. With respect to the first alternative, Meldrum made the following comment about the traders in Harare in the current decade:

The street vendors and flea markets have multiplied in Harare as more and more people have lost their jobs and seek to make a living by selling everything from fruits, vegetables, cigarettes and sweets to shoes and umbrellas. They also sell hard-to-find items such as maize meal at prices that reflect their scarcity. (Meldrum 2005)

The escalation in the number of street vendors in Harare, given the growing rate of poverty in the nation, suggests that the market traders and possibly the crocheters in this study were experiencing significantly increased competition in the sale of their goods. As noted above, the traders had complained that the economic crisis and ESAP in the 1990s resulted in too many traders selling the same goods, which thus reduced overall sales in their businesses. They further noted that those hawking their foodstuffs throughout the city streets were bypassing health inspections, thereby exposing the urban population to health risks. Although the increase in the number of street vendors would cause additional stress and economic strain for these businesswomen, it is highly likely that most of the respondents in this study have continued to operate their enterprises.

With respect to the second option for low-income entrepreneurs listed above, the World Bank and the International Monetary Fund have estimated that as many as 3 million people have left Zimbabwe for South Africa and nations in the Global North during the country's current period of economic and political crisis.[15] Several writers have reported that as many as 3 million Zimbabweans have migrated to South Africa alone. Recently, journalists as well as the leaders of some South African NGOs, such as Sally Peberdy from the Southern African Migration Project, have noted that the earlier numbers of Zimbabweans in South Africa was an overestimate—that the number currently is closer to 800,000 to 1 million Zimbabweans (Biles 2007). Whatever the exact number of migrants might be, the South African Office of Home Affairs has been receiving increased numbers of applications from those seeking asylum in the past few years as poverty and violence have escalated in Zimbabwe.[16]

Throughout this decade's crisis, Zimbabwean traders in food, clothing, and handicrafts have been increasingly engaged in cross-border trade with Zambia and South Africa. Massive unemployment, inflation, and poverty

15. See http://www.irinnews.org/report.aspx?reportid=59180.
16. UN Office for the Coordination of Humanitarian Affairs, September 5, 2007.

have led even more men to cross gender boundaries to become food vendors and cross-border traders. For women and men, cross-border trade is a more lucrative option for keeping their businesses and their families afloat in a period of such extreme crisis, as noted by Peter Moyo, a twenty-eight-year-old Zimbabwean trader selling fruit juices, peanut butter, biscuits, and chocolates in Lusaka:

> Out here life is a lot easier. . . . By bringing in cheap products from Zimbabwe without paying tax, I make enough money to buy many things I need back home. Low costs make it possible for Zimbabwean street vendors to sell their goods at half the price charged by Zambian stores. (reported by the UN Office for the Coordination of Humanitarian Affairs, May 31, 2006)

This and similar stories like it are undoubtedly the case for many of the entrepreneurs in this study. Even those who were not cross-border traders at the time of their interviews are likely to have taken up transnational trade in this period of crisis. Under the current political and economic circumstances in Zimbabwe, it will be very difficult for the businesswomen in this study to realize their dreams for their enterprises; nor can they expect the state to make any improvements in their working conditions. Nevertheless, because of their strong dedication to their businesses and their families—combined with their keen business acumen, creativity, and agency—many of them will likely continue to resist the vagaries of the state and the global economy.

# References

Adomako Ampofo, Akosua, J. Beoku-Betts, W. Njambi, and Mary Osirim. 2004. Women's and Gender Studies in English-Speaking Sub-Saharan Africa: A Review of Research in the Social Sciences. *Gender and Society* 18, no. 6: 685–714.

Afonja, Simi. 1981. Changing Modes of Production and the Sexual Division of Labor among the Yoruba. *Signs* 7, no. 2: 299–313.

Andersen, Margaret. 1997. *Thinking about Women: Sociological Perspectives on Sex and Gender.* Boston: Allyn and Bacon.

Andersen, Margaret, and Patricia Hill Collins, eds. 1992. *Race, Class and Gender: An Anthology.* Belmont, Calif.: Wadsworth.

Assie-Lumumba, N'Dri. 1997. Educating Africa's Girls and Women: A Conceptual and Historical Analysis of Gender Inequality. In *Engendering African Social Sciences,* ed. Ayesha Imam, Amina Mama, and Fatou Sow. Dakar: CODESRIA.

Bango, Bisi, Andy Carlton, Hannes Manndorff, and Walter Reiter. 1999. Microfinance in Zimbabwe: Evaluation of Austrian Support to Microfinance Institutes in Zimbabwe—ILO-SDF, ZWFT, and Zambuko Trust. Final Report, May.

Barnes, Teresa. 1999. *We Women Worked So Hard: Gender, Urbanization, and Social Reproduction in Colonial Harare, Zimbabwe, 1930–1956.* Portsmouth, N.H.: Heinemann.

———. 2002. Virgin Territory? Travel and Migration by African Women in Twentieth-Century Southern Africa. In *Women in African Colonial Histories,* ed. Jean Allman, Susan Geiger, and Nakanyike Musisi. Bloomington: Indiana University Press.

Batezat, Elinor, and Margaret Mwalo. 1989. *Women in Zimbabwe.* Harare: Southern Africa Political Economy Series Trust.

Bay, Edna, ed. 1982. *Women and Work in Africa.* Boulder, Colo.: Westview Press.

Berger, Marguerite. 1995. Key Issues on Women's Access to and Use of Credit in the Micro- and Small-Scale Enterprise Sector. In *Women in Micro- and Small-Scale Enterprise Development,* ed. Louise Dignard and José Havet. Boulder, Colo.: Westview Press.

Biles, Peter. 2007. Zimbabwe Exodus to SA "Lower." BBC News, Johannesburg, September 25.

Black, Jan Knippers. 1991. *Development in Theory and Practice: Bridging the Gap.* Boulder, Colo.: Westview Press.

Blauner, Robert. 1972. *Racial Oppression in America.* New York: Harper & Row.

Blood, Robert, and Donald Wolfe. 1960. *Husbands and Wives: The Dynamics of Married Living.* New York: Free Press.

Blumberg, Rae Lesser. 1995. Introduction: Engendering Wealth and Well-Being in an Era of Economic Transformation. In *Engendering Wealth and Well-Being: Empowerment for Global Change,* ed. Rae Lesser Blumberg et al. Boulder, Colo.: Westview Press.

Bonacich, Edna. 1991. Class Approaches to Ethnicity and Race. In *Majority and Minority: The Dynamics of Race and Ethnicity in American Life,* ed. Norman Yetman. Boston: Allyn and Bacon.

Booysen, Susan. 2003. The Dualities of Contemporary Zimbabwean Politics: Constitutionalism versus the Law of Power and the Land, 1999–2002. *African Studies Quarterly* 7, nos. 2 and 3: 1–31.

Buvinic, Mayra. 1989. Investing in Poor Women: The Psychology of Donor Support. *World Development* 17, no. 7: 1045–57.

Cawthorne, Maya. 1999. The Third Chimurenga. In *Reflections on Gender Issues in Africa,* ed. Patricia McFadden. Harare: Sapes Books.

Chant, Sylvia, and Cathy McIlwaine. 1998. *Three Generations, Two Genders, One World.* London: Zed Books.

Chase-Dunn, Christopher. 1998. *Global Formation: Structures of the World Economy.* Lanham, Md.: Rowman & Littlefield.

Clark, Gracia, ed. 1988. *Traders versus the State.* Boulder, Colo.: Westview Press.

———. 1994. *Onions Are My Husband: Survival and Accumulation by West African Market Women.* Chicago: University of Chicago Press.

Chow, Esther Ngan-ling, ed. 2002. *Transforming Gender and Development in East Asia.* New York: Routledge.

Comte, Auguste. 1875. *The System of Positive Polity,* trans. Frederic Harrison, E. S. Beesley, J. H. Bridges, et al. London.

Daniels, Lisa. 1998. What Drives the Small-Scale Enterprise Sector in Zimbabwe: Surplus Labor or Market Demand? In *African Entrepreneurship: Theory and Reality,* ed. Anita Spring and Barbara McDade. Gainesville: University of Florida Press.

Darkwah, Akosua. 2002. Trading Goes Global: Market Women in an Era of Globalization. *Asian Women* 15: 31–49.

———. 2007. Work as a Duty and as a Joy: Understanding the Role of Work in the Lives of Ghanaian Female Traders of Global Consumer Items. In *Women's Labor in the Global Economy: Speaking in Multiple Voices,* ed. Sharon Harley. New Brunswick, N.J.: Rutgers University Press.

DAWN (Development Alternatives with Women for a New Era). 1995. *Markers on the Way: The DAWN Debates on Alternative Development.* Rio De Janeiro: DAWN.

De Soto, Hernando. 1989. *The Other Path: The Invisible Revolution in the Third World.* New York: Harper & Row.

Downing, Jeanne. 1990. *GEMINI: Gender and the Growth and Development of Microenterprises.* Prepared for Growth and Equity through Microenterprise, Investments, and Institutions (GEMINI). Washington, DC: U.S. Agency for International Development.

———. 1995. The Growth and Dynamics of Women Entrepreneurs in Southern Africa. In *African Market Women and Economic Power,* ed. Bessie House-Midamba and Felix K. Ekechi. Westport, Conn.: Greenwood Press.

Eckstein, Susan. 2002. Globalization and Mobilization: Resistance to Neo-Liberalism. In *The New Economic Sociology: Developments in an Emerging Field,* ed. Mauro F. Guillén. New York: Russell Sage Foundation.

Eisenstadt, Shmuel. 1966. *Modernization: Protest and Change.* Englewood Cliffs, N.J.: Prentice-Hall.

————. 1973. *Tradition, Change and Modernity.* New York: John Wiley & Sons.

Elson, Diane. 1992. From Survival Strategies to Transformation Strategies: Women's Needs and Structural Adjustment. In *Unequal Burden: Economic Crises, Persistent Poverty and Women's Work,* ed. Lourdes Beneria and Shelley Feldman. Boulder, Colo.: Westview Press.

Engels, Friedrich. 1902. *The Origin of the Family, Private Property, and the State,* trans. Ernest Untermann. Chicago: C. H. Kerr & Co.

Evans, Peter. 1979. *Dependent Development.* Princeton, N.J.: Princeton University Press.

Evans, Peter, and John Stephens. 1988. Studying Development since the Sixties: The Emergence of a New Comparative Political Economy. *Theory and Society* 17: 713–45.

Faiola, Anthony. 2008. As Global Wealth Spreads, the IMF Recedes. *Washington Post,* May 24, http://washingtonpost.com/wp-dyn/content/article/2008/05/23/AR2008052303187.html.

Feldman, Shelley. 1991. Still Invisible: Women in the Informal Sector. In *The Women and International Development Annual,* vol. 2, ed. Rita S. Gallin and Anne Ferguson. Boulder, Colo.: Westview Press.

Fernandez-Kelly, Maria Patricia. 1983. *For We Are Sold, I and My People: Women and Industry in Mexico's Frontier.* Albany: State University of New York Press.

————. 1994. Broadening the Scope: Gender and the Study of International Development. In *Comparative National Development,* ed. A. Douglas Kincaid and Alejandro Portes. Chapel Hill: University of North Carolina Press.

Frank, Andre Gunder. 1967. *Capitalism and Underdevelopment in Latin America: Historical Studies of Chile and Brazil.* New York: Monthly Review Press.

Freeman, Carla. 1997. Reinventing Higglering across Transnational Zones: Barbadian Women Juggle the Triple Shift. In *Daughters of Caliban: Caribbean Women in the Twentieth Century,* ed. Consuelo Lopez Springfield. Bloomington: Indiana University Press.

Gabianu, Sena. 1990. The Susu Credit System: An Indigenous Way of Financing Business Outside the Formal Banking System. In *The Long-Term Perspective Study of Sub-Saharan Africa: Economic and Sectoral Policy Issues,* ed. R. Agarwala. Washington, D.C.: World Bank.

Gaidzanwa, Rudo. 1997. Gender Analysis in the Field of Education: A Zimbabwean Example. In *Engendering African Social Sciences,* ed. Ayesha Imam, Amina Mama, and Fatou Sow. Dakar: CODESRIA.

Gordon, April. 1996. *Transforming Capitalism and Patriarchy: Gender and Development in Africa.* Boulder, Colo.: Lynne Rienner.

Green, December. 1999. *Gender Violence in Africa.* New York: St. Martin's Press.

*The Guardian.* 2002. Nigeria: Women Protest Oil Violence. August 28. http://www.cpa.org.au/garchve5/1106nigeria.html.

Hartmann, Heidi. 1982. Capitalism, Patriarchy and Job Segregation by Sex. In *Classes, Power and Conflict: Classical and Contemporary Debates,* ed. Anthony Giddens and David Held. Berkeley: University of California Press.

Hennessy, Rosemary. 1993. *Materialist Feminism and the Politics of Discourse.* New York: Routledge.

Higginbotham, Elizabeth, and Lynn Cannon. 1988. *Rethinking Mobility: Towards a Race and Gender-Inclusive Theory.* Memphis: Center for Research on Women.

Hitchcock, M., and K. Teague, eds. 2000. *Souvenirs: The Material Culture of Tourism.* Burlington, Vt.: Ashgate.

Hochschild, Arlie, with Anne Machung. 1989. *The Second Shift: Working Parents and the Revolution at Home.* New York: Viking Penguin.

Holleman, John F. 1951. Some Shona Tribes of Southern Rhodesia. In *Seven Tribes of Central Africa,* ed. Elizabeth Colson and Max Gluckman. Manchester: Manchester University Press.

Horn, Nancy. 1990. Choice or Necessity? Women Selling Fresh Produce in Harare, Zimbabwe. Paper presented at Annual Meetings of African Studies Association, Baltimore, November.

———. 1991. Redefining Economic Productivity: Marketwomen and Food Provisioning in Harare, Zimbabwe. Paper presented at Annual Meetings of African Studies Association, Saint Louis, November.

———. 1994. *Cultivating Customers: Market Women in Harare, Zimbabwe.* Boulder, Colo.: Lynne Rienner.

House-Midamba, Bessie, and Felix Ekechi, eds. 1995. *African Market Women and Economic Power: The Role of Women in African Economic Development.* Westport, Conn.: Greenwood Press.

ILO (International Labor Office). 1972. *Employment, Incomes and Equality: A Strategy for Increasing Productive Employment in Kenya.* Geneva: International Labor Office.

Inkeles, Alex, and David Smith. 1974. *Becoming Modern: Individual Change in Six Developing Countries.* Cambridge, Mass.: Harvard University Press.

Johnson, R. W. 2007. Zimbabwe, the Land of Dying Children. *London Sunday Times,* January 7.

Johnson-Odim, Cheryl. 1982. Grassroots Organizing: Women in Anti-Colonial Activity in South-Western Nigeria. *African Studies Review* 25, nos. 2 and 3: 137–57.

Kamidza, Richard. 1994. Structural Adjustment without a Human Face. *Southern Africa: Political and Economic Monthly* 7, no. 6: 11–12.

Kanyenze, Godfrey. 2003. The Performance of the Zimbabwean Economy, 1980–2000. In *Twenty Years of Independence in Zimbabwe,* ed. Staffan Darnolf and Liisa Laakso. New York: Palgrave Macmillan.

Katapa, Rosalia, and Magdalena Ngaiza. 2001. Debt in Tanzania: Are Women Silent or Concerned? In *Visions of Gender Theories and Social Development in Africa: Harnessing Knowledge for Social Justice and Equality.* Dakar: AAWORD.

Kazembe, Joyce. 1987. The Woman Issue. In *Zimbabwe: The Political Economy of Transition, 1980–1986,* ed. Ibbo Mandaza. Dakar: Council for the Development of Social Science Research in Africa.

Kilbride, Philip. 1994. *Plural Marriage for Our Times: A Reinvented Option?* Westport, Conn.: Bergin and Garvey.

Kilbride, Philip, and Janet Kilbride. 1990. *Changing Family Life in East Africa: Women and Children at Risk.* University Park: Pennsylvania State University Press.

Kilby, P. 1971. *Entrepreneurship and Economic Development.* New York: Free Press.

King, Elizabeth, and Robert Evenson. 1983. Time Allocation and Home Production in Philippine Rural Households. In *Women and Poverty in the Third World,* ed. Mayra

Buvinic, Margaret Lycette, and Willim Paul McGreevey. Baltimore: Johns Hopkins University Press.

Kwesiga, Joy. 2002. *Women's Access to Higher Education in Africa: Uganda's Experience.* Kampala: Fountain.

Leslie, Joanne. 1987. Time Costs and Time Savings of the Child Survival Revolution. Paper prepared for Rockefeller Foundation / International Development Research Center Workshop on Issues Concerning Gender, Technology, and Development in the Third World, International Center for Research on Women, Washington.

Lewis, Desiree. 2002. Review Essay: African Feminist Studies: 1980–2002. *Gender and Women's Studies Africa.* Available at http://www.gwsafrica/knowledge/africa.

Lips, Hilary. 2005. *Sex and Gender: An Introduction.* New York: McGraw-Hill.

Longwe, Sara. 1989. *From Welfare to Empowerment: The Situation of Women in Development in Africa: A Post-UN Women's Decade Update and Future Directions.* Working Paper 204. Lusaka: Zambia Association for Research and Development.

MacGaffey, Janet. 1986. Women and Class Formation in a Dependent Economy: Kisangani Entrepreneurs. In *Women and Class in Africa,* ed. Claire Robertson and Iris Berger. New York: Africana.

———. 1987. *Entrepreneurs and Parasites: The Struggle for Indigenous Capitalism in Zaire.* Cambridge: Cambridge University Press.

———. 1990. The Endogenous Economy. In *The Long-Term Perspective Study of Sub-Saharan Africa: Economic and Sectoral Policy Issues,* ed. R. Agarwala. Washington, D.C.: World Bank.

———. 1998. Creatively Coping with Crisis: Entrepreneurs in the Second Economy of Zaire (Democratic Republic of the Congo). In *African Entrepreneurship: Theory and Reality,* ed. Anita Spring and Barbara McDade. Gainesville: University Press of Florida.

MacGaffey, Janet, and Remy Bazenguissa-Ganga. 2000. *Congo-Paris: Transnational Traders on the Margins of the Law.* Bloomington: Indiana University Press.

Macharia, Kinuthia. 1997. *Social and Political Dynamics of the Informal Economy in African Cities: Nairobi and Harare.* Lanham, Md.: University Press of America.

Made, Patricia, and Myorovai Whande. 1989. Women in Southern Africa: A Note on the Zimbabwe Success Story. *Issues: A Journal of Opinion* 17, no. 2: 26–28.

Mama, Amina. 1996. *Women's Studies and Studies of Women in Africa During the 1990s.* Working Paper Series. Dakar: Council for the Development of Social Science Research in Africa.

Margolis, Diane. 1993. Women's Movements around the World: Cross-Cultural Comparisons. *Gender and Society* 7. no. 3: 379–99.

May, Joan. 1983. *Zimbabwean Women in Colonial and Customary Law.* Gweru, Zimbabwe: Mambo Press.

Mazumdar, Dipak. 1976. The Urban Informal Sector. *World Development* 4, no. 8: 655–79.

Mbilinyi, Marjorie. 1992. *Review of Women's Conditions and Positions in Tanzania: Issues and Methodology.* Dar es Salaam: Tanzania Gender Networking Programme.

———. 1998. Searching for Utopia: The Politics of Gender and Education in Tanzania. In *Women and Education in Sub-Saharan Africa: Power, Opportunities and Constraints,* ed. Marianne Bloch, Josephine Beoku-Betts, and B. Robert Tabachnick. Boulder, Colo.: Lynne Rienner.

McCormick, Dorothy, and Mary Njeri Kinyanjui. 2007. Industrializing Kenya: Building the Productive Capacity of Micro and Small Enterprise Clusters. In *The African*

*Cluster: Pattern, Practice, and Policies for Upgrading Clusters,* ed. Dorothy Mc-Cormick and Banji Oyeyinka. Maastricht: UNU-INTECH.

McFadden, Patricia. 2001. *Patriarchy: Political Power, Sexuality and Globalization.* Port Louis, Mauritius: Ledikasyon Pu Travayer.

Mead, Donald C. 1999. MSE's Tackle Both Poverty and Growth. In *Enterprise in Africa: Between Poverty and Growth,* ed. Kenneth King and Simon McGrath. London: Intermediate Technology Publications.

Meldrum, Andrew. 1989. Mugabe's Maneuvers. *Africa Report,* May–June, 38–41.

———. 2005. Police in Zimbabwe Arrest 9000 Traders: Street Battles after Stalls Smashed and Goods Seized. *The Guardian,* May 24.

———. 2006. A Tsunami of Demolitions. *New Internationalist,* January 1.

Ministry of Community and Cooperative Development and Women's Affairs. 1981. *Policy Statement.* Harare: Zimbabwe Ministry of Community and Cooperative Development and Women's Affairs.

Moghadam, Valentine. 1997. Women's NGO's in the Middle East and North Africa: Constraints, Opportunities and Priorities. In *Organizing Women: Formal and Informal Women's Groups in the Middle East,* ed. Dawn Chatty and Annika Rabo. New York: Oxford University Press.

———. 1999. Gender and Globalization: Female Labor and Women's Mobilizations. *Journal of World Systems Research* 5, no. 2: 367–88.

———. 2000. *Gender and Globalization: Female Labor and Women's Mobilization.* Occasional Paper 11. Normal: Women's Studies Program, Illinois State University.

———. 2005. *Globalizing Women: Transnational Feminist Networks.* Baltimore: Johns Hopkins University Press.

Moser, Caroline. 1991. Gender Planning in the Third World: Meeting Practical and Strategic Needs. In *Gender and International Relations,* ed. Rebecca Grant and Kathleen Newland. Bloomington: Indiana University Press.

Moyo, Jonathan. 1992. State Politics and Social Domination in Zimbabwe. *Journal of Modern African Studies* 30, no. 2: 305–30.

Munguti, Kaendi, Edith Kabui, and Mabel Isoilo. 2002. The Implications of Economic Reform on Gender Relations: The Case of Poor Households in Kisumu Slums. In *Gender, Economic Integration, Governance and Methods of Contraceptives,* ed. Aicha Tamboura Diawara. Dakar: Association of African Women for Research and Development.

Nash, June, and Maria Patricia Fernandez-Kelly, eds. 1983. *Women, Men and the International Division of Labor.* Albany: State University of New York Press.

Neft, Naomi, and Ann Levine. 1997. *Where Women Stand: An International Report on the Status of Women in 140 Countries.* New York: Random House.

Nethengwe, N. 1999. Cross-Border Dynamics in Southern Africa: A Study of Informal Cross-Border Trade between South Africa and Zimbabwe. MA thesis, University of the Witwatersrand, Johannesburg.

Nyambuya, M. N. 1994. The Social Impact of Cost Recovery Measures in Zimbabwe. *Southern Africa: Political and Economic Monthly* 7, no. 6: 14–15.

Okonjo, Kamene. 1976. The Dual-Sex Political System in Operation: Igbo Women and Community Politics in Southeastern Nigeria. In *Women in Africa: Studies in Social and Economic Change,* ed. Nancy J. Hafkin and Edna G. Bay. Stanford, Calif.: Stanford University Press.

Osirim, Mary J. 1992. Gender and Entrepreneurship: Issues of Capital and Technology in Nigerian Small Firms. In *Privatization and Investment in Sub-Saharan Africa,* ed. Bernard S. Katz and Rexford Ahene. New York: Praeger.

———. 1994a. Women in Business: A Case Study of Small-Scale Entrepreneurship in Southwestern Nigeria. *Sage: A Journal of Black Women* 8, no. 1: 28–38.

———. 1994b. Women, Work and Public Policy: Structural Adjustment and the Informal Sector in Zimbabwe. In *Population Growth and Environmental Degradation in Southern Africa,* ed. Ezekiel Kalipeni. Boulder, Colo.: Lynne Rienner.

———. 1995. Trade, Economy and Family in Urban Zimbabwe. In *African Market Women and Economic Power,* ed. Bessie House-Midamba and Felix Ekechi. Westport, Conn.: Greenwood Press.

———. 1996. Beyond Simple Survival: Women Microentrepreneurs in Harare and Bulawayo, Zimbabwe. In *Courtyards, Markets and City Streets: Urban Women in Africa,* ed. Kathleen Sheldon. Boulder, Colo.: Westview Press.

———. 1997. Trading in the Midst of Uncertainty: Market Women, Adjustment and the Prospects for Development in Zimbabwe. *African Rural and Urban Studies.* 2, no. 1: 43–64.

———. 1998. Negotiating Identities during Adjustment Programs: Women Microentrepreneurs in Urban Zimbabwe. In *African Entrepreneurship: Theory and Reality,* ed. Anita Spring and Barbara McDade. Gainesville: University Press of Florida.

———. 2001. Making Good on Commitments to Grassroots Women: NGO's and Empowerment for Women in Contemporary Zimbabwe. *Women's Studies International Forum* 24, no. 2: 167–80.

———. 2003a. African Women's Entrepreneurship and Cultural Production: The Case of Knitters and Crocheters in Southern Africa. *Contours: A Journal of the African Diaspora* 1, no. 2: 154–70.

———. 2003b. Carrying the Burdens of Adjustment and Globalization: Women and Microenterprise Development in Urban Zimbabwe. *International Sociology* 18, no. 3: 535–58.

———. 2003c. Crises in the State and the Family: Violence against Women in Zimbabwe. *African Studies Quarterly* 7, nos. 2 and 3, http://ucb.africa.ufl.edu/asq/v7.

———. 2007. Creatively Coping with Crisis and Globalization: Zimbabwean Businesswomen in Crocheting and Knitting. In *Women's Labor in the Global Economy: Speaking in Multiple Voices,* ed. Sharon Harley. New Brunswick, N.J.: Rutgers University Press.

Otero, Maria. 1987. *Gender Issues in Small-Scale Enterprises.* Washington, D.C.: U.S. Agency for International Development.

Parrenas, Rhacel. 2000. Migrant Filipina Domestic Workers and the International Division of Reproductive Labor. *Gender and Society* 14, no. 4: 48–64.

Parsons, Talcott. 1966. *Societies: Evolutionary and Comparative Perspectives.* Englewood Cliffs, N.J.: Prentice-Hall.

Parsons, Talcott, and Robert Bales. 1955. *Family, Socialization and Interaction Process.* Glencoe, Ill.: Free Press.

Peberdy, S., and J. Crush. 1998. *Trading Places: Cross-Border Traders and the South African Informal Sector.* Migration Series 6. Cape Town: South African Migration Project.

Peberdy, Sally, and Christian Rogerson. 2000. Transnationalism and Non-South African Entrepreneurs in South Africa's Small, Medium and Micro-Enterprise (SMME) Economy. *Canadian Journal of African Studies* 34, no. 1: 20–40.

Pereira, Charmaine. 2003. Configuring "Global," "National," and "Local," in Governance Agendas in Nigeria. *Social Research* 69, no. 3: 781–804.

Pheko, Mohau. 1999. Privatization, Trade Liberalization and Women's Socio-Economic Rights: Exploring Policy Alternatives. In *Africa: Gender, Globalization and Resistance*, ed. Yassine Fall. Dakar: Association of African Women for Research and Development.

Phimister, Ian. 1988. *An Economic and Social History of Zimbabwe, 1890–1948.* London: Longman.

Phimister, Ian, and Charles van Onselen. 1997. The Labour Movement in Zimbabwe: 1900–1945. In *Keep on Knocking: A History of the Labour Movement in Zimbabwe*, ed. Brian Raftopoulos and Ian Phimister. Harare: Baobab Books.

Portes, Alejandro. 1994. The Informal Economy and its Paradoxes. In *The Handbook of Economic Sociology*, ed. Neil J. Smelser and Richard Swedberg. Princeton, N.J.: Princeton University Press.

———. 1998. On the Sociology of National Development: Theories and Issues. In *Development and Underdevelopment: The Political Economy of Global Inequality*, ed. Mitchell A. Seligman and John T. Passe-Smith. Boulder, Colo.: Lynne Rienner.

Portes, Alejandro, Manuel Castells, and Lauren Benton, eds. 1989. *The Informal Economy: Studies in Advanced and Less Developed Societies.* Baltimore: Johns Hopkins University Press.

Portes, Alejandro, and Patricia Fernandez-Kelly. 2003. "Subversion and Compliance in Transnational Communities: Implications for Social Justice." In *Struggles for Social Rights in Latin America*, ed. Susan Eckstein and Timothy P. Wickham-Cowley. New York: Routledge.

Pyke, Karen. 1994. Women's Employment at a Gift or Burden: Marital Power across Marriage, Divorce and Remarriage. *Gender and Society*, no. 8 (March): 73–91.

Raftopoulos, Brian. 1997. The Labour Movement in Zimbabwe: 1945–1965. In *Keep on Knocking: A History of the Labour Movement in Zimbabwe*, ed. Brian Raftopoulos and Ian Phimister. Harare: Baobab Books.

Raftopoulos, Brian, and Daniel Compagnon. 2003. Indigenization, the State Bourgeoisie and Neo-Authoritarian Politics. In *Twenty Years of Independence in Zimbabwe*, ed. Staffan Darnolf and Liisa Laakso. New York: Palgrave Macmillan.

Reichmann, Rebecca. 1984. *Women's Participation in PROGRESO: A Microenterprise Credit Program Reaching the Smallest Businesses of the Poor in Lima, Peru.* Cambridge, Mass: Accion International–AITEC.

Reinharz, Shulamit. 1992. *Feminist Methods in Social Research.* New York: Oxford University Press.

Robertson, Claire. 1984. *Sharing the Same Bowl: A Socioeconomic History of Women and Class in Accra, Ghana.* Bloomington: Indiana University Press.

———. 1997. *Trouble Showed the Way: Women, Men and Trade in the Nairobi Area, 1890–1990.* Bloomington: Indiana University Press.

Sacks, Karen. 1975. Engels Revisited: Women, the Organization of Production and Private Property. In *Toward an Anthropology of Women*, ed. Rayna Reiter. New York: Monthly Review Press.

Safilios-Rothschild, Constantina. 1990. Women's Groups: An Underutilized Grassroots Institution. In *The Long-Term Perspective Study of Sub-Saharan Africa: Economic and Sectoral Policy Issues*, ed. R. Agarwala. Washington, D.C.: World Bank.

Saito, Katrine. 1991. Women and Microenterprise Development in Zimbabwe: Constraints to Development. Paper presented at Annual Meeting of African Studies Association, Saint Louis, November.

Sanday, Peggy. 1974. Female Status in the Public Domain. In *Women, Culture and Society,* ed. Michelle Rosaldo and Louise Lamphere. Stanford, Calif.: Stanford University Press.

Sassen, Saskia. 1989. New York City's Informal Economy. In *The Informal Economy: Studies in Advanced and Less Developed Countries,* ed. Alejandro Portes, Manuel Castells, and Lauren Benton. Baltimore: Johns Hopkins University Press.

———. 1998. *Globalization and its Discontents.* London: The New Press.

Schatz, Sayre. 1977. *Nigerian Capitalism.* Berkeley: University of California Press.

Schmidt, Elizabeth. 1992. *Peasants, Traders and Wives: Shona Women in the History of Zimbabwe, 1870–1939.* Portsmouth, N.H.: Heinemann.

Schoepf, Brooke. 1992. Gender Relations and Development: Political Economy and Culture. In *Twenty-First Century Africa: Towards a New Vision of Self-Sustainable Development,* ed. Gay Seidman et al. Trenton, N.J.: Africa World Press.

Schumpeter, Joseph. 1959. *The Theory of Economic Development.* Cambridge, Mass.: Harvard University Press.

Scott, Catherine. 1995. *Gender and Development: Rethinking Modernization and Dependency Theory.* Boulder, Colo.: Lynne Rienner Publishers.

Seidman, Gay. 1984. Women in Zimbabwe: Post-Independence Struggles. *Feminist Studies* 10, no. 3: 419–40.

Sithole, B., B. Campbell, D. Doré, and W. Kozanayi. 2003. Narratives on Land: State-Peasant Relations over Fast Track Land Reform in Zimbabwe. *African Studies Quarterly* 7, nos. 2 and 3, http://web.africa.ufl.edu/asq/v7/v7i2a4.htm.

Snyder, Margaret. 2000. *Women in African Economies: From Burning Sun to Boardroom.* Kampala: Fountain Publishers.

Souza, Paulo, and Victor Tokman. 1976. The Informal Sector in Latin America. *International Labour Review* 114, no. 3: 355.

Spring, Anita, and Barbara McDade, eds. 1998. *African Entrepreneurship: Theory and Reality.* Gainesville: University Press of Florida.

Stoneman, Colin. 1989. The World Bank and the IMF in Zimbabwe. In *Structural Adjustment in Africa,* ed. Bonnie K. Campbell and John Loxley. London: Macmillan.

Stoneman, Colin, and Lionel Cliffe. 1989. *Zimbabwe: Politics, Economics and Society.* London: Pinter.

Suda, Collette. 2007. Formal Monogamy and Informal Polygamy in Parallel: African Traditions in Transition. Inaugural lecture, University of Nairobi, Nairobi, October 4.

Sudarkasa, Niara. 1981a. Female Employment and Family Organization in West Africa. In *The Black Woman Cross-Culturally,* ed. Filomina Chioma Steady. Cambridge: Schenkman.

———. 1981b. Interpreting the African Heritage in Afro-American Family Organization. In *Black Families,* ed. Harriette Pipes McAdoo. Beverly Hills, Calif.: Sage.

Summers, Carol. 1991. Native Policy, Education and Development: Social Ideologies and Social Control in Southern Rhodesia, 1890–1934. PhD dissertation, Johns Hopkins University.

Sylvester, Christine. 1991. *Zimbabwe: The Terrain of Contradictory Development.* Boulder, Colo.: Westview Press.

Tendler, Judith. 1989. Whatever Happened to Poverty Alleviation? *World Development* 17 (July): 1033–44.

Turner, Terisa E. 2001. The Land Is Dead: Women's Rights and Human Rights: The Case of the Ogbodo Shell Petroleum Spill in Rivers State, Nigeria. June-July. http://www/africaaction.org/docs01/shel0107.htm.

UNICEF (United Nations Children's Fund). 1993. *The Progress of Nations.* New York: UNICEF.

Van Allen, Judith. 1976. "Aba Riots" or Igbo Women's War? Ideology, Stratification and the Invisibility of Women. In *Women in Africa: Studies in Social and Economic Change,* ed. Nancy J. Hafkin and Edna G. Bay. Stanford, Calif.: Stanford University Press.

Wallerstein, Immanuel. 1974. *The Modern World System: Capitalist Agriculture and the Origins of the European World Economy in the Sixteenth Century.* New York: Academic Press.

West, Michael O. 2002. *The Rise of an African Middle Class: Colonial Zimbabwe 1898–1965.* Bloomington: Indiana University Press.

Young, Kate, Carol Wolkowitz, and Roslyn McCullagh, eds. 1984. *Of Marriage and the Market: Women's Subordination Internationally and Its Lessons.* London: Routledge Kegan Paul.

Yunus, Muhammad. 1999. *Banker to the Poor: The Battle against World Poverty.* New York: Public Affairs.

# Index

*Figures and notes are denoted by f and n following the page number.*

239